Desert Shield at Sea

Recent Titles in
Contributions in Military Studies

Desert Shield at Sea

What the Navy Really Did

Marvin Pokrant

Foreword by Admiral Hank Mauz

Contributions in Military Studies, Number 174

GREENWOOD PRESS
Westport, Connecticut • London

Library of Congress Cataloging-in-Publication Data

Pokrant, Marvin, 1943–
    Desert Shield at sea : what the Navy really did / Marvin Pokrant ;
foreword by Admiral Hank Mauz.
        p.   cm.—(Contributions in military studies, ISSN 0883–6884
; no. 174)
    Includes bibliographical references (p.   ) and index.
    ISBN 0–313–31023–8 (alk. paper)
    1. Persian Gulf War, 1991—Naval operations, American.   2. United
States.   Navy—History—Persian Gulf War, 1991.   I. Title.
II. Series.
DS79.744.N38P645   1999
956.7044'2450973—dc21   98–48907

British Library Cataloguing in Publication Data is available.

Library of Congress Catalog Card Number: 98–48907
ISBN: 0–313–31023–8
ISSN: 0883–6884

First published in 1999

Greenwood Press, 88 Post Road West, Westport, CT 06881
An imprint of Greenwood Publishing Group, Inc.
www.greenwood.com

Printed in the United States of America

The paper used in this book complies with the
Permanent Paper Standard issued by the National
Information Standards Organization (Z39.48–1984).

10 9 8 7 6 5 4 3 2

Approved for Public Release

Work conducted under contract N00014-96-D-0001.

This document represents the best opinion of the author at the time of issue. It does not necessarily
represent the opinion of the Center for Naval Analyses or the Department of the Navy.

Contents

Illustrations

Foreword

As the Seventh Fleet commander in early August 1990, I and my staff (and flagship USS *Blue Ridge*) were back in our homeport of Yokosuka, Japan, after being gone for most of the year up to that point. Our high-priority projects included: working with the Fifth Air Force to refine our joint campaign plan against the USSR; closer cooperation with the Japanese Self-Defense Forces on a variety of fronts; and working closely with commanders in Korea to make the Seventh Fleet a full partner in defense of that peninsula. In developing the campaign plan, asking the right questions of the national intelligence community and pointing them in practical directions of importance to warfighters were major accomplishments. This effort and our strike-planning methodology would later serve us well.

Our involvement with the Central Command had been limited to training of U.S. naval forces as they steamed through the Western Pacific en route to the North Arabian Sea and Persian Gulf. We tried to replicate the kinds of operational challenges they could face in CentCom's area of responsibility. We also provided a great deal of logistics support to naval forces in that area of responsibility. We provided P-3C aircraft for area surveillance, and we supported Commander, Joint Task Force Middle East's (CJTFME's) needs for intelligence collection assets. In early 1989, I had flown to the carrier operating in the North Arabian Sea and then on to Bahrain for talks with Rear Admiral Tony Less, CJTFME. I also helo'd out to a cruiser (USS *England*) operating in the Persian Gulf to see what kind of air defense picture it could maintain. The Gulf was a harsh environment, but the Navy had about 40 years' experience operating there.

On 2 August 1990, I remember hearing about Iraq's invasion of Kuwait and thinking that the then-CJTFME, Rear Admiral Bill Fogarty, was going to be a busy guy. I recall sending him a short personal message offering any possible support. Then began the sequence of events, well documented in this volume, that led to ComSeventhFlt taking over as ComUSNavCent/CTF 150. We still retained our

Seventh Fleet hat but could only watch happenings in the Western Pacific over our shoulder. Our subordinate commands carried the load as best they could, but most of our naval forces were heading to CentCom. Thank goodness Korea, in particular, stayed quiet.

I have several comments about Desert Shield circumstances and events as described in this volume. Foremost in my mind in the fall of 1990 was the question of when and how the war would start. Clearly, the coalition was building strength (and a lot of our activity was aimed at nurturing the coalition). Would Saddam Hussein allow the coalition to get fully established and let us initiate hostilities at the time and places of our choosing? Or would he strike first and get maximum benefit from his forces before they got chewed up? CentCom had some serious vulnerabilities that Saddam could have exploited—overcrowded air bases; thin communications (a satchel charge in the Riyadh PTT would have done a number on our communications there, primarily landline); few ports, with the key ones within easy strike range; a critical desalination plant; little defense against chemical or biological attack; limited logistics sustainability for ground-based forces until late in the build-up period; and so on. The uncertainty as to how and when the war would start shaped some of my key decisions, like how many carriers we needed. It also affected my priorities regarding early Joint Force Air Component Commander strike planning.

As outlined here in *Desert Shield at Sea,* the Navy did have problems with JFACC. While neither I nor my staff doubted the need for centralized control of airpower, there was lack of familiarity with the concept by many in the Navy and lack of appreciation by many in the Air Force regarding Navy strengths and limitations. There was great concern about the closed-door planning process and how Navy sorties were to be used in a campaign plan. We thought we had a lot to contribute to joint air campaign planning, and we saw instances in early iterations of the strike plan where target priorities did not make much sense. Lt. General Chuck Horner and I got along well, and we were usually able to work through problem areas. From my perspective, if the JFACC organization had really been joint, a lot of grief could have been avoided.

As an observation, and based on my experience in the 1980s in NATO Europe, the Mediterranean, the North Atlantic, and throughout Asia, I believe the Navy had become as "joint" as any of the services. Aside from our close association with the Marine Corps, we actively sought opportunities to exercise with the other services, particularly the Air Force. We did so with allies and the numbered Air Forces all over the world. We bought Command, Control, and Communication equipment to facilitate communications between commanders afloat and ashore. We sought to promote interoperability and knock holes through that seeming 100,000-foot wall that divides the land and seas. The Navy had made good progress around the world, but the trouble was that the Ninth Air Force (CentAF/JFACC) was at Shaw AFB with units further spread around the United States. Most Navy warfighters had never even met those who would lead the coalition's air campaign. Whose fault was this? There's enough blame to go around among the JCS, Unified Commands, and the services.

Regarding the best location for ComUSNavCent, my view was (and is) that Riyadh was not the best place to be. With all that was going on in the Gulf during Desert Shield and with what we were planning for Desert Storm, it was inconceivable to me not to have a three-star commander afloat in the Gulf. There were to be five or six rear admirals commanding forces in combat in the same constrained waterspace. There would be all types of air warfare, and airspace management would be difficult. There would be naval actions in the northern Persian Gulf, minesweeping under stressful conditions, Tomahawk salvos, amphibious operations, coordination with allies, continuing concern about Iran's reaction to all this, and the need to respond quickly to the tactical situation. In my view, that could not be done from Riyadh, especially given the command, control, communications and intelligence support we could expect there.

Was there a need for greater and more senior Navy presence in Riyadh? I will take the word of those who were in theater after I left. It does seem appropriate to have had more horsepower there, but not, in my view, another layer of command. I thought General Schwarzkopf was a great leader and believe he and I had a good relationship. His command style was to assign responsibilities to subordinates and let them do their job—although it was obvious he took great and personal interest in how the Army was doing. Where responsibilities overlapped, he was reluctant to take sides. This was evident when there were differences between the Navy and JFACC. I never saw General Schwarzkopf as needing his hand held, either, but having a more senior Navy admiral at his side would have helped, particularly to sort out misunderstandings that might arise. Communications were available to support a dialogue between that senior flag and ComUSNavCent/CTF 150. Would a more senior flag have helped in dealing with JFACC? Maybe, but not, in my view, unless General Schwarzkopf gave that flag a remit of some kind to do so.

Many congratulations are in order. I again want to commend Admiral Stan Arthur and the NavCent staff for the brilliant job they did in the final run-up to war and during Desert Storm. All the sailors and Marines, afloat and ashore, can take great pride in all their achievements, from being first on-scene with sustainable combat power in early August 1990, through sanction enforcement and planning for war, to the air and sea campaigns, and to the retaking of Kuwait City by the Marines. But this was a joint and combined effort in the truest sense. The U.S. Army and Air Force carried the biggest loads, and they did so with unsurpassed skill and professionalism. We all learned lessons that should not be lost. Dr. Marvin Pokrant and the Center for Naval Analyses deserve special praise for digging out those lessons and for taking on controversial issues in the process. I thank them for their competence, dedication, and persistence.

Henry H. Mauz, Jr.
Admiral, U.S. Navy (Retired)

Preface

This is the first of two volumes that describe in detail the role of the U.S. naval forces during operations Desert Shield (Volume I—*Desert Shield at Sea: What the Navy Really Did*) and Desert Storm (Volume II—*Desert Storm at Sea: What the Navy Really Did*). We wrote our account to promote better understanding of these operations and provide insights that might help naval forces contribute even more in future operations. The U.S. Navy has diligently attempted to learn from Desert Shield and Storm. We hope this book will be seen as part of that effort.

We tell our story primarily at the operational level—that of the Commander, U.S. Naval Forces Central Command (ComUSNavCent)—with frequent forays down to the tactical level. We illustrate command-and-control issues through the stories of operations. Where appropriate, we discuss the broader, more strategic-level issues, but only in the context of the impact on the naval operations.

Several themes run throughout the two volumes:

- The operations were dangerous. Brave people risked their lives. That most did not lose their lives does not diminish the risk or their bravery.
- The naval forces faced many difficult challenges and decisions. Although a coalition victory seems assured in retrospect, a quick, low-casualty outcome was not preordained either ashore or at sea. NavCent forces solved many problems only by clever and determined work-arounds.
- One cannot fully understand or appreciate the events of Desert Storm without knowing the events of Desert Shield.
- One cannot completely comprehend command decisions at the operational level without first gaining an understanding of the details of the tactical operations.
- Operations during Desert Shield and Storm exhibited jointness at its best but also were marred by interservice rivalry.

The nature of decisions changed throughout Desert Shield and Desert Storm. During Desert Shield, the Navy was the only service engaged daily in actual operations—the maritime interception operations. Throughout Desert Shield naval forces also conducted defensive patrols to guard against the possibility of a surprise attack by Iraq. During the early days of Desert Shield, described in Part I of this volume, decisions addressed the chaotic events when there seemed to be an imminent threat of an Iraqi invasion of Saudi Arabia. Problems in the maritime interception operations and the defenses had to be addressed as they arose. Decisions made at this time determined how the maritime interception operations would be implemented. There was little time to look far ahead and develop complex plans. In Part II of this volume, we describe decisions made in preparation for defense. As things had settled down a bit, major decisions often dealt with planning, rather than execution of operations. This period also contains a series of moves and countermoves in the maritime interception operations. Part III of this volume deals with the preparation for offensive operations after the president announced a near doubling of U.S. forces to allow the option of driving the Iraqis out of Kuwait.

In contrast, during Desert Storm, as described in *Desert Storm at Sea: What the Navy Really Did,* decisions often concerned execution of previously made plans. An important theme of Desert Storm, however, was the constant need to revise plans to adapt to a rapidly changing situation.

A major goal of this book is to be objective. We describe candidly how command was exercised, how decisions were made, and what alternatives were considered. We attempt to present all sides of each issue fairly in the context of the information available at the time. As much as practical, we keep our judgments out of the narrative and save our opinions for the observations section at the end of Volume II. We hope the reader will find the exceptions obvious.

Another major goal is to present the facts accurately, using primary sources as much as possible. Our main sources include contemporary messages, briefings, other internal staff documents, and logs in the Desert Storm archives at the Center for Naval Analyses. A key source was the author's notes taken while he was the civilian Center for Naval Analyses representative to the ComUSNavCent staff; Vice Admirals Hank Mauz and Stan Arthur gave him access to key meetings and personnel throughout Desert Shield and Storm. We also used the Center for Naval Analyses' fourteen-volume reconstruction report of the naval operations afloat, four-volume reconstruction report of the operations of the Marines ashore, and numerous subsequent in-depth studies on various aspects of the operations. In addition, we interviewed most key participants, all of whom were eager for the accurate story to be told.

We make no pretense of being all-inclusive. Because much vital data necessarily remain classified, we could not relate some interesting and important activities, such as intelligence. In our discussion of air power, we concentrated on the naval contributions to the air campaign, especially those contributions that were unique, and on naval interactions with joint command and control.

Many books and articles have rightfully extolled the role of the U.S. Air Force and Army in Operation Desert Storm. They deserve the acclaim. Like the Air

Force, Army, and Marine Corps forces ashore, the naval forces afloat—both Navy and Marine Corps—played an important role. Though the naval forces were not at the center of events, their story deserves to be told. We leave others to debate who deserves most of the credit for turning the battle-hardened veterans of the world's fourth-largest army into the war-weary conscripts of the world's eighth-largest army. This is the story of the naval forces' contributions to operations Desert Shield and Desert Storm.

SOURCES

The primary sources were the author's personal observations at ComUSNav-Cent headquarters, military messages, official logs, internal briefings and memoranda, CNA reports, and interviews with many key participants. From August 1990 to April 1991, the author was allowed access to almost all meetings at the ComUSNavCent staff. He discussed events and issues with the Battle Watch several times a day, participated in the daily staff briefings and department-head meetings, and also discussed issues with numerous members of the staff as events were occurring. He took detailed notes and was careful to indicate those statements that were direct quotes. These notes were an important source throughout the book and, therefore, are not mentioned as a source for each chapter unless they were the predominant source.

During this period at ComUSNavCent, the author collected many thousands of significant messages. Many of these had the comments of the admiral and various members of the staff. While researching this book, we also had access to the tens of thousands of messages in the CNA Desert Shield and Desert Storm archives. These archives also contain the ComUSNavCent Battle Watch Captain Event Logs and various logs from nearly every ship and command that participated in Desert Shield or Desert Storm.

We interviewed dozens of key participants, many numerous times, while researching this book. These interviews are listed in the Bibliography. In the text, we tried to distinguish between statements made in the midst of events and recollections made later in interviews. CNA reports included both the reconstruction reports (fourteen volumes for the Navy, four volumes for the Marine Corps) and analysis reports that covered specific issues arising out of Desert Storm. To provide perspective, we also used books and articles published by various participants, as well as contemporary newspaper articles.

One of the goals for this book was to cite a source for every statement that was not summary or clearly the author's opinion. Unfortunately, due to the limitations of publication economics, to include the resulting thousands of notes was not practical. Also, many of the sources used are not available to the general public. Therefore, only explanatory notes, sources of direct quotes, and sources of a very few key facts are listed in the notes at the end of each chapter. The notes use short forms of the references. Long forms of the sources are listed in the Bibliography. We have given a bibliographic narrative for each chapter to let the reader know the general types of sources used. A manuscript copy of this book with complete sources will be maintained at the Center for Naval Analyses (CNA). CNA will also maintain a file of the sources themselves.

NOTE TO THE READER

Generally, we follow the *Chicago Manual of Style,* 13th Edition, for transliteration of Arabic place names. We drop ending *h*s and precede place names with the definitive article, *al*, joined to the noun with a hyphen, without indication of the elision used in speech. We make exceptions for Ash Shuaybah and Faylaka Island, because these were the forms used by NavCent forces during Desert Shield and Storm and might not be recognizable to participants if spelled as "al-Shuaiba" and "Falaika." For the names of Iraqi ships we use the spelling in the guide to Iraqi merchant ships issued to NavCent forces, but we generally separate the *Al,* as was commonly done during the operation. For example, we refer to the tanker *Al Fao,* rather than the *al-Faw.* Finally, we refer to the body of water between Iran and Saudi Arabia by its historical name—the Persian Gulf.

For acronyms, we use the definition in the Department of Defense dictionary.

Most events took place in time zone Charlie—indicated by appending the appropriate letter to the time, for instance, 1200C—which is Zulu time (Greenwich Mean Time) plus three hours. Some events took place in time zone Delta, which is Zulu plus four hours.

The word "we" in the text is the editorial "we," and the opinions expressed are solely those of Dr. Marvin Pokrant. They are not necessarily shared by the Center for Naval Analyses or the Department of the Navy.

Acknowledgments

I would like to thank the Honorable Robert J. Murray, President of the Center for Naval Analyses, for the opportunity to write this book.

I owe an enormous debt to Admiral Stan Arthur (Ret.) and Admiral Hank Mauz (Ret.) for giving me access to key meetings during Desert Shield and Desert Storm, for reading drafts of the manuscript, for consenting to my taking an objective view of their decisions, and finally for their encouragement.

I owe a similar debt to those participants who read draft versions of the manuscript—Rear Admiral Bernie Smith, Rear Admiral Tom Marfiak, Rear Admiral Gordon Holder, Captain Tom Connelly, Captain Bunky Johnson (Ret.)—and those who read portions pertinent to their participation—Admiral Hunt Hardisty (Ret.), Admiral Zap Zlatoper, Vice Admiral Bat LaPlante (Ret.), Vice Admiral Connie Lautenbacher, Rear Admiral Cutler Dawson, Captain Denny Morral, Captain Pat Garrett, Colonel Frank Wickersham (Ret.), and Lt. Cdr. Brian Smith. These officers pointed out many early errors of both fact and interpretation. I am grateful to them all and to many other participants, including General Colin Powell (Ret.), General Walt Boomer (Ret.), Admiral Frank Kelso (Ret.), and General Al Gray (Ret.), who graciously consented to be interviewed. Those individuals and others listed in the bibliography, who were interviewed, often at great length and frequently on multiple occasions, played a major role in making this book both realistic and factually accurate. Their encouragement in this project was an inspiration.

I also owe a great debt to my colleagues at the Center for Naval Analyses, whose knowledge of naval warfare in both breadth and depth is unequaled anywhere. The primary reviewer, Captain Peter Swartz (Ret.), was especially valuable because of his prior experience as a Navy officer and his expertise as an analyst. He held me to high standards and pointed out many cases of tortured reasoning, convoluted organization, and places that needed more explanation.

Dr. Jamil Nakhleh and Admiral Bill Smith (Ret.) also reviewed a draft of the manuscript and provided many useful comments. Experts in particular subjects reviewed specific areas. These included Dr. Gregg Adams, Mr. Charlie Chambers, Dr. Larry Hammersten, Ms. Mary Robin Holliday, Mr. Duncan Love, Mr. Barry Messina, Dr. Bill Morgan, Dr. Ron Nickel, Dr. Ralph Passarelli, Dr. Mike Shepko, Dr. Greg Suess, Mr. Paul Symborski, and Ms. Maureen Wigge.

Many other colleagues provided material or ideas that were useful. They included Mr. Richard Brody, Mr. John Keefe, Dr. Jeff Lutz, Dr. Katherine McGrady, Dr. Hung Nguyen, Dr. Dave Perin, Dr. Rob Philipp, Mr. Adam Siegel, Dr. Frank Schwamb, and Mr. William Wallace.

Many others at the Center for Naval Analyses also provided invaluable support. My editor, Ms. Linda Dennis, read the manuscript many times, suggesting numerous improvements in the organization and language. She overcame many of my writing deficiencies. Mr. Allen Austin skillfully drew most of the figures. Others that helped were Ms. Kathy Berens, Dr. Dave Blake, Ms. Alice Brown, Mr. Chris Burton, Mr. George Cottman, Mr. Chester Eiland, Mr. Floyd Freeman, Ms. Beth French, Mr. Ken Gause, Mr. Craig Goodwyn, Ms. Linda Harper, Mr. Jim Higgins, Dr. Tom Hone, Ms. Pam Hutchins, Mr. Ken Kennedy, Dr. Mike Kopp, Ms. Barbara Kuemmerling, Ms. Susan MacDuff, Ms. Pat McGlue, Dr. Igor Mikolic-Torreira, Mr. J. C. Owens, Ms. Julliette Palermo, Mr. Jim Parsons, Dr. Peter Perla, Mr. Ben Regala, Ms. Carol Robinson, Ms. Diane Schug, Dr. Doug Skinner, Ms. Norma Jean Smith, Ms. Alexia Suma, Ms. Jan Weaver, Ms. Marty Weaver, Lt. Tom Wingfield, and Dr. Dave Zvijac. My wife Gail also contributed as a research assistant, fact checker, copyeditor, and critic.

Most of all, I wish to acknowledge the enormous contribution of Ms. Laurie Trader, who was my research assistant, critic, and partner for the first part of the project. Although she started the project with no experience, she learned rapidly and developed into a fine conceptual analyst. Even though, unfortunately, she could not stay until the end of the project, her collaboration made this a much better book.

Fritz Heinzen showed confidence in the value of this work, arranged for Greenwood to examine the manuscript, and showed enormous patience throughout the negotiations. Last, but not least, I want to thank my editor Heather Ruland Staines, copyeditor Pelham Boyer, Lynn Zelem, Production Editor, and the others at Greenwood Press for their patience, skill, and suggestions.

I could not have written this book without the assistance of all these people who were so generous with their time and talent. If this book is good, they deserve much of the credit; any remaining errors of fact or interpretation remain my responsibility and mine alone.

Abbreviations

AADC	Area Air Defense Commander
AAV	Assault Amphibious Vehicle
AE	Ammunition ship
AFS	Combat store ship
AGF	Command ship
AHIP	Army Helicopter Improvement Program
AO	Fleet oiler
AOE	Fast combat support ship
AOR	Replenishment oiler
APAM	Anti-personnel, Anti-materiel
ArCent	U.S. Army Forces, Central Command
ARG	Amphibious Ready Group
ARM	Anti-radiation Missile
ATF	Amphibious Task Force
ATO	Air Tasking Order
AWACS	Airborne Warning and Control System
BB	Battleship
BVR	Beyond Visual Range
C	Charlie time, time zone indicator for Universal time plus three hours
CAFMS	Computer-Assisted Force Management System
CAP	Combat Air Patrol
CATF	Commander, Amphibious Task Force
C-day	Day on which a deployment begins
CentAF	U.S. Central Command Air Forces

CentCom	Central Command
CG	Guided-missile cruiser
CGN	Guided-missile cruiser (nuclear propulsion)
CIA	Central Intelligence Agency
CinC	Commander-in-Chief
CinCCent	Commander-in-Chief, Central Command
CinCPacFlt	Commander-in-Chief, Pacific Fleet
CJCS	Chairman, Joint Chiefs of Staff
CJTFME	Commander, Joint Task Force Middle East
CLF	Commander, Landing Force
CNA	Center for Naval Analyses
CNO	Chief of Naval Operations
ComMidEastFor	Commander, Middle East Force
ComSeventhFlt	Commander, Seventh Fleet
ComSixthFlt	Commander, Sixth Fleet
ComSOCCent	Commander, Special Operations Component, U.S. Central Command
ComThirdFlt	Commander, Third Fleet
ComUSArCent	Commander, U.S. Army Forces, Central Command
ComUSCentAF	Commander, U.S. Central Command Air Forces
ComUSMarCent	Commander, U.S. Marine Forces, Central Command
ComUSNavCent	Commander, U.S. Naval Forces, Central Command
CTF	Commander, Task Force
CTG	Commander, Task Group
CTU	Commander, Task Unit
CV	Aircraft carrier
CVBF	Aircraft carrier Battle Force
CVBG	Aircraft carrier Battle Group
CVN	Aircraft carrier (nuclear propulsion)
CVW	Aircraft carrier air wing

D	Delta time, time zone indicator for Universal time plus four hours
D	Destroyer (some foreign navies)
DD	Destroyer
DDG	Guided-missile destroyer
DDH	Destroyer (Canadian)
DEAD	Destruction of Enemy Air Defenses
DSMAC	Digital Scene-Matching Area Correlation
dwt	deadweight tons

F	Frigate (some foreign navies)
FF	Frigate

FFG	Guided-missile frigate
FS	French Ship
GWAPS	Gulf War Air Power Survey
HARM	High-speed Anti-radiation Missile
HMAS	Her Majesty's Australian Ship
HMCS	Her Majesty's Canadian Ship
HMS	Her Majesty's Ship
HRH	His Royal Highness
HS	Hellenic (Greek) Ship
IFF	Identification, Friend or Foe
JFACC	Joint Force Air Component Commander
JILE	Joint Intelligence Liaison Element
JOTS	Joint Operational Tactical System
JTFME	Joint Task Force Middle East
KARI	Iraqi air-defense system
LCAC	Landing Craft, Air Cushion
LCC	Amphibious command ship
LCU	Landing Craft, Utility
LEDet	Law Enforcement Detachment
LGB	Laser-Guided Bomb
LHA	General-purpose amphibious assault ship
LOI	Letter of Instruction
LPD	Amphibious transport dock (dock landing ship)
LPH	Amphibious assault ship (landing platform, helicopter)
MarCent	Marine Forces, Central Command
MAW	Marine Aircraft Wing
MCM	Mine Countermeasures
MEB	Marine Expeditionary Brigade
MEU	Marine Expeditionary Unit
MidEastFor	Middle East Force
MIF	Maritime Interception Force
Mk	Mark
MV	Merchant Vessel
NavCent	U.S. Naval Forces, Central Command
NavCent-Riyadh	NavCent liaison command in Riyadh

NEO	Noncombatant Evacuation Operation
NGFS	Naval GunFire Support
NLOA	Near-Land Operating Area
NOIC	Navy Operational Intelligence Center
OpOrder	Operation Order
OTCIXS	Officer-in-Tactical-Command Information Exchange System
PERMA	Planning, Embarkation, Rehearsal, Movement, Assault
PhibGru	Amphibious Group
PhibRon	Amphibious Squadron
RHIB	Rigid-Hull Inflatable Boat
RN	Royal Navy
ROE	Rules of Engagement
RPV	Remotely Piloted Vehicle
SEAD	Suppression of Enemy Air Defenses
SEAL	SEa-Air-Land team
SHAPE	Supreme Headquarters Allied Powers Europe
SOC	Special Operations Capable
SOCCent	Special Operations Component, U.S. Central Command
SPEAR	Strike Projection Evaluation and Antiair Research
SPINS	SPecial INstructionS
SuCAP	Surface Combat Air Patrol
T-AH	Hospital ship
TASM	Tomahawk Anti-Ship Missile
TerCoM	Terrain Contour Matching
TLAM	Tomahawk Land-Attack Missile
UAE	United Arab Emirates
USA	U.S. Army
USAF	U.S. Air Force
USCG	U.S. Coast Guard
USCinCCent	Commander-in-Chief, U.S. Central Command
USCinCPac	Commander-in-Chief, U.S. Pacific Command
USCinCPacFlt	Commander-in-Chief, U.S. Pacific Fleet
USMC	U.S. Marine Corps
USN	U.S. Navy
USNR	U.S. Naval Reserve
USNS	United States Naval Ship
USS	United States Ship

WEU	Western European Union
Whiskey-1	CAP station in northern Persian Gulf
Z	Zulu time, time zone indicator for universal time

Part I

Erecting the Shield, 2 August– 17 September 1990

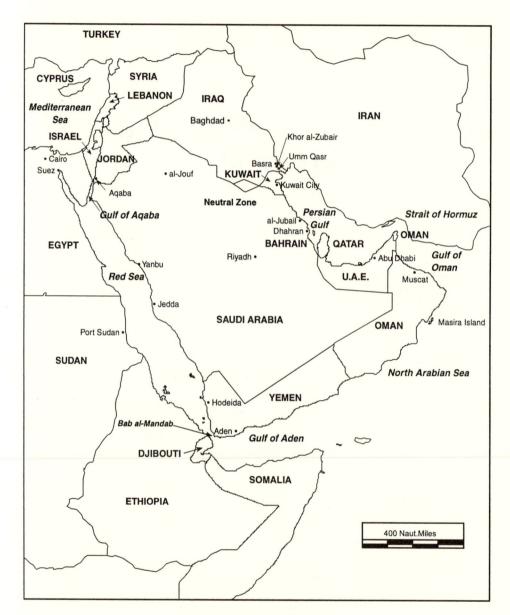

Figure 1–1. The Middle East

Chapter 1

This Will Not Stand

Early on 2 August 1990, Saddam Hussein's Iraqi army, including units of the elite Republican Guard, crossed the Kuwaiti border and invaded its rich neighbor in a well-executed combined-arms attack. In response, the United Nations Security Council passed Resolution 660, demanding that Iraq withdraw from Kuwait. Saddam ignored that demand. More effectively, the United States and other economic powers froze not only Iraq's assets but also Kuwait's, to prevent Iraq from looting Kuwait's foreign accounts.

At the time of the attack, the U.S. Middle East Force, comprising seven surface combatants (destroyers, frigates, and cruisers) plus its flagship, provided a small U.S. naval presence in the Persian Gulf, as it had for more than forty years. A battle group led by the aircraft carrier USS *Independence* (CV 62) sailed in the eastern Indian Ocean, headed for Diego Garcia—a tiny British-owned atoll in the Indian Ocean far from land—for "Weapon Week," a week of exercises intended to hone the battle group's skills. The battle group was then scheduled to proceed to the North Arabian Sea for a regularly scheduled deployment. As one way of signalling long-term commitment to the region, the United States had been keeping a carrier battle group in the North Arabian Sea most of the time since the late 1970s. This was hard duty. Few ports in the region accepted U.S. ships at that time, so these deployments involved sailing around the North Arabian Sea for the better part of a six-month deployment without going ashore. Because training facilities in the area were minimal or nonexistent, crews needed as much training as possible before reaching the operating area (See Figure 1–1).

Within hours of Iraq's invasion, the Chairman of the Joint Chiefs of Staff (CJCS) issued orders for the *Independence* battle group to proceed to the North Arabian Sea without stopping at Diego Garcia. He also ordered the frigates USS *Vandegrift* (FFG 48) and USS *Reid* (FFG 30), scheduled to return home at the end of their deployment with the Middle East Force, to stay until further notice. In the

Mediterranean, the battle group headed by the nuclear-powered carrier USS *Dwight D Eisenhower* (CVN 69) would soon head east for the Suez Canal.

On the weekend of 4–5 August, President George Bush met at Camp David with his advisors, including General Colin Powell, USA, Chairman of the Joint Chiefs of Staff, and General H. Norman Schwarzkopf, USA, Commander in Chief, U.S. Central Command (USCinCCent). Bush sent Secretary of Defense Richard B. "Dick" Cheney, along with General Schwarzkopf and some of his staff, to Saudi Arabia. While they were en route, the *Independence* passed from the command of USCinCPac to USCinCCent. When President Bush returned to Washington from Camp David later on the 5th, he declared to the television cameras that this aggression against Kuwait would not stand.

On 6 August the *Independence* battle group, commanded by Rear Admiral Jerry Unruh, USN, arrived on station in the Gulf of Oman, to operate under the control of the commander of the Joint Task Force Middle East. About the same time the *Independence* arrived on station, Secretary Cheney and General Schwarzkopf met with Saudi Arabia's King Fahd in Jedda and showed him satellite photos of Iraqi troops on the Kuwait-Saudi border, poised to invade his country. After receiving assurances the United States would really commit itself, King Fahd agreed to accept the U.S. military into Saudi Arabia. On this same day, UN Security Council Resolution 661 called for trade and financial sanctions.

On 7 August, the secretary of defense ordered U.S. forces to deploy, named the operation "Desert Shield," and set 7 August as C-day, with H-hour as 1700Z. (C-day is defined as the day on which a deployment operation begins; H-hour is the hour at which it starts. All movements of forces and equipment are tied to this date in the computer database of the time-phased deployment plan.) In accordance with the secretary of defense's guidance, the CJCS issued a flurry of deployment orders. Actually, the lead elements of the deployment had already left the United States, early on the 7th.

On the 8th, the *Eisenhower* arrived on station in the northern Red Sea, having transited the Suez Canal on the previous day. The eight ships in the U.S. Middle East Force remained on station in the Persian Gulf. At 0300, the Ready Brigade of the 82nd Airborne Division began leaving Fort Bragg and Pope Air Force Base in North Carolina. Halfway around the world, ships of Maritime Prepositioning Squadron 2 in Diego Garcia and Squadron 3 in Guam set sail for the Persian Gulf.

OBJECTIVES

President George Bush set the U.S. national policy objectives as:

* Immediate, complete, and unconditional withdrawal of all Iraqi forces from Kuwait
* Restoration of Kuwait's legitimate government
* Security and stability of Saudi Arabia and the Persian Gulf region
* Safety and protection of the lives of American citizens abroad.

Elimination of Saddam Hussein as leader of Iraq, though widely considered desirable, was never explicitly stated as a U.S. goal.

U.S. military objectives during Desert Shield were later stated to be to:

- Develop a defensive capability in the Gulf region to deter Saddam Hussein from further attacks
- Defend Saudi Arabia effectively if deterrence failed
- Build a militarily effective coalition and integrate coalition forces into operational plans
- Enforce the economic sanctions prescribed by UN Security Council Resolutions 661 and 665. (Resolution 665 outlawed all trade with Iraq and authorized force for maritime interception operations.)

Forming and maintaining the coalition would isolate Iraq, avoid the appearance of unilateral American intervention in an Arab dispute, and help sustain U.S. public opinion and internal political support. Establishing and enforcing economic sanctions would offer the possibility of achieving the U.S. goals without bloodshed and, even if not completely successful, would at least sap Iraq's strength prior to warfare. In addition, implied military objectives called for minimizing American casualties and increasing regional stability, which could be achieved only by destroying the Iraqi Republican Guard as a fighting force.

On 10 August, USCinCCent issued his first Desert Shield Operation Order (OpOrder). The USCinCCent mission was to defend Saudi Arabia and be prepared to conduct other operations as directed. The Operation Order summarized the situation by stating that Iraqi forces in Kuwait far exceeded occupation requirements, that they had the capability to attack into Saudi Arabia with three heavy divisions on little or no notice, and that their intent might eventually include seizure of part of Saudi Arabia, including several oil fields. Intelligence estimated, however, that the Iraqis would need considerably more combat power to invade against U.S. forces.

MISSIONS ASSIGNED TO NAVAL FORCES

Marine Corps and Navy forces sometimes serve under a single command. For Desert Shield, there would be separate commands. Commander, U.S. Marine Forces Central Command (ComUSMarCent), would control the Marines ashore. The Operation Order tasked him to be prepared to conduct sustained operations ashore. The Commander, U.S. Naval Forces Central Command (ComUSNavCent), would direct the Navy forces afloat, Navy facilities ashore, and the Marines afloat on the amphibious ships.

The Operation Order assigned the naval forces a wide range of tasks. These included:

- Be prepared to conduct:

- Air defense
- Close air support for ground troops
- Strategic strikes
- Combat search and rescue operations
- Noncombatant evacuation operations
- Amphibious operations
- Mine countermeasure operations
- Support other commands:
  - Make available to the Joint Force Air Component Commander all aircraft sorties in excess of those required for naval warfare tasks
  - Provide naval gunfire support
  - Conduct Maritime Prepositioning Force operations
  - Assist Commander Special Operations Component, U.S. Central Command (ComSOCCent) as required
- Conduct other operations:
  - Protect shipping and ensure freedom of navigation along the sea lines of communications
  - Conduct theater sealift
  - Conduct port security and harbor defense operations
  - Provide sea-based logistics to support ComUSMarCent.

A week later, USCinCCent added another tasking: be prepared to enforce sanctions by conducting maritime interception of shipping to or from Iraq and Kuwait. Initially, these taskings were actually distributed between two naval commands. In the next chapter, we will explain how this came about and was then resolved.

Some of the tasks assigned to the Commander, U.S. Central Command Air Forces (ComUSCentAF), Lt. General Charles "Chuck" Horner, USAF, turned out to be of great import to the naval forces. Horner would serve as the Joint Force Air Component Commander (JFACC), the Area Air Defense Commander, and the Airspace Control Authority. As JFACC, he would plan the strategic air campaign and control Navy and Marine Corps aircraft in some circumstances. In addition, he would establish weapons control measures and fire control procedures.

In other words, USCinCCent gave control of the air to ComUSCentAF. The Air Force had long believed that such unity of command of the air campaign was extremely important. As we will see repeatedly, in carrying out their tasks the naval forces would feel greatly hampered by many of the decisions made by ComUSCentAF.

NOTES

The primary sources for this chapter were military messages. National policy objectives were taken from President Bush's speech of 8 August 1990.

Chapter 2

Selection of ComUSNavCent

Gen. Norman Schwarzkopf could have put a single officer in charge of all naval forces—Navy and Marine—afloat or ashore. He chose not to do this. Instead, Schwarzkopf designated two separate commands, just as the peacetime Central Command (CentCom) had separate Navy and Marine Corps components. USCinCCent's component commanders' peacetime duties included drawing up contingency plans, participating in exercises and war games, and maintaining "corporate memory" of scenarios and "situational awareness" of factors important for likely contingencies in the Central Command. In addition, one of the primary roles of a service component commander was to advise how best to use his forces. Three of Schwarzkopf's service component commanders had served in that capacity prior to Desert Shield: Lt. Generals Walter "Walt" Boomer, USMC (ComUSMarCent), John Yeosock, USA (ComUSArCent), and Chuck Horner (ComUSCentAF). The naval forces were different. For the reader to understand why, we need to relate some history.

Peacetime arrangements for the naval component commander of CentCom were more complex than in other theaters and more complicated than the other service components in CentCom. In the largest unified commands—the Pacific, Atlantic, and European commands—the naval component command had substantial forces assigned to it at all times. Also, the command's primary mission was to support its unified commander. CentCom differed, partly because it had few naval forces permanently assigned. Also, the commander in chief resided in Tampa, Florida, rather than in the theater, where the few permanently assigned naval forces were located.

ComUSNavCent, established in 1983, had a rather small staff and resided in Pearl Harbor. Distance and the time difference between Pearl Harbor and Tampa hampered ComUSNavCent's relationship with USCinCCent. On the other hand, ComUSNavCent had close relations with the Commander in Chief of the Pacific

Fleet (CinCPacFlt), because of physical proximity—ComUSNavCent shared the CinCPacFlt headquarters building on the rim of Makalapa crater—and because ComUSNavCent drew much of its logistics support and many of its forces from CinCPacFlt. As a matter of fact, the first ComUSNavCent, Rear Admiral Stanley "Stan" Arthur, USN, whom the reader will meet again, served simultaneously as the CinCPacFlt Plans Officer during his first year as ComUSNavCent.

In August of 1990, Captain Robert "Bob" Sutton, USN, still a captain but selected as a one-star rear admiral (that is, in the lower half of the rear admiral seniority list), served as ComUSNavCent. Critics charge that the Navy never took CentCom seriously: the Navy assigned a one-star flag officer as the component commander to USCinCCent, whereas the Army and Air Force assigned three-star general officers as component commanders, and the Marine component commander was normally a two-star general. The Navy's long involvement in the Persian Gulf suggests, however, that the situation might be more complex. In any case, a higher-ranking Navy officer was in the theater.

Rear Admiral William "Bill" Fogarty, USN, a two-star rear admiral (that is, in the upper half of the seniority list), commanded both the Middle East Force and the Joint Task Force Middle East (JTFME). The Middle East Force had represented American interests in the Persian Gulf since 1948, operating under its current name since 16 August 1949. In 1990 the Middle East Force typically consisted of five surface combatants plus Fogarty's flagship, the USS *LaSalle* (AGF 3). The flagship spent most of its time at the Mina Sulman pier in Manama, Bahrain. She was painted white, rather than standard Navy gray, to reflect the intense sunlight of the region and so reduce interior temperatures.

On 21 August 1987, to control the expanding force—including non-Navy elements—sent to the Persian Gulf to escort reflagged Kuwaiti tankers in the Persian Gulf (Operation Earnest Will), USCinCCent had established the JTFME. Although the JTFME was designated as a joint task force, in fact Navy officers dominated the staff. The deputy commander was an Air Force officer (Brigadier General Buster C. Glosson, USAF), but of the thirty-six officers on the July 1990 staff roster, twenty-five were Navy, four were Marine Corps, one Army, five Air Force, and one was Coast Guard.

The first USCinCCent Operation Order for Operation Desert Shield, issued on 10 August 1990, reflected the preexisting structure in that it assigned some naval tasks to Commander, U.S. Naval Forces Central Command in Pearl Harbor (Rear Admiral [Select] Sutton—selected for flag rank but not formally promoted) and some to Commander, Joint Task Force Middle East (Rear Admiral Fogarty). Most likely, however, Schwarzkopf had already decided to do things differently.

Just after King Fahd agreed, on 6 August, to accept American forces to defend Saudi Arabia, General Schwarzkopf and some of his subordinates, including Lt. Gen. Chuck Horner and Lt. Gen. John Yeosock, met in Schwarzkopf's hotel room in Jedda. Schwarzkopf's Plans Officer, Rear Admiral Grant Sharp, USN, advised him to have a fleet commander—that is, a Navy three-star admiral—assigned to

CentCom to control the extensive naval forces that would deploy. Shortly thereafter, Schwarzkopf called Admiral Huntington "Hunt" Hardisty, USN, the unified commander of the Pacific region, USCinCPac, to ask his advice on who should command the naval forces in CentCom. After some discussion of the needs and magnitude of the job, they agreed that Schwarzkopf needed a commander of a "numbered" fleet (for instance, Seventh or Sixth) and his staff. But which numbered fleet commander?

ALTERNATIVES FOR COMUSNAVCENT

Admiral Hardisty considered both of the numbered fleet commanders in the Pacific Command: Vice Admiral James "Yank" Dorsey, USN, commander of the Third Fleet (ComThirdFlt) in the eastern Pacific, and Vice Admiral Henry H. "Hank" Mauz, Jr., USN, commander of the Seventh Fleet (ComSeventhFlt), based in Yokosuka, Japan.[1] Several obvious factors favored choosing the commander of the Seventh Fleet. ComSeventhFlt was generally considered to be a warfighter, while ComThirdFlt was regarded as primarily a trainer. During the 1980s, Seventh Fleet had provided forces in support of USCinCCent. Thus, Hardisty felt that ComSeventhFlt and his staff would be operationally more current in the area. Also, the fact that the Seventh Fleet area of responsibility already extended westward across the Indian Ocean to the east coast of Africa would minimize coordination problems.

On the other hand, Seventh Fleet had long-term commitments in northeast Asia that were important to the national interest. For example, its flagship, the USS *Blue Ridge* (LCC 19), was scheduled for a historic port visit to Vladivostok, in the Soviet Far East, in mid-September. Not many things could be more important than improving relations with the Soviet Union. Korea was unsettled and a potential hot spot—especially if the United States left a power vacuum in the area. Was dealing with Saddam Hussein more important than having the Seventh Fleet flagship visit the Soviet Union and otherwise represent U.S. interests in the western Pacific?

Hardisty considered choosing Yank Dorsey and the Third Fleet staff, because that might be less disruptive than choosing ComSeventhFlt. Hardisty considered Dorsey and his staff capable of handling the warfighting job. The primary argument in favor of choosing ComThirdFlt was the lack of political repercussions from Japan and Korea. Though ComThirdFlt and his staff were not as familiar with the Middle East as was ComSeventhFlt, Hardisty believed they could be brought up to speed in a few months.

As will be apparent throughout our narrative, the Navy was always thinking of the long-term problem of sustaining forces in place. Hardisty believed they might be looking at a two-year effort. Thus, he had not only to think about whom to send now but to think ahead to decide which fleet staff he would send as a relief in about six months (the normal length of a Navy deployment), and again six months after

Vice Admiral Hank Mauz. For most of Desert Shield (up to December 1990)
Mauz was Commander, U.S. Naval Forces Central Command and Commander, Seventh Fleet. Navy Photo.

that. After considering the alternatives, Hardisty decided to recommend Mauz and
tentatively planned for ComThirdFlt to relieve ComSeventhFlt after about six
months. Hardisty talked to Admiral Frank Kelso II, USN, Chief of Naval Operations, who agreed with Hardisty's choice of ComSeventhFlt.[2]

Hardisty recommended Hank Mauz and the ComSeventhFlt staff to Schwarzkopf, who approved the choice. Officially, Schwarzkopf had to request Mauz and
his staff from the Chairman of the Joint Chiefs, who in turn would present the
request to the secretary of defense, who would then order USCinCPac (Hardisty)
to deploy Mauz to CentCom. Actually, as we have seen, Schwarzkopf had gone
directly to Hardisty for advice. Schwarzkopf then conveyed this choice to Gen.
Colin Powell, who agreed and said he would clear it with the secretary of defense.
It took a few days for CJCS to send a message to USCinCPac and make it official.

VICE ADMIRAL HANK MAUZ

In Yokosuka, Japan, Vice Admiral Mauz got the first indications that he might
become involved on Wednesday, the 8th of August. Admiral Charles "Chuck"
Larson, USN, CinCPacFlt, called Mauz to tell him he might be chosen as Com-

USNavCent.[3] The same day, Mauz got a second call saying "probably not." Then, on the 10th, Larson told Mauz he was likely to be selected and should start packing. Many on the Seventh Fleet staff cancelled their plans to climb Mount Fuji that weekend. On Sunday, 12 August, CinCPacFlt ordered ComSeventhFlt to deploy Mauz's flagship, the *Blue Ridge,* to the edge of CentCom's area of responsibility, but he could not order either the flagship or Mauz into CentCom's area.

Mauz wanted to fly to the Persian Gulf immediately, but Hardisty did not want Mauz to enter the CentCom area of responsibility until the Joint Chiefs of Staff sent a hard-copy message to make his appointment official. It would be highly embarrassing if Mauz showed up in CentCom only to find out someone had changed his mind. But Mauz, not a patient man, was understandably anxious to get going. Finally, probably in response to a phone call saying the message was on its way, Hardisty agreed Mauz could fly to Diego Garcia and wait there for it.

Mauz's first decision was to take a small battle staff with him to Bahrain in *Peter Rabbit,* his VIP-configured P-3 Orion maritime patrol aircraft (a descendant of the four-engine, propeller-driven Lockheed Electra passenger aircraft).[4] The number of people that could accompany Mauz was limited by the number that *Peter Rabbit* could carry. The rest of the staff would ride the *Blue Ridge* to the Persian Gulf, a journey that would take about three weeks. While en route, without the distraction of having to deal with day-to-day crises, Mauz's Chief of Staff, Captain Bernard "Bernie" Smith, USN, and many of the key staff members, such as the Operations Officer, Captain Robert L. "Bunky" Johnson, Jr., USN, would concentrate on long-range planning for the employment of the naval forces in Desert Shield. Mauz, with his small battle staff, would deal with the expected daily crises and find out what needed to be done. They would stay temporarily on Rear Admiral Fogarty's ComMidEastFor flagship, the *LaSalle.*

On Monday, 13 August, Mauz flew to Diego Garcia in *Peter Rabbit.* Meanwhile, back in Yokosuka, the *Blue Ridge* was a beehive of activity. First, the crew wanted to take care of personal concerns before leaving suddenly on a trip of indefinite duration: things like updating wills and providing powers of attorney to spouses. Also, the *Blue Ridge* had been undergoing maintenance; her boilers were partially dismantled. All day on Monday, 13 August, part of the *Blue Ridge*'s crew reassembled her boilers, while others loaded supplies for a deployment of indeterminate length. Load after load of supplies stacked up on the pier.

After a flight of about ten hours, Mauz arrived in Diego Garcia to spend the night. Although he wanted to fly on to Bahrain early the next day, he was forced to cool his heels in Diego Garcia for twenty-four hours. At last, Hardisty allowed Mauz to continue his journey.[5] When Mauz arrived in Bahrain he intended to spend a day or two looking things over before taking the reins of command from Bill Fogarty. This was not to be.

As soon as Mauz stepped off *Peter Rabbit* onto the tarmac of Bahrain airport on 15 August, he was handed a message from General Schwarzkopf that told him to assume his duties as ComUSNavCent *immediately* upon arrival in Bahrain and take operational control of all U.S. naval forces assigned to USCinCCent.

Schwarzkopf, who would not arrive in-theater for nearly two more weeks, followed this with a more complete message that made the scope of Mauz's authority clear: he would command all assigned naval and sealift forces in CentCom. As Mauz had requested, CJTFME would revert to Commander, Middle East Force, and be under his operational control. The message also assigned Mauz all the mission tasks previously assigned to CJTFME and ComUSNavCent Pearl Harbor (as listed in chapter 1).

What was the background of this person now in charge of all the naval forces afloat? Henry H. Mauz, Jr., had graduated from the U.S. Naval Academy in 1959 and had later earned a postgraduate degree in electrical engineering and a master's degree in business administration. As a junior officer, he had served in destroyers and led river patrol boats in Vietnam. He had commanded an oceangoing minesweeper, the guided-missile destroyer USS *Semmes* (DDG 18), and the guided-missile cruiser USS *England* (CG 22). As a flag officer, he had commanded the USS *America* (CV 66) battle group and Battle Force Sixth Fleet in the Mediterranean during the 1986 air strikes against Libya. But what kind of person was Mauz? Different people saw him in different ways.

Mauz himself thought he was probably as "joint" as any flag officer—he was a graduate of the U.S. Air Command and Staff College, had two tours in NATO Europe (Brussels), and then had begun his first flag tour as Chief of the Operations/Readiness Branch at Supreme Headquarters Allied Powers Europe (SHAPE). He also thought he knew more about carrier operations than any other non-aviator flag officer—he had been Chief of Staff of Commander, Carrier Group One, aboard the USS *Coral Sea* (CV 43), then had commanded the *America* battle group. He saw himself as a "details guy" who enjoyed rolling up his sleeves and delving into minutiae; in practice he tried to resist this impulse every day, because he thought he had a good staff and needed to stay focused on three-star-level issues.

Commander Thomas "Tom" Connelly, USN, the Seventh Fleet Judge Advocate, thought Mauz was brilliant and had a near-photographic memory. According to Connelly, Mauz was a "linear thinker" who could take a stack of documents and read through the pile, making a decision on each document before proceeding to the next one.

Still another side of this complex man is illustrated by his use of his personal resources for the benefit of others. Auditing the account used for receptions and other official entertaining, Connelly noticed that very little money had been spent on Seventh Fleet functions and questioned whether that could possibly be correct. Mauz replied that so little money was allocated for receptions and entertainment that in order to have some available when a ship requested a few dollars to hold a reception for foreign naval officers, he paid for some ComSeventhFlt receptions out of his own pocket, so that they could be done properly. Mauz also routinely bought "official" gifts for foreign dignitaries. He did all this quietly, with most of the staff never realizing that he was paying for it personally.

At least one sailor thought Mauz, more than any other admiral in the Navy, cared about the common sailors. Years after Mauz left Seventh Fleet, this sailor, who had served on the *Blue Ridge,* still remembered how Mauz once had gone down to the mess deck (where the crew ate meals), stood behind the steam table, and dished out mashed potatoes to the sailors. When presented with a staff proposal for a ship's schedule, Mauz invariably asked, "Does this meet the happy-sailor criterion?" By that, he meant that he wanted every ship on a six-month deployment to visit a port that the junior sailors would find entertaining at prices they could afford. Thus, Singapore was fine for the officers but too expensive for the enlisted people.

Many thought Mauz discouraged people from telling him bad news; he had a reputation for "killing the messenger." Yet, when the author, as the Center for Naval Analyses representative on Mauz's staff, paid his reporting-in call on him, Mauz's parting comment was that one of the author's duties was to "tell the emperor when he doesn't have any clothes." When confronted with something he didn't want to hear, Mauz sometimes responded "Bullshit!" and conveyed an attitude that discouraged dissent; yet a few days later, he could forcefully argue the point he had rejected so emphatically.

During the long months the staff spent in the Persian Gulf, Mauz would play bridge for an hour or so a few nights a week. Staff gossip held that the admiral won every time, because the game always continued until he was ahead—and besides, Mauz kept score. It was true that Mauz rarely lost, and he did keep score, but the author never detected a single error. Mauz had an extremely fine ability to visualize the hands that he couldn't see. Also, he usually got the best achievable result from the cards that he played. He played quickly and had little patience with those who played slowly.

Mauz seldom showed mercy toward those who played poorly. Once during the previous summer one of his old friends, an extremely successful lawyer holding a prestigious position, had joined the game for a few nights. Unfortunately, this lawyer's many talents did not include playing bridge well. For months afterwards the staff would chortle, remembering the admiral repeatedly admonishing his friend to "get them puppies off the street" when the distinguished lawyer once again failed to draw trumps.

To Lieutenant Steve Hardgrave, USN, Assistant Logistics Officer on the staff, Mauz was someone on whom you could play a joke. Once during the *Blue Ridge's* stay in Bahrain, Captain James C. "Cutler" Dawson, USN, the ComUSNavCent Plans Officer, went to one of the stalls in the Manama *suq* (market area) and bought a rug that depicted dogs playing pool. One night Hardgrave sneaked into Mauz's cabin (which also served as his office) and substituted this rug for the rather expensive Persian rug Mauz had recently purchased. Mauz laughed when he saw the rug and pointed it out to visitors for the next several days.

Mauz had a knack for discovering things people did not want him to see. All numbered fleet commanders like to visit ships during exercises to judge their states of readiness. During the Team Spirit exercise in the spring of 1990, Mauz had visited a cruiser during an antisubmarine warfare event. This multipurpose ship could contribute to a variety of missions but is generally considered an antiair warfare asset because of its extremely sophisticated Aegis combat direction system. As usual, the ship's officers planned a tour to show him everything they considered important. In the midst of the tour, Mauz asked why they didn't go down a particular passageway; the tour guide explained to the admiral that the planned tour did not include that area. Mauz insisted, went down the passageway, and wandered into the sonar room. He asked the men there how things were going, and they replied "great." Mauz asked whether they were finding any submarines; the answer was a somewhat subdued, "Well-l-l, no." "Why not?" Mauz then asked. A few more questions determined that the sonar had been shut down so that technicians could conduct preventive maintenance that was done every thirty days. Conducting preventive maintenance during a submarine vulnerability period meant that the crew would not get the advantage of one of its all-too-few training opportunities. This sent a message that the commanding officer of the ship did not consider antisubmarine warfare to be very important. The commanding officer soon learned that Mauz considered antisubmarine warfare to be quite important.

Mauz was tactically aggressive. While Deputy Chief of Staff for Operations and Plans at the headquarters of the Pacific Fleet, Mauz commanded the "Blue" (U.S.) side in many war games examining a global war against the Soviet Union. He always sought to seize the initiative. He constantly argued against imagining the enemy to be "ten feet tall." For example, during the war games he always moved the Pacific Fleet's carriers forward early in the war, even into the Sea of Japan, so he could strike the enemy, although this exposed the carriers to attack. As we shall see later in our story, Mauz was also willing to go against conventional wisdom and bring a carrier into the Persian Gulf.

When Mauz took command, he faced a number of problems. Before we examine these problems, let us describe some of the U.S. Navy's prior involvement in the area.

PREVIOUS NAVAL INTERACTIONS IN THE MIDDLE EAST

To understand some of what the naval forces did during Desert Shield and Desert Storm, one must understand previous events involving the United States, Iraq, and Iran. Iran in particular had many reasons to hate the United States, and thus the United States had good reason to fear suicide attacks from Iran. Iraq, on the other hand, might well have believed that it could take on the United States Navy and come out on top. Therefore, let us review some of the salient events involving the Navy in the Middle East over the previous decade.

- On 24 April 1980, helicopters took off from the USS *Nimitz* (CVN 68), operating in the North Arabian Sea, in an unsuccessful attempt to rescue American hostages held by Iran.
- In October 1983, a fanatical suicide bomber killed 241 Marines by driving a truck full of explosives into the Marine barracks in Beirut.
- On 17 May 1987, during the "tanker war" part of the Iran-Iraq War in the Persian Gulf, an Iraqi Mirage F-1 launched two Exocet missiles that struck the frigate USS *Stark* (FFG 31). The missiles badly damaged the *Stark* and killed thirty-seven Americans. Evidently the Iraqis were trying to attack an Iranian tanker. In part because the *Stark* did not expect the Iraqis to be trying to attack a U.S. ship, she did not react as quickly as one might have hoped.
- From July 1987 to December 1988, U.S. ships escorted reflagged Kuwaiti tankers to protect them from attack by Iran (Operation Earnest Will).
- On 21 September 1987, U.S. Army OH-58D helicopters flying from the frigate USS *Jarrett* (FFG 33) caught the *Iran Ajr* laying mines in the shipping channel off the coast of Bahrain and attacked it with rockets. U.S. Navy Special Operations forces (SEALs) boarded the vessel and photographed the evidence.[6]
- On 8 October, Army helicopters operating off Navy ships responded to Iranian fire from four speedboats by attacking them—sinking one and capturing two.
- U.S. Navy forces attacked two Iranian oil platforms used as military outposts.
- On 12 February 1988, an Iraqi aircraft attacked the destroyer USS *Chandler* (DDG 996), evidently by mistake. There was no damage.
- On 14 April 1988, the frigate USS *Samuel B Roberts* (FFG 58) hit a mine, suffered severe damage; several men were injured. The United States was convinced that Iran had laid the mines.
- On 22 April 1988, the United States retaliated for the mining of the *Samuel B Roberts* with Operation Praying Mantis. During a series of engagements, U.S. naval forces neutralized two gas-oil separation platforms manned by Iranian forces and used to coordinate attacks against merchant ships. Navy aircraft attacked Iranian Boghammar speedboats. When the Iranian ships fired missiles at U.S. ships and aircraft, U.S. forces sank two Iranian ships and left a third dead in the water.
- On 3 July 1988, the Aegis cruiser USS *Vincennes* (CG 49), believing she was about to be attacked, shot down an Iranian civilian airbus, killing 290 people.

Each of the three countries—Iran, Iraq, and the United States—undoubtedly learned something from these incidents. The airbus incident almost certainly intensified the Iranians' hatred of Americans—and the U.S. Navy in particular. The Iranians had previously demonstrated their willingness to do things Americans considered foolhardy. The fear that some crazed Iranian fanatic or bereaved relative of an airbus victim would attempt a suicide mission against the U.S. Navy underlay many NavCent plans and actions during Desert Shield and Desert Storm. On the positive side, the Iranians should have been impressed, and ideally deterred, by the capabilities demonstrated by the U.S. Navy. The Iraqis, on the other hand, had had fewer interactions and may not have been so impressed by the American capabilities, especially in the case of the *Stark*. They probably also noticed that mines caused the Americans serious problems. For its part, the U.S.

Navy had learned that many of its weapon systems and tactics worked quite well. The reader will again encounter many of these ships, weapons, and tactics in our discussion of Desert Shield and Storm. Finally, the U.S. Navy came away with a determination never again to be caught by surprise like the *Stark*.

PRIMARY CONCERNS OF THE NAVAL FORCES AFLOAT

Iraqi Threat

First, the naval forces afloat were concerned about the Iraqi threat. Certainly, the Navy had confidence that unless caught by surprise, it could win most tactical battles by making any attacker pay a high price for an attack against a U.S. Navy ship. But the Navy realized that in the political arena, if an enemy could damage a U.S. ship and kill a substantial number of sailors, he would claim a political victory. Also, one of the primary arrows in the defense's quiver is that a strong defense usually does not have to destroy every single attacker; killing a few usually causes the remaining attackers to turn around without pressing their attack vigorously. But this defense does not work against missiles; nor does it work against suicidal fanatics. Thus, the defense has to be nearly perfect—an exceedingly difficult task.

Here are some highlights of the types of threats Iraq could array against the U.S. Navy:

* Aircraft capable of firing antiship missiles.
* Silkworm antiship missiles fired from ground launchers.
* Patrol boats capable of firing antiship missiles.
* Suicidal attacks by aircraft or boats.
* Mines.
* Terrorists.
* Chemical attack—In the Iran-Iraq War, Iraq had used nerve agents (tabun, sarin, and GF), as well as the blister agent mustard, and was thought to be developing persistent and semipersistent nerve agents and a hallucinogen.
* Biological attack—Intelligence assessed Iraq as having anthrax and botulin toxin and the technological ability to develop the use of these agents as weapons.

Immediate Tasks for Naval Forces

Vice Admiral Mauz's message to General Schwarzkopf on his first full day in-theater reveals that three tasks were uppermost in his mind—enforcing the sanctions, conducting area defense of the Persian Gulf, and bombing the Iraqis if they attacked. These three areas of potential contribution to the USCinCCent strategy tie in with three of the four major task areas assigned to ComUSNavCent early in Desert Shield. Soon the fourth area, amphibious operations, would come to the fore.

Enforcement of economic sanctions would prevent Iraq from obtaining supplies or equipment by sea. In addition, Iraq's only significant export, oil, could be shipped in large quantities only by sea or pipeline. Preventing the export of oil could keep Iraq from earning the foreign exchange necessary to buy military equipment that might be shipped over land. Enforcement of UN sanctions also had an important subsidiary effect—it lent legitimacy to American actions and thus helped form the coalition. (Chapters 3 and 4 describe the initial stages of the maritime interception operations to enforce the UN sanctions.)

Effective air defense and control of the sea would allow unhampered deployment and supply of U.S. and coalition forces. That such control is usually taken for granted does not make it less valuable. Although the airlift brought a great many troops to the area quickly, 85 to 95 percent of the tonnage sent to the theater arrived by sea. Finally, control of the air over the Persian Gulf and Red Sea could provide air defense for the flanks of the forces in Saudi Arabia. (Chapter 5 recounts the initial arrangements for air defense.)

If Iraq invaded Saudi Arabia, both carrier-based U.S. Navy aircraft and ground-based Marine aircraft could provide close air support. Gunfire from ships could provide heavy artillery support near the coast. (Chapter 5 relates initial plans for close air support.)

Finally, control of the sea would enable the United States to threaten or execute an amphibious landing in the rear of Iraqi troops advancing south into Saudi Arabia. (Chapter 6 discusses early developments in this area.)

To carry out these tasks, ComUSNavCent would use the following forces in-theater or en route as of 16 August:

- The Middle East Force in the Persian Gulf, commanded by Rear Admiral Bill Fogarty
- The *Independence* battle group in the North Arabian Sea, commanded by Rear Admiral Jerry Unruh
- The *Eisenhower* battle group in the northern Red Sea, commanded by Rear Admiral Thomas "Tom" Lynch, USN
- The *Saratoga* (CV 60) battle group, commanded by Rear Admiral George N. "Nick" Gee, USN, which would relieve or join the *Eisenhower* battle group
- Maritime patrol aircraft operating out of Masira, Oman
- The battleship USS *Wisconsin* (BB 64), commanded by Captain David Bill III, USN
- Amphibious Group Two (PhibGru Two), commanded by Rear Admiral John "Bat" LaPlante, USN, consisting of thirteen ships with the 4th Marine Expeditionary Brigade (4th MEB), commanded by Major General Harry W. Jenkins, Jr., USMC, embarked
- Mine countermeasures ships and helicopters
- Maritime Prepositioning Squadron 2, with four ships from Diego Garcia unloading at al-Jubail with equipment and supplies for 7th Maritime Expeditionary Brigade (7th MEB)
- Maritime Prepositioning Squadron 3, with four ships from Guam en route to al-Jubail with equipment for 1st Maritime Expeditionary Brigade (1st MEB)
- Two hospital ships: the USNS *Mercy* (T-AH 19) and USNS *Comfort* (T-AH 20).

KEY DECISIONS AFFECTING THE NAVAL FORCES

One of the objectives of this book is to highlight decisions, whether made by a naval commander or someone else, that had major impact on naval operations. We point out how some decisions worked out well or poorly, often for totally unanticipated reasons. We attempt to distinguish clearly information known at the time from facts that came to light later, and we try to judge a decision maker solely on the knowledge available to him at the time. During the period up to 17 September 1990, key decisions affecting the naval forces included:

- Location of headquarters for ComUSNavCent (discussed below)
- Basic organizational structure (discussed below)
- Amount of force to use in enforcing UN sanctions (chapters 3 and 4)
- USCinCCent's decision to appoint a Joint Force Air Component Commander with broad powers, and his decision to use an Air Tasking Order (chapter 5)
- USCinCCent's decision to restrict U.S. naval forces from going into the northern Persian Gulf (chapter 6).

Location of ComUSNavCent Headquarters

Vice Admiral Mauz decided to locate his headquarters on board a ship based in Bahrain—initially the *LaSalle*, later the *Blue Ridge,* when she arrived on 1 September. This decision has been widely criticized. As with all decisions, identifying the relevant circumstances at the time of the decision is crucial to understanding. Locating ComUSNavCent headquarters on a flagship provided instant communications, a command center, berthing, and office space. This choice kept ComUS-NavCent and his staff close to the fleet to provide leadership and to gauge the state of things in the area where battles might be fought. On the other hand, locating ComUSNavCent headquarters in Riyadh would have, first, maximized the ability to advise General Schwarzkopf on the best employment of the naval forces and, second, allowed frequent face-to-face interactions between the ComUSNavCent staff and other staffs. Lack of an adequate deployable communications suite, however, might have made such a location difficult (some say impossible).

The various actors had different ideas about what the ComUSNavCent staff would do, but the author has located no evidence that anyone said *at the time the decision was made* ComUSNavCent should be located in Riyadh. At the time Schwarzkopf was not in the theater, and the ComUSNavCent staff had only "guesstimates" as to when he might come. Rear Admiral Sharp (Schwarzkopf's Plans Officer) has said he knew of no discussion about having the fleet commander anywhere but on a ship. Mauz, Hardisty, and Sharp all agreed that putting a Navy flag officer in Riyadh as liaison for ComUSNavCent was an obvious thing to do. All realized there would be coordination problems but deemed the presence of a Navy flag-level (one or two-star) liaison officer sufficient to solve the problem.[7] Mauz decided to stay on a ship rather than go to Riyadh, and Schwarzkopf did not disagree.[8]

After the war, Mauz said he felt that locating his headquarters in Riyadh would have removed the fleet commander from his communications and his forces. He questioned how he could have conducted training, for example, if he had been distant from the fleet and could not talk to his forces. As for communications with USCinCCent, Mauz reported that initially he talked to General Schwarzkopf several times a day.

CinCPacFlt ordered Rear Admiral Timothy W. "Tim" Wright, USN, the commander of Carrier Group Three, to deploy to Riyadh for approximately ninety days for duty as Mauz's representative in Riyadh. Contacted on a trip across the United States with his wife, Wright was told almost nothing about his mission except that a Navy admiral was needed in Riyadh. Wright decided to take six of his staff members with him. They left Alameda, California, on 16 August and flew to Riyadh, arriving late on the 17th. Wright, a one-star admiral and an experienced naval aviator, would represent NavCent's interests in Riyadh at the flag level. Mauz designated Wright's organization as NavCent-Riyadh.[9] In addition, Captain Ray "Sully" Sullivan, USN, and his Fleet Coordination Group, from Seventh Fleet, went to Riyadh to coordinate the details of daily air operations with JFACC. This group had considerable experience coordinating Navy and Air Force air operations in Japan and Korea.

Thus, Mauz could rely on two experienced people and their staffs to represent NavCent's interests to CinCCent and JFACC. Several very smart and experienced people did not predict the way in which the naval operations actually evolved. Mauz evidently did not appreciate that Schwarzkopf's personal style of command meant that a one-star flag officer was in the *outer* circle and not a participant in major decisions. Although Wright saw Schwarzkopf every day in meetings and had a chance to raise issues, he never had a one-on-one session with Schwarzkopf and was not in on key decisions. As the pros and cons of this decision are complex and can best be discussed in view of events that occurred later, we defer full discussion of it to the observations section at the end of Volume II. There we examine in detail the information available at the time, alternatives to the decision, pros and cons of the location chosen, and what happened that caused people to later criticize this decision.

Command-and-Control Organization

Vice Admiral Mauz retained his "hat" as ComSeventhFlt, with an area of responsibility that stretched more than a third of the way around the world, from the east coast of Africa to the middle of the Pacific. In CentCom, Mauz wore two hats: CTF 150 (the fleet commander) and ComUSNavCent, one of the USCinCCent's service component commanders. Under Mauz, the command generally called itself CTF 150 when talking to subordinate commands, to emphasize its warfighting role; when talking to higher authority or other component commanders, the staff would generally use the designator ComUSNavCent. In some theaters, two different people serve as the CinC's service component and the fleet commander. Table 2–1 depicts the organization Mauz chose for his command.[10]

Vice Admiral Mauz had asked General Schwarzkopf to disestablish CJTFME, because it no longer served any useful purpose. With Schwarzkopf directing the overall operation and separate Army, Marine Corps, and Air Force subordinate commands, having a Joint Task Force no longer made sense. Schwarzkopf readily agreed.

Mauz retained the Middle East Force, designated CTG 150.1, for most warfighting functions inside the Persian Gulf. Under this hat, Rear Admiral Fogarty would control only the half-dozen or so ships of the Middle East Force, augmented by the battleship *Wisconsin* when it arrived. Under a second hat, CTG 150.2, Fogarty would be the commander of the U.S. Maritime Interception Force. For this job, his authority would extend outside the Persian Gulf to ships operating in the North Arabian Sea and Red Sea, but only for interception operations. Rear Admiral (Select) Sutton's Naval Logistic Support Force provided naval logistic support throughout the CentCom area of responsibility, medical support, defense of naval facilities ashore (including explosive ordnance disposal, port security and harbor defense, and mobile diving and salvage), mobile sea-based logistics support to ComUSMarCent if required, naval cargo handling, and port group operations. Mauz also tasked Sutton to be prepared to support amphibious operations and joint logistics over the shore.

Mauz designated two carrier task groups, one for the Red Sea and one for the eastern side of the theater. The name given to CTG 150.4—Commander CVBG North Arabian Sea—reveals the usual operating mode, in which carriers stayed out of the Persian Gulf. That would soon change. In the Red Sea, the *Eisenhower* battle group approached the end of its six-month deployment. Unless Iraq attacked, the *Saratoga* battle group would relieve it. In early September, Mauz agreed with the commander of Sixth Fleet to alternate two battle groups on the west side of the theater, with one operating in the Red Sea while the other sailed in the Mediterranean. This would maintain a naval presence in the Mediterranean most of the time as Sixth Fleet wanted, give both battle groups experience in operating in the environment of Desert Shield, and also give the crews a break, with visits to Mediterranean ports. Because the Mediterranean was outside USCinCCent's and ComUSNavCent's area of responsibility, Mauz could not talk directly to the battle group in the Mediterranean without violating the chain of command. Yet he needed to keep the battle group informed of developments. In early September, the European chain of command agreed to allow Mauz to designate the Mediterranean battle group as CTG 150.9 while it was in the Mediterranean so he could talk to it about strike planning and coordination issues.

Mauz might have placed the North Arabian Sea battle group commander in charge of the Amphibious Task Force, but he chose to keep the amphibious ships

Table 2-1
Desert Shield Organization of ComUSNavCent

Command	Task designator	Person	Location
Commander, U.S. Naval Forces Central Command	CTF 150	Vice Adm. Mauz	USS *Blue Ridge*
Command Liaison Group	CTG 150.0	Vice Adm. Mauz	USS *Blue Ridge*
U.S. Naval Forces Central Command Riyadh	CTU 150.0.1	Rear Adm. Wright	Riyadh
U.S. Naval Coordination Group Riyadh	CTU 150.0.2	Capt. Sullivan	Riyadh
Commander, Flagship Unit	CTU 150.0.3	Capt. Henderson	USS *Blue Ridge*
Commander, Middle East Force	CTG 150.1	Rear Adm. Fogarty	USS *LaSalle*
Commander, U.S. Maritime Interception Force	CTG 150.2	Rear Adm. Fogarty	USS *LaSalle*
Commander, U.S. Naval Logistics Support Force	CTG 150.3	Rear Adm. (S) Sutton	Bahrain
Commander, CVBG North Arabian Sea	CTG 150.4	Rear Adm. Unruh	USS *Independence*
Commander, CVBG Red Sea	CTG 150.5	Rear Adm. Lynch later Rear Adm. Gee then Rear Adm. Mixson	USS *Eisenhower* USS *Saratoga* USS *Kennedy*
Commander, U.S. Amphibious Task Force	CTG 150.6	Rear Adm. LaPlante	USS *Nassau*
Commander, U.S. Maritime Prepositioning Force[a]	CTG 150.7	Rear Adm. Clarey	Bahrain
Commander, U.S. Landing Force	CTG 150.8	Maj. Gen. Jenkins	USS *Nassau*
Commander, CVBG Med	CTG 150.9	Various	

Source: ComUSNavCent 171642Z AUG 90, Task Designators.

a. On 12 September, after the MPF ships finished unloading and the USMC Maritime Prepositioning Force (MPF) forces were ashore and established under the operational control of ComUSMarCent, ComUSNavCent disestablished the MPF, CTG 150.7.

as a separate force. CTGs 150.6 and 150.8 constituted the two parts of the amphibious assets: Commander, Amphibious Task Force (CATF), and Commander, Landing Force (CLF, pronounced "Cliff")—a Navy admiral and a Marine general, respectively. They embarked on the same ship, the amphibious assault ship USS *Nassau* (LHA 4), so they could coordinate plans for an amphibious assault. At this time they had just left the United States and would not arrive in-theater for several weeks.

BLUE RIDGE ARRIVES IN-THEATER

When Vice Admiral Mauz departed Japan with his small battle staff to fly to Bahrain, he left the rest of his staff and his flagship behind to join him later. After frantically getting ready to sail all day Monday, 13 August, the *Blue Ridge* sailed from Yokosuka, Japan, on 14 August and headed at high speed for Subic Bay in the Philippines. While en route, her crew prepared to go to war. Gas masks were issued to everyone on the 15th. All personnel were advised to buy long-sleeved shirts (for flash-burn protection) if they did not already have some. After loading more supplies in Subic Bay, the *Blue Ridge* sailed again on 20 August. Before she sailed, eight more staff members were selected to fly to Bahrain and join the admiral.[11]

About noon on 1 September, the *Blue Ridge* arrived at Mina Sulman pier in Manama, Bahrain, after a long journey at high speed. Meanwhile, Mauz had been hosting a congressional delegation on the *LaSalle*. The staff had given the delegation a thorough briefing on the situation, especially on enforcement of the sanctions, and a tour of part of the ship. Congressman Dan Rostenkowski looked out from the flag bridge as the *Blue Ridge* arrived and docked on the opposite side of the pier from the *LaSalle,* with her bow pointing toward the shore. Rostenkowski commented that after Pearl Harbor everyone had questioned why the battleships were pointed the wrong way.[12] Later that day, the battle staff transferred to the *Blue Ridge*.

The next day, Mauz hosted another congressional delegation. Commander Wayne Perras, USN, Mauz's Intelligence Officer, prepared the briefing, but Mauz himself presented it. Captain Dawson, the ComUSNavCent Plans Officer, thought that was a good choice, because Mauz conveyed to the congressmen that the commander of the naval forces knew what he was doing. The congressmen were badly jet-lagged, and the conference room in which this meeting was held was fairly small for the large group of people. It was 107 degrees outside; the conference room, directly beneath the main deck and filled with people, was hot and stuffy. During the briefing, one congressman asked Dawson if there was a latrine on the ship. As Dawson led him down the passageway toward the head, the congressman threw up on Dawson's back. He apologized profusely, cleaned up in the head, and gamely went back into the briefing. Dawson thought this incident was indicative of how important this congressman and the rest of the delegation considered the

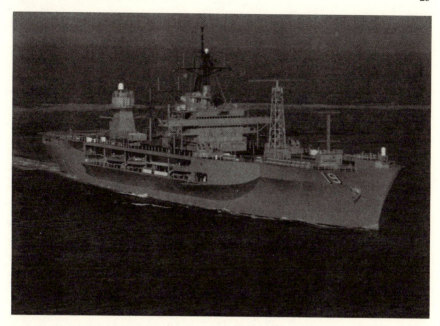

USS *Blue Ridge*. The command ship of U.S. Naval Forces Central Command and Seventh Fleet provided mobile communications, command center, office space, berthing, messing, and a helicopter pad for the admiral and his staff. Navy Photo.

briefing. The delegation seemed impressed that the staff knew what it was doing, particularly with regard to the maritime interception operations.

NOTES

Interviews with participants (including Hardisty, Mauz, Sharp, Kelso, Dawson, Wickersham, and Wright) were the primary sources for events related to the selection of ComUSNavCent and early decisions. Messages were also used. Palmer's books were the primary sources for historic events. The description of Mauz came from his staff and the author's own observations.

1. In the summer of 1990 the unified commander in the Pacific, USCinCPac, commanded naval forces (PacFlt), air forces (PacAF), and Army forces (ArPac). In turn, CinCPacFlt commanded two fleets: Seventh Fleet and Third Fleet. In 1996, USCinCPac would often exercise command by designating the commander of Seventh Fleet to command a Joint Task Force, bypassing CinCPacFlt.

2. Admiral Kelso recalled the choice as being between ComSeventhFlt and ComSixthFlt.

3. CinCPacFlt is the naval component commander under the unified command, USCinCPac, and the common superior of ComThirdFlt and ComSeventhFlt.

4. Seventh Fleet staff members chosen to travel with Mauz included the Plans Officer (Captain James C. "Cutler" Dawson, Jr., USN), who would act as Mauz's Executive Assis-

tant; the Fleet Marine Officer (Colonel Frank Wickersham III, USMC); the Intelligence Officer (Commander Wayne Perras, USN); a strike expert as the Air Operations Officer (Captain R. E. "Bo" Smith, USN); the Judge Advocate, who would be in effect the acting Operations Officer (Commander Thomas "Tom" Connelly, USN); the Communications Officer (Commander James "Jim" Carroll, USN); the staff SEAL (Commander Ed Bowen, USN); the officer who handled air coordination for joint and combined operations (Captain Ray "Sully" Sullivan, USN); an expert on data links (Lt. Commander Keith Adolphson, USN); a strike planner (Commander Stu Ashton, USN); and the Assistant Public Affairs Officer (Lieutenant Kevin Wensing, USN), to act as Mauz's Flag Lieutenant. ComSeventhFlt Battle Staff Organization, Memorandum from Chief of Staff, 12 August 1990.

5. Hardisty later thought he probably received a phone call saying that a hard-copy message was on the way.

6. "SEAL" is an acronym for SEa-Air-Land team.

7. Vice Admiral Dorsey later said he suggested at some point (timing unclear) that he be sent to CentCom to work under Mauz, either as his liaison in Riyadh or as his fleet commander while Mauz was in Riyadh, at Mauz's choice. Private communication with Vice Adm. Yank Dorsey.

8. Wickersham says Mauz and his battle staff discussed the advantages and disadvantages of locating his headquarters in Riyadh, but Dawson later did not remember this.

9. Wright was never NavCent Forward. Rear Admiral Sharp, Schwarzkopf's Plans Officer, was designated ComUSNavCent Forward on 9 August. Sharp never played a significant role in NavCent activities, and the position of ComUSNavCent Forward disappeared when Mauz issued his command organization on 17 August.

10. A message sent nine hours earlier differed in four respects: CTG 150.2 was commander of the Maritime Quarantine Force rather than of the Interception Force; CTG 150.7 was CLF; CTG 150.8 was MPF; CTG 150.9 was Commander, U.S. Maritime Preposition MAGTF.

11. These included the fleet surgeon (Captain Ken Andrus, USN), the Air Force liaison officer on the staff (Lt. Colonel Don Rupert, USAF), an air operations officer (Lt. Commander Mark Suycott, USN), a command-and-control officer (Lt. Commander J. D. Aishman, USN), the civilian Center for Naval Analyses representative on the staff (the author), the assistant logistics officer (Lt. Steve Hardgrave), and a reservist (Commander John Duck, USNR).

12. Actually, the author knows of no one who ever asked that question. Nor does it seem that it would have made any difference, since the USS *Nevada* was the only battleship that managed to get under way that day.

Chapter 3

Sanctions

In addition to deploying military forces to supplement the Middle East Force already present in the Persian Gulf, the United States undertook a parallel effort to implement economic sanctions. On 2 August 1990, President George Bush issued an executive order freezing Iraqi and Kuwaiti assets. On 6 August, the United Nations Security Council passed Resolution 661, which imposed trade and financial sanctions on both Iraq and occupied Kuwait. These sanctions served as a tool to achieve the national policy goals listed in chapter 1.

WHY SANCTIONS?

Historical View of Sanctions

Dating back to the Greeks in 432 BC, sanctions have been a preferred foreign policy tool that demonstrates resolve, deters, and punishes. As an alternative to military force, sanctions provide a country a way to demonstrate its resolve to the target country and to the world. Sanctions also attempt to deter others from future similar behavior. That is, the entire world community witnesses the success or failure of the sanctions as they are used to punish violations of international law or aggression. From the military point of view, sanctions hinder the opposition's ability to obtain additional equipment, supplies, and spare parts for its war effort. A final, unspoken reason for imposing sanctions is that they are politically acceptable and relieve the pressure to take direct military action immediately.

Do sanctions ever work? It depends on the type of behavior to be altered. Hufbauer, Schott, and Elliott, in their comprehensive case study analysis of sanctions, conclude that in the 116 cases they examined from World War I through the Gulf War, 34 percent were successful. An important caveat applies here, however. Their success ratings depend upon the type of behavior to be modified: military operations, political policies, or punishment for a specific incident. As a general rule, the larger and more complicated the dispute, the less likely sanctions were to be successful. Hufbauer and his colleagues estimated that when the goal was to impair military potential or otherwise change an adversary's policies in a major way, sanctions succeeded only about 20 percent of the time, whereas for more modest goals, sanctions proved to be more successful.[1] Unfortunately, the coalition had quite ambitious goals.

Sanctions and Iraq

Many conditions seemed to auger well for the success of the sanctions against Iraq:

- Iraq was in a weak position:
  - Iraq depended heavily on the export of a single commodity—oil—that was in abundant supply from alternative sources and that was bulky, thus requiring it to be exported by ship or pipeline.
  - Iraq needed to import almost all other commodities—food, military spare parts, and technological goods.
  - Iraq had few foreign currency reserves with which to buy needed imports and no source of credit.
  - No "black knight" stood ready and willing to help.[2] Iraq could count only on "black pawns," such as Jordan. They could help, but not significantly.
  - Iraq had little time to learn evasion techniques or to mobilize domestic support, because the United States and the UN implemented sanctions quickly (including freezing Iraqi assets).
  - The sanctions comprehensively covered imports and exports, financial aid (official and private credit sources), and services.
- The coalition held a strong position:
  - The majority of the world supported the sanctions.
  - Cutting off oil imports from Iraq would not hurt the coalition, because of available alternative supplies.
  - Cutting off exports to Iraq would have minimal impact on the coalition, because they were only a small portion of coalition exports.

On the other hand, some factors cast doubt on whether sanctions would succeed:

- The coalition was asking for severe modifications in Iraq's behavior—the unconditional withdrawal from Kuwait would be humiliating for Saddam Hussein and might cause him to fall from power.
- Iraq was not a U.S. ally, and it is traditionally harder to alter the behavior of an unfriendly nation.
- Iraq had some resources:
  - Iraq had several possible "black pawns" to assist it in evading sanctions. Jordan, Iran, and Turkey all share long borders with Iraq.

- Iraq had managed to steal from Kuwait an estimated one-half billion dollars in gold and hard currency.[3]
- The United States needed to hold the coalition together for an extended period of time, which, given the group's diversity, would not be an easy task.[4]
- The leaders of Iraq seemed unlikely to be moved by the suffering of the Iraqi people.

The situation had certain aspects of an irresistible force applied to an immovable object. Many factors strongly favored the success of the sanctions. Considering the severe alteration in Iraq's behavior the world was demanding, however, it should not be surprising that the sanctions failed to force Iraq out of Kuwait. Nonetheless, because Iraq had so many factors going against it, Hufbauer and colleagues predicted in December 1990 that sanctions backed by the threat of military action would persuade Iraq to leave Kuwait.[5]

ENFORCING SANCTIONS

Overall, one could reasonably hope that the sanctions would be successful. ComUSNavCent's role was to enforce sanctions at sea and do so in such a manner as to build and maintain the coalition. At this time, the Iraqi merchant fleet consisted of about forty-two ships, twenty of which were tankers.

Iraq, almost landlocked, possesses only three ports—Basra (the principal port), Umm Qasr, and Khor al-Zubair—as shown in Figure 3–1. In addition, Iraq has three crude-oil loading terminals—al-Faw, Khor al-Amaya, and Mina al-Bakr—in the far northern Persian Gulf. The only access to these Persian Gulf facilities from the North Arabian Sea and Indian Ocean passes through the Strait of Hormuz. In addition to exporting oil by sea, Iraq at the time used pipelines through Saudi Arabia and Turkey. Iraq obtained many of her much-needed imports by transshipping them through Jordan's port of Aqaba, at the end of the Gulf of Aqaba, an arm of the Red Sea. Given the geography, two natural chokepoints affect Iraqi sea trade—the Strait of Hormuz and the Strait of Tiran leading into the Gulf of Aqaba.

Iraq should have been a relatively easy target for enforcement. The majority of UN member states supported the UN sanctions against Iraq. In particular, Saudi Arabia and Turkey shut down the pipelines; even Jordan agreed to support the sanctions (as long as they did not interfere with its trade). Normally, each country is responsible for ensuring that its citizens do not trade with the target country. Because oil is fungible and easily transferred, however, a single renegade country can break the sanctions on exports. To counter this possibility, the United States wanted to be aggressive and act quickly to enforce the sanctions with military force. The United States believed it had the right to do so under Article 51 of the UN Charter and, specifically for this crisis, UN Security Council Resolution 661. Other countries, especially the Soviet Union, did not consider Article 51 sufficient. They wanted to wait and see whether sanctions would work without the use of force. If voluntary compliance did not work, the UN could explicitly authorize

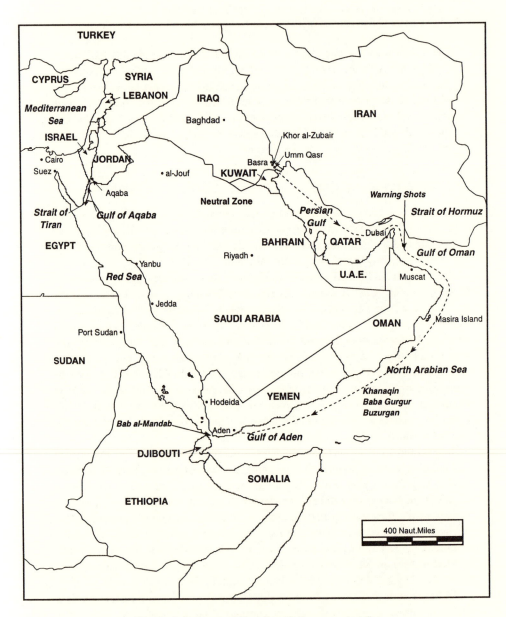

Figure 3–1. Areas of Sanction Enforcement at Sea

the use of force. Despite this opposition, the United States decided to go ahead. It was now up to ComUSNavCent to enforce the sanctions at sea and simultaneously sustain the growing coalition.

OPERATION ORDERS

On 11 August 1990, the Chairman of the Joint Chiefs of Staff (CJCS), Gen. Colin Powell, issued the Alert Order for a maritime interdiction operation to enforce an economic quarantine on Iraq. Three important points in this message were:

[For] all ships perceived to be proceeding to Iraq or an Iraqi-controlled port or trans-shipment points to Iraq or Iraqi-controlled ports, or carrying prohibited material from Iraq or an Iraqi-controlled port, a visit and search will be made to verify the perception.

Ships which, after being intercepted, signal their intention to proceed to ports in nations which do not support Iraq may be released without visit or search.

Empty vessels proceeding to Iraq or an Iraqi-controlled port will be diverted.[6]

The first CJCS Execute Order directed that the Maritime Quarantine Force Operations begin on 16 August 1990. A second CJCS Execute Order replaced the word "quarantine" with "interception" and changed the name of the operation to the Maritime Interception Force Operation. It also delayed enforcement of the sanctions for twenty-four hours. The words were altered because of the belligerent connotation of terms such as "quarantine" and "embargo." The use of other terms, such as "blockade," was a concern as well. Whereas a blockade is "a belligerent act which could involve the deliberate and unprovoked capture and even destruction of ships running the blockade," interception means "diverting ships" found to be or believed to be violating the sanctions. Therefore, the term "blockade" was not used.

The USCinCCent Operation Order authorized the use of force to enforce maritime interception operations against designated units.

With regard to the multinational coalition, the naval forces from other countries that participated would operate under their national commands. Australia, Canada, the United Kingdom, the Netherlands, Pakistan, and France were dispatching forces but had not yet committed themselves to participating.

Vice Adm. Hank Mauz, ComUSNavCent, might have kept direct control of the maritime interception operations for himself, but as it was expected to require a great deal of coordination, he decided to let Rear Adm. Bill Fogarty, ComMidEastFor, and his staff handle the details. This would allow Mauz to concentrate more on warfighting.

Fogarty had two hats. As CTG 150.1, he commanded the Middle East Force of about half a dozen ships inside the Persian Gulf; as CTG 150.2, he commanded U.S. maritime interception operations throughout the theater. For interception operations inside the Persian Gulf, Fogarty could use the forces assigned to him as CTG 150.1. For operations outside the Persian Gulf, he would use forces permanently assigned to the Red Sea and North Arabian Sea battle groups. Each battle group would typically assign two ships on a rotating basis to Fogarty's tactical control for interception operations, but the ships would still report to the battle group commander for other warfare tasks. The full power of the battle group would be available for contingencies. If Fogarty and the battle group commander could not agree on the details, Mauz would adjudicate the dispute. (This never became necessary.) One person in each battle group, typically the attached destroyer squadron commander, was designated as a local Maritime Interception Force commander, who reported to Fogarty for interception operations and continued to report to the battle group commander for other operations. This seemingly convoluted command-and-control setup is fairly standard for the Navy and worked well during Desert Shield and Storm.

A Commander Middle East Force (ComMidEastFor) Operation Order went into further detail, supplying the exact wording and sequence of events for communicating with suspect vessels. The original ComMidEastFor Operation Order, dated 17 August, established the patrol areas and the details of how to intercept vessels and to determine whether a visit and search was required. The first communication with a suspect ship would announce that the "U.S. intends to exercise its right to conduct a visit and search of your vessel under international law." The American ship would then request that the suspect vessel stop immediately and prepare to receive an inspection team. If the vessel refused to comply, the U.S. ship was to use warning shots. Authorization for warning shots had to come from ComMidEastFor, Rear Admiral Fogarty. If the situation required immediate action, however, the on-scene commander was authorized to use "warning shots/minimum force." The phrase "disabling fire" was not used. If, on the other hand, the ship agreed to stop, the U.S. ship was to respond with questions about her port of origin, destination, and cargo. In later versions of the Operation Order, these questions came first, to determine whether a visit and search was required.

Because of Iraq's geographic location and its dependence on the port of Aqaba, Jordan, ComMidEastFor established patrol areas in the northern Red Sea to monitor activity in the Strait of Tiran. ComMidEastFor established other patrol areas in the Gulf of Oman and in the Persian Gulf.

Over time, the ComMidEastFor Operation Order went through numerous revisions, primarily as to what and how to communicate with suspect ships. The second ComMidEastFor Operation Order, dated 19 August, clarified some of the wording of the original, but both orders clearly state that Fogarty could authorize warning shots and the use of minimum force. Force, however, would not be used lightly. ComMidEastFor's Operation Order warned:

During this period of heightened tensions it is imperative to scrupulously adhere to the rules of engagement. Commanders should be sensitive to the fact that the first shot fired may start the war.[7]

Was the United States ready to disable ships if necessary?

THE FIRST INTERCEPTIONS

Uncertainty about Iraq's intentions and the fragility of the coalition made the initial intercepts crucial. The United States worried about an Iraqi retaliation if one of its merchant ships was fired upon. Building and sustaining the coalition was a major objective. Another concern was the image presented to the public. Public support for the U.S. actions was necessary to the success of the maritime interception operations and Desert Shield. If the United States could not gather and maintain domestic public support, it would be hard to sustain the coalition. As Secretary of State James A. Baker III later stated,

For better or worse, there was a synergistic relationship between the international coalition and domestic support. The stronger the coalition, the easier it was to generate consensus at home. Likewise, the more domestic support we had, the more the President was put in a commanding position vis-à-vis other governments.[8]

The first three interceptions illuminate this potential problem. The definition of an intercept is "making contact with a ship to determine whether it must be turned away or otherwise diverted, and diverting that ship if required." The Iraqi oil tanker *Al Fao* was the first intercept. The guided-missile frigate USS *John L Hall* (FFG 32) intercepted her in the Red Sea on 17 August while the Iraqi tanker was en route from Aden, Yemen, to Yanbu, Saudi Arabia. The Saudis denied her permission to enter the port, and the *Al Fao* headed back toward Aden.

The cruiser *England*, as part of the Middle East Force, was active in patrolling the Persian Gulf waters for vessels trying to circumvent the UN sanctions. The *England* made the first interception in the Persian Gulf—the Iraqi ships *Al Abid* and *Al Bayaa,* on 17 August. These two ships claimed to be empty and refused to stop. Vice Admiral Mauz contacted Gen. Norman Schwarzkopf, who was still in Tampa, Florida. Schwarzkopf, after reviewing the Operation Order and the UN resolutions, found nothing to support a view that empty ships returning to Iraq would be exporting "ill-gotten goods from Kuwait" or obtaining "supplies for its war effort." Schwarzkopf directed Mauz to allow the ships to continue their course: "There's no use starting World War Three over empty tankers." A few hours later, General Powell told Schwarzkopf that Secretary of Defense Dick Cheney believed Schwarzkopf had failed to follow orders. Schwarzkopf responded with, "Now that you've made it clear what you want, the next tanker that comes through, we'll blow it away."[9]

An additional factor in the decision not to stop these ships was that the ships reported they needed to maintain course and speed because they had only a one-day supply of food and water; thus, there were humanitarian considerations. Contrary to Schwarzkopf's statement in his autobiography, however, the Operation Order at this time specified that even empty ships were not to be allowed to sail to Iraq.

THE FIRST BOARDING AND FIRST DIVERSION

The *England* achieved another first, conducting the first boarding of a suspect vessel. On 18 August she intercepted her third merchant ship, the *Heng Chun Hai*, a 29,316-dwt Chinese cargo ship heading south in the Persian Gulf, away from Iraq.

A team from the *England* boarded the *Heng Chun Hai* without incident and searched the ship. The boarding team learned that the *Heng Chun Hai* was carrying fertilizer to a port in China. In accordance with the current Operation Order, the *England* directed the *Heng Chun Hai* to return to her port of origin, Khor al-Zubair, Iraq. Higher authority overruled the *England*. Because the *Heng Chun Hai* was not an Iraqi ship, was not carrying oil, and had been loaded prior to the sanctions, she was allowed to proceed to Qing Dao.

The *Heng Chun Hai* was the first ship successfully boarded, but it was not diverted. The first ship to be diverted was the Cyprus-flagged cargo ship *Dongola* in the Red Sea. The *Dongola*, carrying caustic soda and aluminum sulfate, was en route from Sudan to Aqaba, Jordan, when she was intercepted by the guided-missile destroyer USS *Scott* (DDG 995). The *Dongola* agreed to return to her port of origin without the necessity of a visit and search. Here, a verbal warning was sufficient to enforce the sanctions.

The *Dongola*'s diversion angered the governments of Jordan and Sudan, which claimed the ship was to ferry eight hundred Sudanese refugees who had fled to Jordan from Kuwait and wanted to return to Sudan. The Sudanese foreign minister warned that the United States was setting a dangerous precedent. The United States responded that the ship could continue its voyage provided she submitted first to inspection and carried only the Sudanese and their luggage.

These initial intercepts indicated potential problems enforcing the sanctions. The United States had allowed empty tankers to return to Iraq, and Iraq warned of "grave consequences" for the United States if it continued interfering with its merchant ships.

DISABLING FIRE

On 17 August two outbound Iraqi tankers, the *Khanaqin* (35,338 dwt) and the *Baba Gurgur* (36,397 dwt), were intercepted by the frigates *Reid* and USS *Robert G Bradley* (FFG 49), respectively. These interceptions were delayed until the 18th so they could take place during daylight hours. Also, on the same day, the *England* intercepted another outbound Iraqi tanker, the *Buzurgan*. ComUSNavCent planned to deal with the *Khanaqin* first, then the *Baba Gurgur*, and finally the *Buzurgan*. The guided-missile destroyer USS *Goldsborough* (DDG 20), attached to the *Independence* carrier battle group in the North Arabian Sea, would come over and relieve the *Reid* so that she could return to her patrol station inside the Persian Gulf.

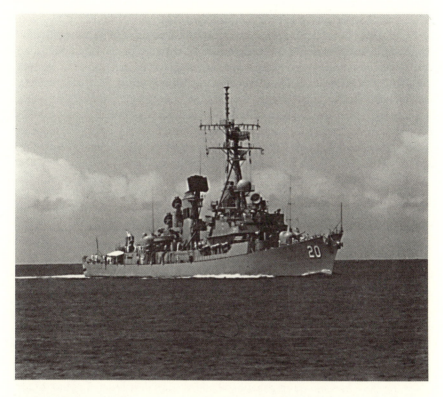

USS *Goldsborough*. This guided-missile destroyer was nearly ordered to disable the Iraqi tanker *Khanaqin*. Later her crew took over the Iraqi merchant ship *Zanoobia*. Navy Photo by OS2 John Bouvia.

The *Reid* began the interception while the *Khanaqin* was in Iranian territorial waters in the Persian Gulf, heading toward the Strait of Hormuz (Figure 3–1 shows the *Khanaqin's* track). Her story was that she had departed from Basra, Iraq, en route to the North Arabian Sea to dispose of "dirty ballast" and then to steam back into the Persian Gulf to Dubai, UAE. The ports of embarkation and debarkation were both reported as Basra, Iraq. The *Reid* was unable to confirm whether the *Khanaqin* was carrying cargo or "dirty ballast."

The *Reid* directed that the *Khanaqin* either submit to a visit and search or return to her port of origin, Basra. The master opted for the latter and requested ten minutes to contact the ship's owner. The *Reid* agreed to wait but asked that he turn about in the meantime. The master agreed, and the *Khanaqin* altered her course. Shortly after this, the master told the *Reid* the company had directed him to go Aden, Yemen, for provisions.

In the meantime, the *Reid* requested permission to fire warning shots, and the *Goldsborough* closed in, repeating a verbal warning to stop. The *Khanaqin* refused to alter her outbound course or to slow.

Permission having been granted, the *Reid* fired three 25 mm rounds across the *Khanaqin*'s bow. The *Reid* then again issued a verbal warning. The master pleaded that he was en route to Aden for provisions and bunkering, that his vessel was not a warship, and that he had citizens of other countries on board. (The commanding officer of the *Reid* reported that the Iraqi skipper sounded terrified over the radio. Reportedly, masters of Iraqi ships were under orders not to stop or be diverted on pain of death for them and their families.) The *Reid* fired three 76 mm rounds as additional warning shots. The master again stated his intent to maintain course and speed, and the crew of the *Khanaqin* donned their lifejackets.

The *Reid* reported that the *Khanaqin* had refused to stop and the *Reid* intended to proceed in accordance with the Operation Order. But Rear Admiral Fogarty told the frigate to await further instructions while continuing to trail the *Khanaqin* and to issue verbal warnings. As the tension increased, Fogarty asked for confirmation that the *Khanaqin* was full; the *Reid* and the *Goldsborough* both reported she was. The *Goldsborough* relieved the *Reid,* who returned to her station in the Gulf.

Vice Admiral Mauz had the authority to disable uncooperative ships if necessary, but he contacted General Schwarzkopf anyway and asked whether higher authority really wanted him to shoot at a civilian ship. As Cdr. Tom Connelly, the ComUSNavCent Judge Advocate, noted, the rules of engagement provided guidance, but when the threat is not imminent, an on-scene commander will discuss the situation with higher authority.

Mauz tried to force USCinCCent and higher authority to make a decision about disabling the *Khanaqin,* saying that he would shoot unless ordered not to. Mauz and Schwarzkopf each had phones in both ears; Mauz was talking simultaneously to his subordinates and to Schwarzkopf, while Schwarzkopf talked to Washington with his second phone. Mauz pointed out that one could never be sure that one would merely disable a ship rather than sink it or cause it to explode. Furthermore, if he damaged a tanker, the United States "bought" the ship and would have to find somewhere to tow it; no local ports were likely to welcome a leaking oil tanker. Mauz also worried about the impact on the sensitive effort to build a coalition. If the United States was perceived to be attacking unarmed ships for no valid reason, the coalition would fall apart. In contrast, his autobiography conveys the impression that Schwarzkopf's primary concern was not to start the war prematurely.

We presume Schwarzkopf talked to General Powell, Chairman of the Joint Chiefs of Staff, who in turn probably passed the issue to the National Security Council Deputies Committee. Richard Haass, then special assistant to the president for Middle East affairs and a member of the Deputies Committee, believed that if the United States disabled a vessel or two without much loss of life, it would not be a grave matter. The concern was defending Saudi Arabia, and disabling a merchant vessel or two would not provoke Iraq into attacking Saudi Arabia. Similarly, Admiral David Jeremiah, USN, Vice Chairman of the Joint Chiefs of Staff and the JCS member of the Deputies Committee, added that the National Security Council principals had been told disabling one or two ships might be necessary.

Later in the afternoon of 18 August, Mauz and Schwarzkopf again discussed disabling the *Khanaqin*. Finally, Schwarzkopf told Mauz, "Yep, go ahead and do it."[10] Mauz directed *Goldsborough* to get in position to fire and issue one more warning; if the *Khanaqin* did not agree to a visit and search, the *Goldsborough* would fire warning shots across the stern and then announce that had been the final warning. If ignored, she would fire into the stern. Capt. Cutler Dawson, Mauz's acting Executive Assistant, sensed that Mauz just did not feel right about firing to disable a civilian ship, feeling that the Americans had been good and noble people up to then. Also, daylight was running out, presenting a danger to both the civilians on the *Khanaqin* and the *Goldsborough* sailors that might have to rescue them. Mauz suggested to Schwarzkopf they wait until morning—the *Khanaqin* was still going to be there. This decision was to have far-reaching implications, though Mauz later claimed it was simply a "tactical" matter.

As night fell in the Persian Gulf, it was midday in Kennebunkport, Maine. President George Bush, Secretary of Defense Dick Cheney, national security adviser Brent Scowcroft, and Gen. Colin Powell met on the patio of the president's house. Secretary of State James Baker, in Colorado, was on the telephone. Either way, they faced political risks. If they let the *Khanaqin* go, they risked looking like "wimps." If they disabled it, however, they risked looking bad in the eyes of the world. Bush was uneasy—he did not want to seem weak-kneed so soon after starting to enforce the sanctions. For his part, Baker wanted to get the coalition involved. He argued that keeping the Soviets in the coalition required getting a UN resolution authorizing force. Bush reluctantly agreed to give him a few days. In spite of his uncertainty, Bush decided to run the political risk and let the ship go because, if it became necessary to look tough, they could shoot at *Khanaqin* later or another ship in a few days. Until the United Nations acted, the maritime interception operations were suspended.

The *Baba Gurgur*, a 36,397-dwt Iraqi product carrier (a ship designed to carry finished oil products from a refinery to distribution points), was intercepted the same day as the *Khanaqin*, 18 August, en route to Aden. Despite an Associated Press article stating the *Baba Gurgur* was en route to pick up refined oil, ComUS-NavCent had evidence suggesting she was already loaded with it. The *Robert G Bradley* trailed the *Baba Gurgur*, which refused to respond to bridge-to-bridge radio communication or to three 25 mm shots across her bow.

Had the *Khanaqin* been disabled, the *Baba Gurgur* would have been next. After the first round of warning shots, further action, such as 76 mm warning shots, was delayed until the following morning, with surveillance continuing through the night. The plans being developed focused on what to communicate to the ship and the best way to disable her while minimizing collateral damage. One person thought that the Army OH-58D helicopters embarked on some NavCent ships would be the best way to disable the *Baba Gurgur*. Because disabling authority was rescinded during the night, however, nothing happened.[11] The *Buzurgan*, intercepted by the *England* on this same eventful day, also refused to stop. This action, however, never progressed to the warning-shot stage. Eventually, the *Baba Gurgur* joined the *Buzurgan*. NavCent ships followed both vessels as they sailed toward Aden.

While the *Goldsborough* and *Robert G Bradley* trailed the three Iraqi ships toward Aden, the ComUSNavCent staff became frustrated by what it regarded as an excessive number of questions by officers on the USCinCCent staff in Tampa, who did not seem to understand naval operations. For instance, the ComUSNav-Cent staff had told the USCinCCent staff that contact on the Iraqi ships would be reestablished by a helicopter that would launch at dawn. Early the next morning, a staff officer from the USCinCCent staff (then in Tampa where it was late at night) called and asked for the status of the helicopter. On being told by the Com-USNavCent watch officer that the helicopter had not launched yet, the USCinCCent staff officer asked why not, since it was now past dawn there. On being told it was not light yet, the officer retorted that his calculations indicated it was past dawn. When the ComUSNavCent watch officer said that he had just looked outside and it was definitely not light, the USCinCCent officer eight thousand miles away adamantly insisted that his calculations showed that it was light.

The fact that *Khanaqin* was headed for Aden imposed a deadline for disabling her. The *Goldsborough*'s orders directed her to break off once the *Khanaqin* entered Yemeni territorial waters outside the port. Thus, while the politicians in Washington and New York worked on what would be UN Resolution 665, the sailors on the *Goldsborough* remained in position and ready to disable the *Khanaqin*—awaiting only the word. ComUSNavCent thought they might receive permission to disable any day. During the night of 23 August, the *Khanaqin* reached the mouth of Aden's port and anchored until daylight; the following day she entered the harbor. The *Khanaqin*, *Baba Gurgur*, and *Buzurgan* would not be disabled. It had been a false start.

Several times on 18 August Mauz had permission to disable *Khanaqin* but chose not to do so precipitously. In his book, former Secretary Baker addresses the importance of the crucial decision not to disable the *Khanaqin*:

If we [had] boarded or sunk that ship, I believe we never would have gotten the Soviets to come with us on that resolution authorizing military action to enforce the trade embargo, as well as subsequent ones that permitted military force to eject Iraq from Kuwait. The coalition might well have collapsed right then and there.[12]

NOTES

Historical background on sanctions came mainly from the book by Hufbauer et al. Details of the operation orders came from messages. The descriptions of the first interceptions relied mostly on messages, logs, and interviews with Mauz, Dawson, and Connelly. Articles by Delery and Moore added a few details. Perspective on events back in Washington was provided by interviews with Haass, Jeremiah, and Powell. Books by Schwarzkopf and Baker provided their perspectives. The description of the meeting in Kennebunkport came from an interview with Powell and the book by Baker.

1. Hufbauer, Schott, and Elliott, *Economic Sanctions Reconsidered,* 93.

2. The term "black knight" is taken from the Hufbauer, Schott, and Elliott study.

3. This was the Intelligence estimate. Salinger and Laurent have said an unofficial source estimated Iraq stole a billion dollars worth of gold and three billion in foreign currency, in addition to many sellable goods.

4. In his book, former Secretary of State James Baker describes the linkage problem: Iraq and its allies wanted to link the aggression against Kuwait with the Arab-Israeli conflict. Baker successfully kept the two issues separate.

5. Hufbauer, Schott, and Elliott, *Economic Sanctions Reconsidered,* 93–95, 112.

6. CJCS Washington DC 111700Z AUG 90, Operation Desert Shield Alert Order.

7. CoMidEastFor 171046Z AUG 90, Multinational Maritime Interception Operations [Order].

8. Baker, *The Politics of Diplomacy,* 333.

9. Schwarzkopf, *It Doesn't Take a Hero,* 372–3.

10. Interview with Adm. Hank Mauz, 14 March 1996.

11. Yemen allowed *Baba Gurgur* to enter her port but did not allow her to unload her cargo.

12. Baker, *The Politics of Diplomacy,* 287.

Chapter 4

After the False Start

On 19 August, following the *Khanaqin* affair, the United States in effect suspended the maritime interception operations pending passage of a UN Security Council resolution explicitly authorizing the use of force to enforce the economic sanctions against Iraq.

Bush administration officials still claimed a willingness to enforce sanctions, but vaguely.

Our forces are authorized to intercept. . . . We want to continue to work both by voluntary means and by naval means, if necessary, to see to it that the sanctions are enforced.

Secretary of Defense Cheney

We intend to enforce the sanctions, but we want to give them every opportunity to turn around and change course.

White House Press Secretary Marlin Fitzwater[1]

Meanwhile, the *Goldsborough* and *Robert G Bradley* continued to trail the three Iraqi tankers headed toward Aden, expecting to take action as soon as the UN Security Council passed the resolution.

RESUMPTION OF MARITIME INTERCEPTION OPERATIONS

When President Bush asked the British prime minister, Margaret Thatcher, to wait for a UN resolution authorizing the use of force, she admonished him, "Don't go wobbly on me." Bush asked her to give the UN a little time; if a resolution was not passed, they would go ahead with enforcing the sanctions. (Richard Haass later insisted that Thatcher made this comment to Bush at this time, not when they met in Colorado earlier in August.)[2]

The proposed UN Security Council resolution encountered a few difficulties, however. First, some Third World countries believed they were being pressured into putting a UN umbrella over naval operations already being conducted by the United States, Britain, and France. The other two sticking points were China and the Soviet Union—both permanent members of the Security Council, thus having veto power over any UN Security Council resolution. As long as China did not invoke its veto power, the United States would not object to an abstention. China finally declared that if it did not vote for the resolution, it would not vote against it.

The Soviet Union, with two concerns, remained a problem. First, it maintained that unless widespread abuse of the sanctions existed, the Security Council should refrain from endorsing military action. The Soviet foreign minister, Eduard Shevardnadze, told Secretary of State James Baker that the Soviets could convince Saddam Hussein to withdraw unconditionally from Kuwait and asked for five days to do so. Baker relayed the request to President Bush, who reluctantly agreed to hold off the UN Security Council vote until 25 August. (News of this delay did not reach ComUSNavCent.) On 24 August Baker received word from Shevardnadze that the Soviets had been unable to convince Saddam Hussein and accordingly would support the resolution, with "certain amendments." The Soviets wanted the term "minimum force" to be clearly defined.

By a 13-0-2 vote (Cuba and Yemen abstaining) on 25 August, the UN passed Resolution 665. To appease the Soviets, instead of the term "minimum force" the resolution called on countries "deploying maritime forces to the area to use such measures commensurate to the specific circumstances as may be necessary . . . to halt all inward and outward maritime shipping." This landmark resolution, allowing individual navies to maintain their autonomy in enforcing the sanctions, marked the first time the United Nations had authorized military action without a UN flag or UN command and control.

As the UN vote approached, Gen. Norman Schwarzkopf, USCinCCent, ordered Vice Adm. Hank Mauz, ComUSNavCent, to plan a "multinational mugging"—supposedly Gen. Colin Powell's words—to resume the interception operations, with British, French, and American ships simultaneously stopping about four Iraqi ships. At the practical level, however, ComUSNavCent found the proposal much too difficult to coordinate.

Thus, the maritime interception operations, which began on 17 August 1990, were suspended on 19 August and resumed on 25 August. The St. Vincent–flagged *Zorba Express* was one of the first merchant ships intercepted when the operation resumed. En route from Jedda, Saudi Arabia, to Aqaba, Jordan, she was intercepted by the guided-missile destroyer USS *Sampson* (DDG 10), boarded, and searched. As no discrepancies were found, the *Zorba Express* was cleared to proceed.

The maritime interception operations resumed in earnest. At the strategic policy level, the issue of using minimum force to enforce the sanctions was settled with the passage of UN Security Council Resolution 665—the threat was in place.

On the tactical level, however, clarity was lost. In that he no longer had authority to disable ships, Mauz understood that higher authority (USCinCCent and CJCS) was withholding full implementation of interception operations. Mauz communicated this understanding up the chain of command via his daily Situation Report. Higher authority, on the other hand, interpreted this point differently. Powell, CJCS, sent a message to Schwarzkopf confirming that Mauz held authority for warning shots but that Powell held disabling authority. Schwarzkopf added that if a situation arose where Mauz deemed it necessary to disable a ship, he need only ask permission. In theory and in the minds of "Washington," it appeared to be straightforward. In practical terms on-scene, however, this arrangement could easily lead to problems if a disabling decision needed to be made quickly.

EMPTY IRAQI SHIPS

U.S. decision makers debated what to do with empty ships returning to Iraq. Some, such as Secretary of Defense Cheney, wanted to stop and inspect all Iraqi ships. Others, such as Vice Admiral Mauz, argued that the objective of the sanctions was to deprive Iraq of the economic value of its commerce and that an empty ship had no economic value to Iraq. Later, some, such as Capt. Bernie Smith, the ComUSNavCent Chief of Staff, would suggest that these empty ships might have a potential military value to Iraq—as indeed eventually proved to be the case. Initially, as noted in chapter 3, General Schwarzkopf had decided to allow empty Iraqi ships to return to Iraq unmolested, but General Powell, passing along Secretary Cheney's objections, demanded such ships be stopped in the future. This policy changed on 27 August, when General Powell stated that empty vessels should be allowed to proceed after verifying that they were empty by stopping and searching them, but that General Schwarzkopf could allow obviously empty vessels to proceed without being searched. Schwarzkopf passed this discretionary authority to Mauz.

The *Al Qadisiyah*, a large Iraqi tanker (157,690 dwt), was intercepted by the frigate USS *Reasoner* (FF 1063) on 31 August outside the Strait of Hormuz. The *Al Qadisiyah* answered the bridge-to-bridge calls with the information that she was in ballast and en route to Basra, Iraq. On being told to stop, the master of the Iraqi ship pleaded that he had to switch fuel type to slow down and had engineering problems; he wanted to contact the owners for instructions. After an hour or more, the ship slowed to six knots; her owners then told her to speed up and proceed to Basra. The *Reasoner* continued surveilling the *Al Qadisiyah* until daylight the following day. With USCinCCent concurrence, ComUSNavCent released the *Al Qadisiyah* without boarding, because she was riding high in the water. The same day, personnel from the USS *Biddle* (CG 34), a guided-missile cruiser, boarded and searched the *Al Karamah* in the Red Sea—the first boarding of an Iraqi ship. This small Iraqi tanker (12,882 dwt) was in ballast and operating with an all-Iraqi crew. Found not to be violating the sanctions, she anchored inside Jordanian waters. Coalition forces continued to monitor her location.

USCinCCent revised the Operation Order on 1 September 1990. The revision mainly refined the previous order but contained a few significant changes. In particular, the revised order formalized the policy on intercepting empty ships. The Operation Order gave Mauz the authority to waive a visit and search if a vessel was "obviously empty." In addition, the revised Operation Order specified:

- All ships that were inbound to or outbound from the port of Aqaba were to be intercepted. That is, all ships were to be queried and suspect ships boarded.
- Mauz had authority to designate diversion ports.
- Iraqi ship masters were to be offered "safe haven" (to counter Saddam Hussein's threat of harming them or their family for allowing the ship to be searched) before the disabling threat. (Of course, this would not protect their families.)
- The Chairman of the Joint Chiefs of Staff (CJCS) held authority for disabling fire.

ZANOOBIA

So far, the United States had failed to divert a single Iraqi ship. With the latest Operation Order revision, many of the gray areas had been cleared up, and UN Resolution 665 allowed the use of minimum force (or rather, "such measures commensurate to the specific circumstances as may be necessary . . . to halt all inward and outward maritime shipping"). On 4 September the *Goldsborough*, operating in the Gulf of Oman, intercepted the *Zanoobia*, an Iraqi merchant ship of 3,549 dwt bound from Sri Lanka to Iraq.

If past patterns ran true and Iraq remained obstinate, would the United States back down as it had with the *Al Abid, Al Bayaa,* and *Al Qadisiyah,* or would it risk starting the war early and potentially damaging the coalition by firing on a civilian ship? The *Zanoobia* would prove to be an interesting interception for a couple of reasons. First, she was not a tanker, so causing pollution with disabling fire was not an issue. Second, the master, without evasion, admitted to carrying prohibited cargo (a thousand tons of tea) bought by Iraq and en route to Basra. This presented a clear case of violating the UN sanctions. Third, the *Zanoobia* was suspected of carrying mines—so this incident was not just a case of U.S. resolve to prevent the Iraqis from drinking their tea.

It was *Zanoobia*'s location at a military pier in early August that prompted the suspicion that she was carrying mines. Later, a helicopter from the cruiser *Antietam* (CG 54) had observed a black spherical object being lowered into its hold. Upon seeing the helicopter, the crew had covered numerous items on the deck and gone inside the ship. Because of a 1984 incident in which a Libyan merchant ship had been believed to have mined Red Sea shipping lanes, the concern was that the *Zanoobia* could do the same. The *Zanoobia* had then sailed to Sri Lanka.

On 2 September 1990, a Navy P-3 maritime patrol aircraft flying out of Masira, Oman, had detected the *Zanoobia* in the Indian Ocean headed in the direction of the Persian Gulf. The *Goldsborough* gained contact on the *Zanoobia* on 4 September and began querying her via bridge-to-bridge radio calls. The *Goldsborough* started with basic information gathering. Here this interception differs from the previous ones like those of the *Khanaqin* and *Baba Gurgur*. The *Goldsborough* began by asking such questions as: "What is your flag and registry? What is your destination? What is your port of origin and last port? What is your international call sign? What is your cargo?" In contrast, the previous method can be summed up as "Your vessel is subject to a visit and search; stop your vessel."

The watch officer cooperated with the inquiry, stating that his ship was an Iraqi merchant vessel carrying tea from Colombo, Sri Lanka, en route to Basra, Iraq. The *Goldsborough* issued a warning that the vessel should slow and prepare to be boarded and searched. The *Zanoobia* did not respond. After a second warning, she requested time to get the master to the bridge. The master claimed he needed twenty minutes to slow.

At this point, the master was offered the option of diverting to a neutral port, thus avoiding a visit and search. The master declined, stating that the United States was welcome to visit and search the ship but that his orders were to go to Iraq. The master, it appears, did not understand the implication of the option. The *Goldsborough* repeated it once more to ensure that he understood the situation—he would not be allowed to proceed to Iraq. He again welcomed the visit and search but reiterated his intention to continue on to Iraq.

The *Zanoobia* slowed and readied for the boarding party. Prior to sending the visit and search party, the *Goldsborough* obtained a count of twenty-five crew members on the *Zanoobia*. The most important instruction from the *Goldsborough* was for the *Zanoobia* to alter her course. The master agreed without objection. If *Zanoobia* had continued on its previous course, she would have entered Iranian territorial waters.

The *Goldsborough* launched her gig (the commanding officer's boat) to take a fourteen-member boarding party led by a member of the United States Coast Guard Law Enforcement Detachment (USCG LEDet) and an assistant boarding officer, the Executive Officer of the *Goldsborough*.

Just as the boarding party came alongside the *Zanoobia*, USCinCCent ordered the boarding terminated; for political reasons, USCinCCent wanted to delay the boarding to make it a multinational affair. ComUSNavCent pointed out that the *Zanoobia* was only twenty nautical miles from Iranian territorial waters and got the order reversed. The *Goldsborough* directed the boarding party to continue. A security team guarded the crew while a sweep team escorted the boarding officer to the bridge. Once on the bridge, the boarding officer identified himself and detailed how the boarding party would inspect the ship. He reviewed the ship's documents, and the party began to search the ship.

The boarding officer again offered the diversion option, and the master's reply was simple: "I don't have any port; I am going to Basra." The next offer was to assist in finding safe haven for the master, but this too was refused. To make sure there was no confusion, the boarding officer asked if the master had heard the notice to mariners regarding the UN sanctions and the shipping limitations. The master nodded that he had and that he knew he was carrying prohibited cargo. His response: "I know, but I was ordered to go to Iraq."[3]

Presumably believing the master was under threat from the Iraqi government, the boarding officer repeated the offer of safe haven. This second offer offended the master; for the first time, but not the last, he became clearly agitated. In the meantime, the search team found the thousand tons of tea. If *Zanoobia* would not divert of her own free will, the United States would use force. The *Goldsborough* sent four additional crew members to assist in taking custody of the *Zanoobia*.[4]

At this point the master began to argue, and the mood became tense. It appears that he did not understand why, after cooperating with the visit and search, he could not continue on to Basra. After a period of angry silence, the master reluctantly excused his first officer from the bridge, who left with a look of great relief on his face. He was escorted to the salon, where the remaining crew had been moved.

Another heated exchange occurred when the boarding officer asked the master to order his helmsman to step away from the helm. The master replied that force would have to be used, because he would not do it. When a member of the boarding party displayed handcuffs, the master acquiesced and ordered the helmsman to step back. An American helmsman turned the *Zanoobia* toward Muscat, Oman. The United States had taken over the *Zanoobia*, without incident or injury.

The master insisted that he be allowed to contact his company on the radio. The boarding officer denied this request and told the master that the U.S. command would notify his company. (Actually, the master's request was denied because a linguist was not available; there was no way to control what the master would say, and there was still a fear of retaliation and of starting the war prematurely.) The master then asked to send a message to his company which, after review, the *Goldsborough* sent:

Kindly note the U.S. Navy force [*sic*] my vessel to alter course to Muscat. Many U.S. commandos boarding at 0730 hours. And by force have altered course, await your advice. Regards, Master.[5]

While en route to Muscat, arrangements were made for the *Zanoobia*'s crew to follow their normal eating and sleeping schedule as much as possible. They were allowed to pray at their normal times (which included the required bathing beforehand). Under the supervision of the boarding party engineers, who had taken over the ship's engineering spaces, an Iraqi engineer remained in the engineering room to answer any questions.

While the boarding party monitored the crew members, American diplomats ashore in the region were negotiating what to do with the *Zanoobia*. USCinCCent directed the boarding party to bring the *Zanoobia* to a position fourteen miles off Mina Qaboos (the port of Muscat, Oman) on the morning of 5 September.

The Omani government had previously agreed to accept diverted ships, but now with an Iraqi ship on the way, it balked. At first, the Iraqi ambassador to Oman asked that the United States tell the *Zanoobia* to return to Sri Lanka. The American embassy representative refused and told the ambassador to pass the message directly to the *Zanoobia* himself. (Because the boarding party debarked from the *Zanoobia* before the Iraqi ambassador embarked, we do not know what he said.) The *Zanoobia* then departed the area and headed in the general direction of Sri Lanka. The *Zanoobia* actually went to Bombay, India, arriving on 8 September, but never docked in the port, sailing on 22 September. She declared she was headed for Umm Qasr, Iraq, but ComUSNavCent Intelligence assessed that to be unlikely, since she was believed to be still carrying the same cargo. Intelligence estimated she was en route Aden, Yemen, with an estimated date of arrival of 29 September. We shall encounter the *Zanoobia*'s tea again in chapter 8.

Several procedural aspects of the *Zanoobia* interception contributed to its success. The professionalism of the boarding party in explaining the situation and instructing the master and his crew promoted cooperation. Showing respect for their culture and their own chain of command lent itself to a cooperative environment and thus reduced the need to use force. Despite the master's objections and although the crew appeared to be slightly nervous, they cooperated. At one point in the salon they asked if they were hostages. The security personnel answered "no." When a U.S. Navy P-3 overflew the ship, the first officer commented, "He has been following us for four days. He is our friend. Every day he calls us on the radio and says good morning and asks about our health."[6] Second, the boarding party and additional crew accommodated the reasonable wishes of the Iraqi crew.

The U.S. Coast Guard LEDets proved to be a valuable contribution to the maritime interception operations, because of their expertise in countersmuggling, shipping documentation, and maritime law gained through their counterdrug operations. Ten LEDets, each consisting of one officer and three enlisted personnel, deployed during this period—six to the Red Sea and four to the North Arabian Sea.[7]

The *Zanoobia* was the first Iraqi ship boarded and forcibly diverted. The interception was done without warning shots or threats of disabling. It is unclear whether the Iraqi ships had been told to cooperate with the coalition warships. The *Zanoobia* interception seems to indicate some cooperation—she allowed a boarding without shots being fired. On the other hand, the safe-haven option, added to counter Saddam Hussein's threat of killing family members of Iraqi ships' masters cooperating with the United States, had not worked.

THE COALITION

The *Zanoobia* voyage turned out to be the last Iraqi attempt to carry on normal trade through the Persian Gulf.[8] To build on this success, the multinational coalition needed to coordinate its efforts. To this end, a multinational maritime interception operations conference was held in a hotel in Manama, Bahrain, on 9–10 September 1990. Twenty countries attended: the United States, the United Kingdom, France, Denmark, Norway, the Netherlands, Greece, Canada, Italy, Spain, Belgium, Australia, Portugal, Argentina, Kuwait, Saudi Arabia, Qatar, the United Arab Emirates, Oman, and Bahrain. Topics of discussion included patrol areas, communications, rules of engagement, logistics, diversion ports, and intelligence sharing. The participants resolved all issues related to these topics and outlined a schedule of monthly conferences to update and revise as necessary.

France, then head of the Western European Union (WEU), wanted to use the WEU structure to lead the coalition, but only Italy supported this idea. The other nations supported the structure already in place. That is, the United States would be the leader of the maritime interception operations, but each country would have autonomous control over its ships and its specific rules of engagement (ROE), as we will see with the next intercept. By the end of September, forty-two ships from ten countries had joined approximately sixty American ships in-theater.

Other international issues were resolved at this time as well. From the beginning of the maritime interception operations, Egyptian territorial waters had been a problem. Generally, interceptions were authorized on the high seas but not inside territorial waters, unless there were prior arrangements. The Egyptian government would not allow intercepts to take place in its waters. Also, Egypt was not at war with Iraq; therefore, closing the Suez Canal to Iraqi ships would be a treaty violation.

An agreement was made in principle on 28 August and confirmed in a formal message to ComUSNavCent on 6 September. The Egyptians requested that the NavCent ships not conduct intercepts in the Gulf of Suez; the Egyptians would do that. Most important, two NavCent ships at a time would be given diplomatic clearance for an Egyptian port visit any time during a period of several weeks. These ships could enter Egyptian territorial waters under the guise of this clearance and intercept ships in Egyptian territorial waters south and east of the point where the Gulf of Suez and the Gulf of Aqaba come together. On 6 September, the frigates USS *Elmer Montgomery* (FF 1082) and USS *Thomas C Hart* (FF 1092) were cleared to enter the Adabiya, Egypt, area from 7 to 22 September.

TARIK IBN ZIYAD

Small packages, which might contain items contributing to Iraq's nuclear or biological program, could be smuggled into Iraq hidden on a ship, even a ship not carrying any substantial cargo. Thus, the decision to allow "obviously empty" vessels to proceed could be dangerous. ComUSNavCent now had the authority to decide whether to allow "obviously empty" vessels to proceed without an inspection. On 12 September, the *Reasoner* intercepted the *Tarik Ibn Ziyad*, a 118,139-dwt Iraqi tanker, in the North Arabian Sea south of Oman. She claimed to be in ballast, and the *Reasoner* observed that she was riding high in the water. The decision was made to clear her without a boarding, but one of the ComUSNavCent battle watch officers, Commander Carradean "Dean" Brown, USN, thought this was peculiar, because of the concern over small packages; he persuaded ComUS-NavCent to initiate action against the *Tarik Ibn Ziyad*. *Reasoner* personnel boarded the *Tarik Ibn Ziyad* and confirmed she was in ballast. The boarding crew could not inspect her tanks, because they were filled with nitrogen to guard against explosions. The Iraqi ship was allowed to proceed. The coalition had exercised its right to inspect even "obviously empty" Iraqi ships, and an Iraqi ship had once again allowed a boarding without the necessity of warning shots.

AL FAO

Back on 17 August, the Iraqi tanker *Al Fao* had refused to stop for inspection while headed from Aden, Yemen, to Yanbu, Saudi Arabia, where she was denied entry. Now she sailed in the Gulf of Oman headed for the Persian Gulf and Iraq (see Figure 4–1). The last two Iraqi ships encountered had stopped and been reasonably cooperative. Would the *Al Fao* continue this trend, or would she refuse to stop as she had done in August? Tension heightened when intelligence warned that Iraqi military personnel might be on board some ships.[9]

With the help of a U.S. Navy P-3 maritime patrol aircraft, the frigate USS *Brewton* (FF 1086) gained contact and first queried the *Al Fao* on 14 September at 0119D. (In the Gulf of Oman, time zone Delta, Zulu plus four hours, was used.) Anticipating a difficult boarding, the *Brewton* went to General Quarters. The *Al Fao* responded to the bridge-to-bridge communications and answered questions. She had left Aden, Yemen, on 9 September and was en route to Basra, Iraq, with an estimated date of arrival of 16 September. She had a crew of thirty-five and carried ballast, no cargo. In accordance with the Operation Order, the *Brewton* advised the *Al Fao* of her intent to conduct a visit and search. The master of the *Al Fao* responded by saying he had to contact his company. Initially, no one answered, possibly because this action occurred on a Friday, which is the Moslem Sabbath. At noon the ship's master was still trying to contact the owners. Contacting the company was regarded as a delaying tactic; if a ship was near entering territorial waters, delay could cause complications. (In this case, territorial waters would become an issue, though not immediately.) In fact, however, this delay would give the Australian frigate HMAS *Darwin* (FFG 04) time to arrive on the scene and make this a multinational effort.

At this time, as noted, Vice Admiral Mauz held the authority for warning shots, but the Chairman of the Joint Chiefs held the authority for disabling fire. By coincidence, General Powell was in the theater, visiting the battleship *Wisconsin* that day. Because the *Al Fao* was two hours away from Iranian territorial waters, Mauz asked USCinCCent for permission to disable the *Al Fao* if necessary. The reply was "Wait, out."

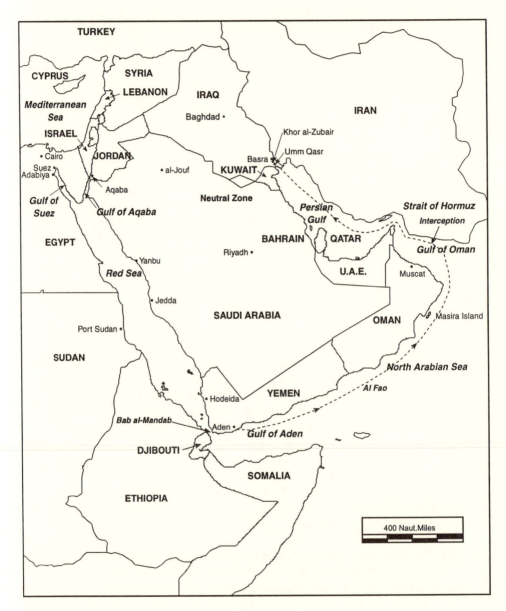

Figure 4–1. *Al Fao*

After hours without communication from the *Al Fao*, the *Brewton* again issued the instruction for it to prepare for a U.S. inspection team. The *Al Fao* wanted another thirty minutes. Minutes later, ComUSNavCent received reports that Iraqi troops were overrunning the embassies in Kuwait. Rear Admiral Fogarty told Mauz they had to try to stop the *Al Fao,* in view of events in Kuwait. They agreed to use .50-caliber, then five-inch warning shots, and then .50-caliber and five-inch gunfire to disable. The *Brewton* went through all the prescribed verbal warnings. She told the master that the United States would assist him in finding safe haven if he wished, but this was "strongly" refused. The *Brewton* told the *Al Fao* she could avoid a visit and search if she chose to divert to a nonprohibited port. The master of the *Al Fao* continued to request more time to contact his company.

The *Darwin*, now on-scene, offered her support for the intercept, and both ships used helicopters for surveillance. Taking note of the proximity to Iranian territorial waters, the *Brewton* directed the *Al Fao* to alter her course; the captain replied that he needed to "draw out a track," but the ship showed no signs of changing course. The *Brewton* and *Darwin* were discussing guns when Fogarty directed the *Brewton* to interpose herself so as to "shoulder" the *Al Fao* away from Iranian waters. Later, someone on the ComUSNavCent staff noted that as *Al Fao* displaced about eighty-nine thousand tons, and the *Brewton* at most displaced about 4,200, having the *Brewton* "shoulder" the *Al Fao* seemed neither prudent nor realistic. We do not know how much "shouldering" the *Brewton* did, but it evidently had no effect.

Although the intercept had begun before dawn, only thirty-five minutes now remained until sunset, and the *Al Fao* was only eleven nautical miles from Iranian territorial waters. Fogarty, with Mauz's concurrence, directed the *Brewton* to fire warning shots and invited the Australians to participate. Because there was no official multinational interception force command structure, the United States could not order the Australians to fire warning shots but only "invite" them. The *Brewton* fired warning shots across the bow of the *Al Fao,* along with a verbal warning to stop immediately, both of which failed to convince the *Al Fao* to stop. The *Al Fao's* responses to the warning shots were that she was not stopping because of a boiler problem, and that there was no inert gas in her tanks and therefore she could explode if fired upon. The master requested ten to fifteen more minutes to stop. The *Darwin* now fired a burst of .50-caliber warning shots. The master yet again requested more time to slow.

On the *Blue Ridge,* in contrast to his view during the *Khanaqin* affair, Vice Admiral Mauz did not mind trying to stop a ship after dark using .50-caliber fire. Although .50-caliber fire was unlikely to disable a ship, it was much less likely to cause unintended damage than the five-inch gunfire that would have been used in the *Khanaqin* incident. Nevertheless, as Mauz sat in his command center he did not seem anxious to shoot a civilian ship. Finally, he noted that none of the warnings explicitly had stated that a ship would be allowed to proceed if she were found not to be carrying prohibited material. He said, "If we tell him that and he still does not stop, that is kind of an admission that he might be carrying something, and I would not feel so bad about shooting him." This was passed to the *Al Fao,* with no effect.

The *Al Fao* was now only five miles from Iranian territorial waters. *Al Fao* said she would need thirty minutes to stop. Mauz directed that she be told "request turn toward open sea while slowing." A staff officer passed down the chain of command what he thought the admiral intended, to grant the *Al Fao* thirty minutes to slow only if she turned toward the open sea. Mauz did not like this; he thought this wording painted him into a corner. In any case, after the instruction passed through ComMidEastFor, the words ComUSNavCent overheard on the radio the local interception commander tell the *Brewton* were quite different from the words used by either Mauz or the staff officer, though the general meaning seemed the same.[10] Mauz, however, did not intervene.

The master of the *Al Fao,* having finally communicated with his company, agreed to stop and allow a boarding. Once his engines stopped, the *Brewton* again requested the *Al Fao* to turn toward the open sea. The master responded by stating that his instructions from the company were to stop but not to turn.

The Australian frigate HMAS *Adelaide* (FFG 01) and the British destroyer HMS *York* (D 98) joined the interception and stationed themselves two and three miles, respectively, ahead of the *Al Fao* in case she started her engines again. The *Al Fao* came to a stop only four miles from Iranian territorial waters. At the suggestion of his civilian operations analyst, Mauz gave the *Brewton* the option of having the *Al Fao* lay to overnight and boarding in the morning, rather than risking a night boarding of a ship that might have Iraqi military personnel on board. The *Brewton* replied that the boarding would begin at once.

Once on board, the American and the Australian boarding parties, including the USCG LEDet, confirmed the *Al Fao* was in ballast. She was cleared to continue her voyage to Basra. Curiously, the ComUSNavCent battle watch was not aware of the participation of the *Adelaide* and *York*. The people on-scene had coordinated their participation without direction from higher authority.

The United States and the coalition forces demonstrated their resolve in boarding the *Al Fao*. The *Al Fao*'s delaying tactics had effectively slowed things down but had not stopped the boarding. Also, the coalition continued to improve its techniques. As in the *Zanoobia* incident, the Coast Guard LEDet was a valuable asset to the boarding party, and using the *Al Fao* chain of command (controlling the crew through its own officers) proved to be an effective way to control the Iraqi crew. Ships' helicopters kept an eye on the *Al Fao* and provided cover for the boarding parties. Most important, the interception of the *Al Fao* was the first multinational interception.

Maritime interception operations procedures during early September were much smoother than during August, but the interceptions were still challenging at times. In August, the decision to disable the *Khanaqin* had dragged on until sunset. Fortuitously, sunset precluded disabling the ship safely. The *Al Fao* interception started before dawn yet went on all day and turned into a cliff-hanger, with the *Al Fao* stopping only four miles from Iranian territorial waters. It had taken nearly two hours for ComUSNavCent to obtain permission to disable the *Al Fao* if necessary. Because ships move slowly, there was time enough to refer the decision all the way back to Washington. Nevertheless, given the constraints of territorial waters, time was not an unlimited resource. If any of these ships had been intercepted closer to territorial waters, taking two hours to get permission to disable would have been too long. It sometimes seemed that a Parkinson's Law of maritime interception operations decreed that the time needed to make a decision inevitably consumed all the time available.

Both the *Zanoobia* and *Al Fao* cooperated, in that they eventually accepted boarding parties, but both interceptions took considerable effort. Thus far, each interception had been unique, and it was difficult to determine a trend. On the one hand, up to 30 August no Iraqi ship had accepted a boarding party; since then, however, all four Iraqi ships had accepted boarding parties. This seemed to indicate a trend toward cooperation. On the other hand, the Iraqis could not be described as cooperative, because they continued to use delaying tactics—wanting to call their owners, change fuel, deal with engineering problems. The last ship, the *Al Fao,* had delayed the most. Would Iraqi resistance increase or decrease? So far, permission to disable had been granted to ComUSNavCent for only two tankers, the *Al Fao* and *Khanaqin*, neither of which were disabled. How long could this last if the Iraqis resisted future boardings? The move-countermove game of Iraqi resistance and coalition responses continues when we resume the story of the maritime interception operations, in chapter 8.

NOTES

Events on the resumption of the maritime interception operations drew on an interview with Haass, articles by Moore and Goshko, and Baker's book. Details of the UN resolution come from the State Department's *Dispatch*. Sources for issues concerning empty Iraqi ships included messages, an interview with Mauz, and Schwarzkopf's book. Details of the interceptions of the Iraqi ships came from messages, especially the after-action reports from the ships making the interceptions.

1. Molly Moore, "U.S. Delays Action against Iraqi Tankers," *Washington Post,* 20 August 1990.

2. Interview with Richard Haass, 24 August 1995.

3. USS *Goldsborough* 051800Z SEP 90, MV *Zanoobia* Interception After Action Report 001.

4. A "boarding party," not a "prize crew," took "custody" of the ship. Use of the term "prize crew" was forbidden because it implied a state of war.

5. USS *Goldsborough* 040915Z SEP 90, Unit SitRep/*Goldsborough*/016E/SEP, *Zanoobia* Message to Owner.

6. USS *Goldsborough* 051800Z SEP 90, MV *Zanoobia* Interception After Action Report 001.

7. Another ten LEDets would deploy from October to February, and five deployed in March 1991.

8. The purpose of the *Ibn Khaldoon*'s voyage in December 1990, which we will describe in chapter 12, was propaganda rather than normal trade.

9. This intelligence was originally entered into the ComUSNavCent battle-watch log as applying specifically to the *Al Fao,* but this was later corrected to be a general warning.

10. The lesson is that when the exact words are deemed important, one must pass the wording in advance in a message (as was done with all the warnings in the ComMidEastFor Operation Order), painstakingly ask that the exact words be read back, or skip several layers in the chain of command.

Chapter 5

Air Power

So that his forces could go to war on short notice, Vice Adm. Hank Mauz, Com-USNavCent, had to organize them quickly to conduct area air defense, strike operations, and amphibious operations. Each warfare area presented its own unique challenges. Chapter 6 discusses amphibious plans. In this chapter, we describe the initial situation and early plans for employing air power. To put this into perspective, we first try to give the reader a feel for the atmosphere of August 1990, by describing some of the intelligence that NavCent received.

INTELLIGENCE

Years after the overwhelming victory of Desert Storm, we find it exceedingly hard to remember the grave concern over a potential Iraqi attack into Saudi Arabia in August 1990. Vice Adm. Tim Wright, the first NavCent-Riyadh, recalls that in Riyadh at that time Saddam Hussein and his army were thought to be twenty feet tall. Intelligence estimated the Iraqis would need anywhere between four hours and three days to reach Riyadh if they attacked. When the author arrived at the MidEastFor flagship *LaSalle* on 21 August with the second advance contingent of the ComUSNavCent staff, the Intelligence Officer told him that Iraq could come down any time it wanted and take over Saudi Arabia: "We are all prisoners of war. All they have to do is come and collect us. Fortunately, the *LaSalle* can get under way." The *LaSalle* kept steam up continuously and was under two hours' notice to get under way. [1]

The Iran-Iraq peace agreement of late August 1990 had serious implications for naval forces in the Persian Gulf. Saddam Hussein announced that Iraq would accept Iran's conditions for settlement of their eight-year war. This would free up to twenty-five Iraqi infantry divisions and three heavy divisions for the Saudi Arabian front. Intelligence concluded that Iraq could attack south into Saudi Arabia, capture Dhahran air base and the Saudi oil fields, and still have enough forces to secure its flank effectively. Iraq could "capture Riyadh, should Baghdad deem it necessary."[2]

Another intelligence summary contained several items of direct interest to the Navy. First, at least five Mirage F-1 fighters had deployed to Shaiba airfield in southeastern Iraq, from which F-1s had frequently staged attacks into the Persian Gulf during the Iran-Iraq War. Also, Iraq had captured six Kuwaiti patrol boats capable of firing Exocet missiles.

A 26 August intelligence report concluded that the fact that the Iraqis had not yet constructed permanent defenses showed that they intended either to move forward into Saudi Arabia or retreat back into Iraq. The report allowed, however, that Iraq's failure to build defenses also might be due to utter contempt for its opponent.

An intelligence summary of 28 August reported 142 naval mines at Ras al-Qulaya naval base in Kuwait. It concluded that these mines were probably intended for use against an amphibious assault into Kuwait. Intelligence thought Iraq would not mine international waters because that would risk provoking a military reaction, but it cautioned that Iraq had the capability to conduct offensive mining covertly if it decided to be confrontational.

In early September, the Navy Operational Intelligence Center (NOIC) noted that immediately upon seizing Kuwait Iraq had placed forces along the eastern coast to oppose any amphibious assault. NOIC characterized Iraq's defense as positional, with prepared strong points and second-echelon mobile armored forces.

Intelligence messages inundated both the ComUSNavCent and battle group staffs, especially during these early days. Many different agencies back in the United States apparently sent any data they had on Iraq. Multiple agencies reported on the same topic, sometimes with different data or conclusions. Worse, agencies included summaries of information from other agencies; the recipient, overwhelmed with redundant reports, could not identify which was the primary or most recent source. Toward the end of August, ComUSNavCent Intelligence directed these agencies not to send everything to everybody in NavCent, but to send it only to ComUSNavCent, who would act as a clearinghouse.

Many reports contained only unevaluated intelligence. In one twelve-hour period, ComUSNavCent received twenty-one information reports from one agency. Some of these were useful, but many told what some source with no special insight or knowledge thought about the situation. Most of these opinions seemed useless to an operational commander.

Vice Admiral Mauz thought that USCinCCent Intelligence products amounted to just "cutting and pasting," rather than true fusion of intelligence, as Naval Intelligence personnel tried to do. Mauz thought his Intelligence Officer, Cdr. Wayne Perras, knew more about how to do intelligence summaries than anyone at USCinCCent.

Many other intelligence reports dealt with narrow technical issues. Reports of Iraqi capabilities that could potentially be extremely difficult to counter flooded the ComUSNavCent staff.

Navy laboratories in the United States played their part by assessing the technical details and implications of reported Iraqi capabilities. Often they ran tests to determine the implications. In other cases, they made theoretical assessments of, for example, the vulnerability of battleship magazines to Iraqi missiles.

The four World War II battleships brought back in the 1980s provided unique capabilities. Because shallow waters prevented ships from getting close to the coast, the Navy's five-inch guns could not reach many coastal areas of Saudi Arabia and Kuwait. Only the battleships' sixteen-inch guns, with their twenty-three-mile range, could reach the shore and inland. The battleships could fire a broadside of nine three-thousand-pound shells more than twenty miles, do it again less than a minute later, and continue for hours. Also, these seeming dinosaurs were relatively invulnerable to modern weapons. Because most modern combat ships do not have much armor plating, state-of-the-art missiles such as Exocet generally emphasize precision over warhead size. Thus, most believed that modern weapons could not severely damage the battleships, which had been built to take hits from sixteen-inch shells. A platform the enemy thinks he cannot harm is a valuable asset.

Thus it came as a shock when the Naval Sea Systems Command assessed that shaped-charge warheads on Iraqi antiship cruise missiles and rocket-propelled antitank weapons could, under certain circumstances, penetrate a battleship's armor and detonate its magazines. By filling all fuel and ballast tanks on the third deck, a battleship could neutralize the antitank weapons, but not the cruise missiles. An amplifying message assessed the odds of "battleship magazine mass detonation" from a shaped-charge cruise missile warhead as one in a hundred for a single hit. "Battleship magazine mass detonation" describes what happened to the USS *Arizona* at Pearl Harbor in 1941. One chance in a hundred seems remote, but a 1990 battleship carried well over a thousand sailors. Blowing up a battleship and killing a thousand Americans would certainly be a great victory for Iraq.

Iraq possessed chemical weapons and had used them both on Iran and on its own people. U.S. intelligence believed Iraq also possessed biological weapons, including anthrax and botulism. Experts from Washington visited the *Blue Ridge* and briefed the ComUSNavCent staff about the effectiveness of some of these substances and countermeasures:

- Two hundred kilograms (440 lb) of sarin, a nerve agent, could contaminate 0.16 sq km (a square four hundred meters on a side).
- Two hundred kilograms of VX1, another nerve agent, could contaminate 0.85 sq km (a square more than nine hundred meters on a side).
- Two hundred kilograms of anthrax could contaminate 3,700 sq km (a square more than sixty kilometers [about thirty-seven miles] on a side).

- One could be vaccinated against anthrax, but there was not enough vaccine to go around, which might create a panic.
- One could be vaccinated against botulism, but the treatment required several years to take effect.
- Anthrax responds well to penicillin, but there are no symptoms until it is too late, and there is no way to detect exposure. Anthrax is 100 percent fatal. An exposed person would get better after phase 1; phase 2 sets in on the fifth day after exposure and kills victims in twenty-four hours.[3]

A gas mask and two cartridges, as well as a head-to-toe chemical warfare suit, were issued to each person on the ComUSNavCent staff. All the military people had been trained in the use of these items, but everyone now went through refresher training to be sure they knew how to use everything. The antidote kit for exposure to nerve gas was not handed out until the eve of the war—more on that in chapter 15.

Thus, in late August American intelligence depicted Iraq as having formidable weapons and as capable of capturing the oil fields in northeast Saudi Arabia and perhaps Riyadh. Intelligence considered an Iraqi attack quite possible, if not likely. Projecting U.S. military attitudes on Iraqis probably enhanced the expectation of an Iraqi attack. If American military officers had commanded Iraq's military and observed the growing coalition buildup in Saudi Arabia, they would have attacked to gain the initiative and capture many of the ports and airfields needed to complete the coalition buildup.

The intelligence picture implied that NavCent forces had to prepare to meet a surprise attack at any time. Thus, the greatest challenge was in air defense, because of the short reaction times. Also, there was always the memory of the devastating Iraqi Exocet missile attack on the *Stark* in 1987.

AIR DEFENSE

Prior to August 1990, the Iraqi air force had demonstrated substantial proficiency (for a Third World military) that contradicts the widespread post–Desert Storm perception that the Iraqi military consisted of incompetent bumblers. During the Iran-Iraq War, Iraq had gained an enormous amount of invaluable experience attacking ships in the very same waters in which NavCent forces would operate. Iraqi aircraft had made an estimated 252 successful attacks on ships. Though most of the attacks were against unarmed ships, they gave the Iraqis more real-world, recent, successful experience attacking ships than anyone else in the world had.

The Iraqi targeting process, however, lacked sophistication by American standards. In a typical attack, F-1 aircraft had flown southeast from Iraq following the Saudi Arabian coastline and then turned east into the central Persian Gulf. Upon arriving in their assigned area, they had turned on their radar and fired at the first large target they detected. The Iraqis had accidently attacked the *Stark* that way.

Now, with most merchant traffic gone from the western parts of the central and northern Persian Gulf, any target they picked up was likely to be a coalition ship.

Most impressive—especially for a Third World country—Iraq had conducted one-third of its strikes during the Iran-Iraq War at night. It also made several strikes at extended ranges. Using air-to-air refueling, it had attacked as far as the Strait of Hormuz. Thus, it threatened the entire Persian Gulf.

Not only did the Iraqis have recent experience, they also possessed enough naval attack aircraft to allow strikes with considerable force:

- Strike variants of the French Mirage F-1 that could carry Exocet missiles
- Chinese-made Badger long-range bombers that carried air-launched Chinese Silkworm missiles
- Falcon 50s modified to carry Exocet missiles
- Soviet Su-24 Fencers capable of attacking ships
- SA-321 Super Frelon French-made helicopters that could carry Exocet missiles.

About forty Iraqi aircraft could deliver Exocet antiship cruise missiles. The Exocet missile, an extremely capable, sea-skimming missile that can be fired about forty miles from the target, had demonstrated its effectiveness in the Falkland Islands War and in the attack on the *Stark*. On the other hand, while the slow and easy-to-detect Badgers represented only a modest threat, the large warhead on the Silkworm missile could cause major damage.

In addition to coalition combatant ships, potential Iraqi targets in the Gulf included normal merchant shipping, U.S. Military Sealift Command vessels supporting the buildup in the theater, port facilities where ships unloaded the equipment and supplies for the buildup, and oil platforms off the coast of Saudi Arabia and the United Arab Emirates (UAE). In addition, Iraqi aircraft might fly over water and then turn inland to attack American and coalition forces ashore.

In August 1990, one of Vice Admiral Mauz's priorities was to provide area air defense in the Persian Gulf. Effective area defense would protect targets in the Gulf as well as provide flank defense for forces on the ground, most of which were near the Persian Gulf side of the Saudi Arabian peninsula. Air defense in the Red Sea area also concerned Mauz, but the chances of an Iraqi attack there were considerably less than in the Persian Gulf. The possibility that Iran also might attack U.S. ships—especially after the Iran-Iraq peace settlement—compounded the air-defense problem in the Persian Gulf. Alternatively, Iraqi aircraft might use Iranian airspace for an attack approach.

NavCent forces could not simply shoot at anything that looked like a threat. As a counterpoint to the quick reactions needed to avoid a repeat of the *Stark* attack, the incident in which the *Vincennes* had shot down a civilian Iranian airbus was a powerful reminder of the severe penalty for a *single* incorrect identification (and the *Vincennes* incident had occurred in a situation with relatively few aircraft in the area). Airspace management and identification of aircraft would prove to be vital, unending tasks.

Mauz tasked Rear Adm. Bill Fogarty, Commander, Middle East Force (Com-MidEastFor), to provide air defense in the Persian Gulf, as CTG 150.1. Initially, Fogarty had only a few guided-missile cruisers and depended on CentAF and Saudi Airborne Warning and Control System (AWACS) E-3A aircraft to provide warning. Then, the Aegis cruiser *Antietam* detached from the *Independence* battle group and entered the Persian Gulf to bolster air defense there. NavCent forces realized they needed information from the AWACS aircraft, but several aspects of the cooperation required concerned them. At this stage, the AWACS aircraft covered the northern Persian Gulf from an orbit over northeastern Saudi Arabia but did not cover the area continuously (more on this in chapter 9). Furthermore, communications between naval ships and the AWACS were often tenuous.

Effective air defense required combat air patrol (CAP) fighter aircraft to orbit over the northern Persian Gulf continuously, ready to counter any Iraqi attack. Starting on 10 August, *Independence* aircraft flew CAP in the Persian Gulf. Because the *Independence* sailed in the Gulf of Oman, these aircraft had to get permission to overfly Oman and the UAE. Even then, it was 330 miles to the CAP station in the central Persian Gulf. The *Independence* alternated two F-14s with two F/A-18s. Each aircraft was airborne for four and one-half hours. These CAP missions relied extensively on in-flight refueling from CentAF KC-10 or KC-135 tanker aircraft. Moving the *Independence* into the Persian Gulf would solve this problem, but at this time Vice Admiral Mauz would not do so unless conditions became dire. Mauz said he would probably bring the *Independence* into the Gulf if the Iraqis attacked into Saudi Arabia and drove U.S. forces back. (The last U.S. aircraft carrier to operate in the Persian Gulf had been the USS *Constellation* [CV 64] in 1974.)

From outside the Gulf, the *Independence* could not provide twenty-four-hour-a-day coverage for long. On 22 August, F/A-18s of the Third Marine Aircraft Wing (3rd MAW) started arriving at Sheikh Isa airfield in Bahrain. On 24 August, they started covering "Whiskey-1"—the CAP station in the northern Persian Gulf—in an excellent example of interservice cooperation. Thereafter, a section of fighter aircraft (two aircraft) covered Whiskey-1 continuously, twenty-four hours a day, for more than five months, from late August until the CAP station moved farther north during the war.

Later, Canadian CF-18s operating out of Qatar joined the Americans in flying CAP over the northern Persian Gulf. Initially, Mauz had some questions about whether their rules of engagement allowed them to shoot Iraqi aircraft attacking American ships or required them to ask Ottawa for permission. The answer came back quickly that the Canadians could do essentially everything the Americans could do. U.S. Marine and Canadian aircraft operated together during the succeeding months until 17 January 1991, when 3rd MAW shifted to support MarCent forces ashore. Often, CAP station Whiskey-1 had one Marine aircraft and one Canadian aircraft sharing the coverage.

Many nervous moments ensued during the next five months. For example, at the 8 September ComUSNavCent staff meeting, the Intelligence Officer reported that on the night of 6–7 September an Iraqi aircraft had flown over the northern Persian Gulf. At one point, it had been within sixteen minutes' flight time of Exocet launch range to the nearest U.S. ship. Furthermore, the Intelligence Officer reported that the ComUSNavCent staff had never gotten real-time information on the event; they had found out in an intelligence daily summary. The Saudi AWACS had evidently held contact, but word never got to the ComUSNavCent staff.

The responsibility for providing forces on the ground with flank defense against air attack involved a real expenditure of effort. For instance, in late August Saudi Arabia became concerned about a threat of attack by Iraqi aircraft operating from Port Sudan, in Sudan, across the Red Sea from Jedda. To allay Saudi fears of the threat to Jedda and Mecca (about forty miles inland from Jedda), USCinCCent in Tampa directed ComUSNavCent to move the Aegis cruiser USS *Philippine Sea* (CG 58) from the northern Red Sea to the central Red Sea, off the coast from Jedda. In response, Capt. Cutler Dawson, acting as Mauz's executive assistant at the time, said fine, but it would take the *Philippine Sea* eight to twelve hours to get there. The USCinCCent action officer back in Tampa demanded, in all serious-ness, to know why the cruiser could not be there within thirty minutes—it was only two inches on the map!

In the Persian Gulf, Mauz and his staff worried that Iraqi aircraft needed to fly only about a hundred miles over water to reach Exocet launch range against coa-lition ships operating near the port of al-Jubail. These ships included the Maritime Prepositioning Force and sealift ships going to al-Jubail to unload. This left a reac-tion time of only a very few minutes. To increase the reaction time, and the com-fort factor, NavCent forces needed the early warning that AWACS could provide. On 26 August, Fogarty's staff met with Major General Thomas Olsen, USAF, and part of the CentAF Forward staff. The ComMidEastFor officers stressed the crit-icality of uninterrupted AWACS coverage of the northern Persian Gulf to provide warning time.

The naval forces did not operate independently in providing air defense of the Persian Gulf. The USCinCCent Operation Order designated Lt. Gen. Chuck Hor-ner, ComUSCentAF, as the Area Air Defense Commander, though Horner dele-gated many of the details to Olsen. When Mauz travelled to Riyadh shortly after he arrived in-theater, he called on Olsen. Mauz felt Olsen did not appreciate NavCent's air-defense needs or capabilities; when Mauz had referred to having an Aegis cruiser as the Persian Gulf air defense commander, Olsen had taken offense, saying *he* was the air defense commander.

As such, Olsen provided air defense for the entire theater. Defending the direct attack routes from Iraq to Riyadh and the Dhahran air base in Saudi Arabia undoubtedly concerned him most. He designated ComUSNavCent as the sector Area Air Defense Commander for the Persian Gulf and Red Sea areas. Mauz, in turn, passed the responsibility for the two regions to the Red Sea battle group commander and to Fogarty, respectively. ComUSCentAF also defined the system by which tactical electronic data links would tie all the local air defenses together. Because the Navy and Air Force had different systems, capabilities, philosophies, procedures, and perceived needs, NavCent and CentAF personnel had different views on how best to organize the theater data links. The ComUSNavCent staff strongly opposed the proposed theater data link system but did not get its way. Subsequently, the ComUSNavCent staff worried almost continuously that it did not get a full picture of the information available from the AWACS.

STRIKE WARFARE

During these early days of Desert Shield, several aspects of strike warfare concerned Vice Admiral Mauz:

- Close air support to the U.S. Marines ashore if the Iraqis invaded Saudi Arabia
- Plans for the offensive strike operations that evolved into the air campaign of Desert Storm
- Establishment of the Joint Force Air Component Commander (JFACC)
- The Air Tasking Order (ATO)
- The struggle to get NavCent Tomahawk cruise missiles included in the JFACC strike plans.

Plans for Close Air Support

During Desert Shield, both offensive and defensive air campaigns were planned. After the war, attention focused on the offensive air campaign actually executed in Desert Storm. In the early days of Desert Shield, however, much of the attention went to the immediate problem of a defensive air campaign for use if Iraq attacked Saudi Arabia.[4]

In early August, the *Independence* and *Eisenhower* battle groups, operating in the North Arabian Sea and Red Sea, respectively, developed strike packages to provide close air support if needed. They put aircraft and aircrews on alert and worked on arranging for CentAF tankers to support the strikes. Initially, the *Independence* set a thirty-minute alert—that is, readiness to launch a strike on thirty minutes' notice. Later, this time frame was relaxed to sixty minutes; even this was hard to maintain when it went on for days on end. Aircraft loaded with ordnance and parked on the flight deck could not be used for anything else and made other flight-deck operations nearly impossible. On 13 August, the alert time was relaxed to six hours.

As noted, it was in late August that Vice Admiral Mauz stated that he would probably bring the *Independence* into the Persian Gulf if the Iraqis invaded Saudi Arabia and the coalition ground forces had trouble stopping them. This bold plan would greatly decrease the range to the targets and increase the number of attack sorties per day that the *Independence* could throw into the battle.

On 20 August, Rear Adm. Thomas Lynch, commander of the *Eisenhower* battle group, expressed concern that CentAF forces were not adequately supporting his air wing with airborne refueling and AWACS. He preferred KC-10 tankers to KC-135 tankers. Potential practice time had been lost because his aircraft and the CentAF tankers had failed to rendezvous. Lynch sent Mauz a strong message asking for his personal involvement to get things on track.

Owing to our critical dependence on external tanking assets and the difficulty of refueling with KC-135 tankers, I cannot assure you with confidence that we can successfully meet our assigned tasking until we refresh additional pilots. . . . The complex coordination issues involved with AWACS and KC-135 tanker interoperability, timing and location make it unlikely that we can successfully execute on the first attempt. We desperately need to practice how we intend to blunt an Iraqi offensive.[5]

For months to come, even after the *Saratoga* battle group, commanded by Rear Adm. Nick Gee, replaced the *Eisenhower* battle group on 26 August, coordinating with CentAF AWACS and tankers would remain a ComUSNavCent priority.

In strike training, the first priority was maintaining aircrew proficiency. At this time, the air wings thought aircrew proficiency required practice flying low-level, overland routes. It took a great deal of staff work to obtain permission from Oman and Saudi Arabia to fly low-level routes regularly over their territory. (The irony of expending all this effort to practice flying low-level strike profiles will become apparent to the reader in Volume II, when we discuss early strikes during Desert Storm.)

The second priority was rehearsing the strike plans in what are termed "mirror-image" strikes—practice runs that duplicate as well as possible the distance, flight profile, bomb load, bomb delivery tactics, and coordination with fighters, tankers, and defense-suppression aircraft. For example, a 26 August message from the commander of the Red Sea battle group outlined how he would use a mirror-image strike to test such aspects of the plans as ordnance breakout, buildup, load, and launch. He intended later to conduct a second test, using CentAF tankers in an overland strike to check the timing.

The plan to defend against an Iraqi attack remained in place until Desert Storm began. But as time went on, emphasis shifted to plans for an offensive air campaign. Even in the early days, there was always the thought of going offensive eventually.

Offensive Strike Plans

Initially, there were multiple U.S. military efforts at planning a deep strike campaign. Some planning began in Washington, in the Air Force Staff's Checkmate group, under Colonel John Warden III, USAF, and it was later transferred to the theater of operations. Several Navy officers participated in the Checkmate group. They monitored the planning and offered suggestions but were not in decision-making positions. Commands in the CentCom theater also planned strikes.

The *Independence* battle group received its first Desert Shield target list (nineteen Iraqi targets) from the pre-Mauz ComUSNavCent, still at Pearl Harbor, on 2 August. The *Independence* received on 8 August a second target list with thirty-one targets, twelve of which were in Kuwait. The number of targets on the revisions of the master lists given to the *Independence* grew to 111 on 19 August, 133 on 24 August, and 151 on 3 September. The 3 September target list differed significantly from the previous lists. Initially, each carrier had tried to plan missions for every likely target, which resulted in the intelligence people being inundated with multiple requests for targeting materials (photos and such) on each target. Then, USCinCCent directed that all intelligence requests to support targeting should go through him so he could prioritize them and avoid overlaps. (In fact, JFACC strike planners in Riyadh routinely went direct to Washington to get intelligence rather than through USCinCCent or USCentAF Intelligence organizations in Riyadh.) By this time, planning in Riyadh had gained primacy over planning on the carriers and planning begun in Washington.

Instant Thunder

Planning in Washington moved into high gear when, on 8 August, Gen. Norman Schwarzkopf requested the help of the Air Force Staff in planning options for air strikes. Colonel Warden, who had written a book on strategic air campaigns, led the Checkmate group in devising a plan called Instant Thunder (in deliberate contrast to the Rolling Thunder campaign of the Vietnam War). Warden's theory focused on hitting "centers of gravity" deep in enemy territory. The primary targets were the enemy's command, control, communications, and decision-making capability—often collectively referred to as "leadership" targets. Of second importance were the facilities that supported enemy military and economic production. National infrastructure, such as transportation facilities, came third. It was not considered moral to strike population and food sources—the fourth priority—nor would it be very effective. Significantly, at the bottom of Warden's list were the enemy's military forces; their function was to protect the other targets, and they were not considered important.

Instant Thunder had several elements that were a reaction to what Air Force officers perceived as the bad experience in the Vietnam War. Throughout modifications to the plan during the next five months, these features remained:

- Attacks on the enemy's leadership from the opening hours of hostilities (as opposed to exempting sets of targets or the enemy's capital)
- A high tempo of strike operations from the start (as opposed to gradual escalation)
- No bombing pauses to seek diplomatic solutions.

Most naval aviators generally agreed with these features. (The last feature was a political, not military, decision of course but the military leadership convinced the political leadership this was important and planned the air campaign with the assumption there would be no bombing pauses.)

Warden briefed the outlines of Instant Thunder to Schwarzkopf in Tampa on 10 August. On 17 August, Warden presented a more detailed version of the Instant Thunder plan to Schwarzkopf and the USCinCCent staff in Tampa. Major General Robert B. Johnston, USMC, Schwarzkopf's Chief of Staff, suggested that USCinCCent spend a longer time destroying Iraq's air defenses before attacking all targets deep inside Iraq. Warden's team objected; Schwarzkopf did not pursue Johnston's suggestion. Whereas Warden thought Instant Thunder was a recipe for victory, Schwarzkopf saw it as a way to reduce Iraqi strength prior to a ground war. Nevertheless, air power advocates would be given the best chance ever to show whether air power could win a war all by itself. At the end of the briefing, Schwarzkopf directed Warden to go to Riyadh to brief the plan to Lt. General Horner, his air component commander and USCinCCent Forward—the acting CinC in-theater.

Things did not go well in Riyadh. The 1986 Goldwater-Nichols Defense Reorganization Act had strengthened the unified commands, such as CentCom, in part to stop the service staffs in Washington from interfering in operations. (One of the bad features of the Vietnam War had been that civilian and military officials in Washington often picked targets.) Horner thought that he and his ComUSCentAF staff should have devised the plan. Schwarzkopf had gone outside his command to ask for help from Washington, and Horner resented the interference. The briefing took place on 20 August. Horner did not like it; he thought it naive and academic. He had serious concerns about an Iraqi ground attack, and, among other things, he thought Instant Thunder did not address that problem. Horner felt that Warden had presented him with a list of targets and a way of categorizing those targets, but not a plan for an air campaign. Furthermore, Horner later said, he thought Warden failed to respond appropriately to legitimate questions. In any case, Horner sent Warden back to Washington but kept some of his team in Riyadh to work on a USCentAF plan. Horner needed someone in whom he had greater confidence to plan the air campaign.

On the morning of 22 August, as the author of this book ate breakfast in the flag mess of the *LaSalle* for the first time, the white-haired Air Force general who was Deputy Commander of the Joint Task Force Middle East (JTFME) had breakfast on the *LaSalle* for the last time. Schwarzkopf had disestablished JTFME on 16 August, in his message designating Mauz as ComUSNavCent. That meant the Air Force general was out of a job. He was not despondent, though, because he had another job—one of the best any Air Force officer could hope to get. Brig. Gen. Buster Glosson would direct the air campaign and its planning as USCentAF Director of Campaign Planning. As he packed his belongings, Glosson seemed almost giddy with excitement. He declared that a person could climb the flagpole in this war. As he left his stateroom, he predicted this would be the war that air power won.

On the previous day, Lt. Colonel Dave Deptula, USAF, one of Warden's team who had stayed in Riyadh, had briefed Glosson on Instant Thunder. Glosson evidently thought more was needed than the six-day plan of Instant Thunder, but he liked many aspects of it, especially the idea of attacking Baghdad from the start. Glosson and Deptula revised Warden's plan and got Horner's acceptance on 26 August. From then on, the "Black Hole" in Riyadh, as Glosson's operation became known, was the primary planning node for the air campaign.

Up to this point, the Navy had had almost no involvement in the macro aspects of the planning. NavCent-Riyadh, Rear Admiral Wright, who had arrived in Riyadh in mid-August, had not been included in any of Colonel Warden's briefings of the Instant Thunder plan. Alerted by a call from the Navy Staff in Washington, Vice Admiral Mauz asked Wright to find out about Instant Thunder. At the evening USCinCCent meeting in Riyadh, Wright asked what those present could tell him about Instant Thunder. This request created quite a stir, but he was given the information.

Wright found out that the Instant Thunder plan had a good many aircraft going to downtown Baghdad on the first night, including NavCent's A-6s, because they could carry so many bombs. Wright thought this was unnecessarily risky; there were other ways to get those targets on the first night. One could send the A-6s there after neutralizing the Iraqi air-defense system.

When Mauz learned of the Instant Thunder plan, he thought it was nonsense. It was aggressive—he liked that. He was unhappy, however, that Horner and Glosson planned merely to suppress, not destroy, Iraq's air defenses and intended to strike Baghdad on the first day, without adequate preparation. He thought the target list was mostly silly. He considered it ridiculous to send old, relatively slow, and nonstealthy Navy A-6s over Baghdad on the first night, before any effort to suppress Iraqi defenses, to bomb targets such as the Baath Party Headquarters. To Warden, government buildings were symbolic leadership targets; to the Navy they were office buildings that were empty at night. Mauz questioned sending A-6s over Baghdad at night to hit empty buildings; he recalls Air Force officers responding by "challenging the Navy's manhood." To Mauz, that was not the issue at all. He was willing to send A-6s over Baghdad for worthwhile targets. Mauz did not like the lack of effort to negate Iraqi threats, such as the Mirages, that might attack NavCent ships. Nor was he pleased with the small amount of effort that would be devoted to knocking out Iraq's air defenses. Some other targets—military headquarters buildings, chemical storage areas, air bases—were logical and expected. Primarily, he thought the plan lacked a way to prioritize and sequence targets—precisely the things he and his staff had learned to do over the previous year as ComSeventhFlt.

Mauz as Air Campaign Planner

Of his accomplishments as ComSeventhFlt, Vice Admiral Mauz took the most pride in developing what he believed were the first concrete, executable strike plans for use in the Far East in the event of a global war with the Soviet Union. Previously, the plans had been quite vague. Furthermore, the Seventh Fleet's previous plans and the corresponding 5th Air Force plans had been developed without either consulting the other. Mauz claimed to have coordinated his planning with the 5th Air Force. Although, in retrospect, this plan represented the last great, dying gasp of the now-obsolete Maritime Strategy, it also provided Mauz and his staff with enormous experience in real-world air campaign planning.

His strike plan began with a "DEAD" (pronounced "Dee-Add") campaign. In strike jargon, "SEAD," a term long in use, means suppression of enemy air defenses, that is, to use decoys, jamming, antiradiation missiles, and other means to degrade surface-based enemy air defenses *temporarily,* long enough for the bomb-dropping aircraft to reach their targets. Mauz's DEAD stood for *destruction* of enemy air defenses (radars, missile batteries, command centers, control vans), so that one would not have to suppress the same defenses day after day. Seventh Fleet's strike campaign against the Soviet Union in the Far East had envisioned a week or more of DEAD at the start. Then, when the enemy had little or no air defense left, the bombers would attack the real targets, such as leadership, military production, transportation. In the absence of air defenses, the weight and intensity of the main attack would be much greater. Mauz felt that his, and his staff's, experience in devising a strike campaign against the Soviet Union in the Far East had given them invaluable experience. He thought his staff had something important to contribute to strike planning and that Air Force parochialism, not only in Washington but also in Riyadh, was preventing them. Mauz said that initially the CentAF strike planners would not let the Navy into the room. He was frustrated.

On 30 August, Brigadier General Glosson returned to the *LaSalle* to brief Mauz. Mauz forcefully argued for a DEAD campaign to roll back Iraqi air defenses. Glosson was noncommittal.

On 3 September, Schwarzkopf approved Glosson's plan. Many details of the plan would change over the ensuing four months, but the basic emphasis on attacking leadership targets did not change. Tension between air-power advocates and the ground-oriented commanders remained. Glosson, like Colonel Warden, had a different view than did Schwarzkopf about what the plan would accomplish. Like Warden, Glosson hoped that air power alone could defeat Iraq.

Tension also remained between SEAD and DEAD advocates. Mauz had not seen in the ComUSCentAF plan any details of the connectivity within the Iraqi air-defense system. This was the kind of analysis Mauz and his staff had learned to do for their strike campaign against the Soviet Union. SPEAR (Strike Projection Evaluation and Antiair Research)—an Office of Naval Intelligence tactical support organization—had analyzed the Iraqi air-defense system in great detail. SPEAR personnel came to the theater in September and presented their findings. (After the war, the Gulf War Air Power Survey, commissioned by the Secretary of the Air Force, concluded that SPEAR had provided one of the most accurate prewar analyses of Iraq's capabilities and that this was because it was one of the few intelligence organizations that combined individuals with intelligence and operational backgrounds.)

Commander Perras, Mauz's Intelligence Officer, added in-theater knowledge and drew up complex charts describing how if particular nodes were knocked out, other nodes could not function and so did not need to be attacked. Vice Admiral Mauz invited Lt. General Horner down and showed him the construct of Iraqi air defenses. Horner seemed impressed but was noncommittal. Mauz later felt that the strike plans were changing in accordance with NavCent's suggestions. The original Instant Thunder plan, with limited emphasis on dismantling Iraq's air-defense system, evolved by January 1991 into the Desert Storm plan that included a major effort to destroy Iraq's air-defense system in the first few hours of the war. These changes were consistent with the arguments made by Mauz and SPEAR.[6]

Joint Force Air Component Commander

Few subjects raise as much disagreement and emotion among U.S. military officers as that of controlling air power. We do not attempt to give the entire history here or to resolve all the conflicts, but we do describe briefly a few issues.

Many officers in the U.S. Air Force believe that air power can be decisive but only if it is applied with unity of effort. Further, that unity of effort requires unity of command—one person in command of all air assets—which allows a coherent strike campaign that consistently attacks the primary objectives. If a situation requires concentration of all available air power in one sector of the theater, perhaps due to an enemy attack, the one person in charge can redirect efforts expeditiously. If the situation dictates that all strike assets in the theater be concentrated on one type of target, that too can be done quickly. By having the option of using the platforms and weapons of all services against any target in the theater, the person in charge can optimize how these air assets are distributed. These Air Force officers believe that many mistakes had been made in the application of air power during the Korean and Vietnam conflicts.[7] In those cases, Navy, Air Force, and Marine Corps aircraft had not been commanded by the same person. Within the Air Force, however, officers have differences about whether air power is best employed strategically or in support of the tactical surface forces.

Naval officers generally agree that air power should be applied with unity of effort. To most naval officers, however, unity of effort means that air power must be closely integrated with the surface forces (Marines on land, ships at sea). They believe one person should be in charge of all assets—air, sea, and ground—in each sector of a battlefield to coordinate the efforts of all. The Marine Corps' Marine Air-Ground Task Force, the Navy's carrier battle groups, and the Navy-Marine Corps amphibious assault arrangement illustrate how the two services combine the air arm with surface forces in one organization to achieve unity of effort.[8] The Air Force position brings surface and air forces under the same command only at the operational CinC level; naval forces do so at a lower, tactical echelon of command.

With the publication of "Joint Doctrine for Theater Counterair Operations (From Overseas Land Areas)" in 1986, the Air Force position prevailed. This publication was written during the Cold War, when air campaign planning focused on the central front of Europe and on Korea. The joint publication suggested that a CinC should normally appoint a Joint Force Air Component Commander. A so-called 1986 Omnibus Agreement, however, exempted most Marine air assets, because of their unique connection with the Marine Air-Ground Task Force. Although Vice Admiral Mauz, along with many others, embraced the idea of a central *planner* for the air campaign and was willing to accept tasking from the JFACC, many Navy officers never really accepted the idea of JFACC as a *commander*. They believed JFACC was merely a joint force air *coordinator*. As a coordinator, he could not command any naval air sorties. JFACC was merely the person who checked that two aircraft were not bombing the same target. He also would "deconflict" sorties to make sure aircraft did not run into each other. For example, Adm. Chuck Larson (CinCPacFlt) sent a message to Mauz saying that both he and Adm. Hunt Hardisty (USCinCPac) supported the JFACC concept, but only "as a coordinator, not a commander." Mauz thought it did not make much difference whether JFACC was called a coordinator or a commander. He would have objected if Lt. General Horner had tried to command Navy aircraft on the carriers, for example by specifying bomb loads; early on, however, Horner told Mauz he had no intention of commanding Navy aircraft.

Many NavCent officers thought they knew a better way. In part, they did not like the Air Force controlling Navy aircraft. They feared that an Air Force general, not understanding naval warfare and ordering naval air sorties somewhere at a crucial time, would deprive the fleet of its air and surface defense. Less dramatically, they just did not think the Air Force understood naval capabilities well enough to use naval aircraft to the best advantage in the national effort. Their better way was for the unified CinC to assign various commands geographic portions of the theater where each would have primary responsibility for strikes. This method had been used in Vietnam, where it had been termed "route packages." (This term is misleading, in that it is not ingress and egress routes that are apportioned but broad target areas.)

Route packages are a decentralized way to fight an air campaign. The commands for geographic portions of the theater decide, with the CinC's guidance, what targets to strike and how and when to conduct the strikes. The decentralization of this scheme greatly reduces the communications demand and avoids the problems of a commander from one service misusing assets from another service due to lack of understanding of their capabilities and limitations. Tactically, concentration on one area of the theater allows mission planners and air crews to become familiar with targets, terrain, and defenses in that area. The route-package method fits nicely with the Navy's battle groups, which provide "one-stop shopping" for strike operations.[9] Carrier battle groups have an intelligence section, mission planners (mostly aviators), ordnance, support aircraft, and attack aircraft.

The Navy officers feel they can understand the CinC's objectives well enough to pick out the most lucrative targets to strike, given their own capabilities and limitations, as well as ensure the defense of the fleet and civilian shipping at sea and in port.

Shortly after Mauz arrived in the theater, he called on Horner in Riyadh. They discussed plans to stop an Iraqi invasion of Saudi Arabia, alert states for aircraft, and similar practical issues. Mauz suggested that with the large number of aircraft arriving in-theater, Horner might want to think about assigning area responsibilities—at least in the near term—to keep things as simple as possible in the hectic early days before all the forces arrived. Mauz did not use the term "route packages," but Horner so interpreted him. He said he would resign before he accepted route packages; he thought they had killed people in Vietnam. Mauz thought to himself that what had killed aviators in Vietnam was not route packages but sending aircraft repeatedly to the same stupid targets picked by Washington.

One argument against route packages is that they do not allow quick concentration of effort in one geographic area of the battlefield, or on a particular type of target across the entire theater. Also, route packages would have restricted the choices for the best way to attack certain targets. For example, during Desert Storm, NavCent aircraft did not have bunker-busting weapons; CentAF aircraft did. If route packages had been used, this argument goes, bunkers in the NavCent's area could not have been attacked effectively, or special arrangements would have been necessary for CentAF aircraft to take out the bunkers in the NavCent's sector. The counterargument is that anyone can be brought into a route package.

Nevertheless, USCinCCent Operation Order 1 named ComUSCentAF as JFACC and directed ComUSNavCent to make available to JFACC all sorties "in excess of those required for naval warfare tasks." An exception was made to allow Marine aircraft to support MarCent under normal circumstances, but ComUSMarCent was also directed to make his excess sorties available to the JFACC. Interestingly, nobody defined "excess sorties." So, in effect, each component commander could provide as many or as few sorties to the strategic air campaign as he thought he could spare from his own primary needs. If NavCent and MarCent wanted to play a role in the central air campaign directed by JFACC, however, they would have to supply sorties to JFACC. As far as we know, Horner never directly challenged either ComUSMarCent or ComUSNavCent to declare more sorties "excess."

In addition to naming Horner as JFACC, General Schwarzkopf also appointed him as Area Air Defense Commander and Airspace Control Authority. Thus, Horner was in charge of almost all theater air operations except for sorties in direct support of NavCent or MarCent.

JFACC played a number of roles:

- One section of JFACC (the Black Hole) did overall planning for the strike campaign.

- During Desert Storm, JFACC decided which aircraft would strike which targets each day.
- JFACC controlled day-to-day air operations and could exercise tactical control of NavCent and MarCent sorties.

As previously noted, ComUSNavCent played only a minor role in Desert Shield and Storm strike campaign planning, despite experience in planning the naval air campaign against the Soviet Far East. Rear Admiral Wright states that he realized soon after arriving in Riyadh that the majority of the strike campaign planning would take place in the Black Hole in Riyadh, but he thought that Mauz was not initially convinced of that.[10] Two Navy officers participated in the Black Hole strike planning as the representatives of the carrier battle groups. We shall see how the perception that much of the strike planning for NavCent aircraft should be done on the carriers persisted all the way into Desert Storm.

The second JFACC function listed above—deciding which aircraft would strike which target each day—did not come fully into play until Desert Storm. Therefore, we defer much of the discussion of that function until we get to Desert Storm, in Volume II. But the system for implementing this aspect of JFACC was put into place early in Desert Shield. Instead of using the methodology suggested by the joint publication for developing an air schedule, CentAF—9th Air Force before Desert Shield—adopted the 9th Air Force Computer-Assisted Force Management System (CAFMS). CAFMS, an interactive set of computers tied together primarily with landlines, allowed squadrons to offer to attack targets on the list and thus interactively build an Air Tasking Order (ATO). CAFMS was not a universally accepted system, not even within the Air Force; other parts of the Air Force used systems that were similar but differed in the details. Naval commanders did not have the computers that constituted this or any similar system and did not have enough communication capacity to use CAFMS on their ships. Thus, they started out as second-class participants.

During Desert Shield, day-to-day air operations comprised mostly training flights and defensive patrols. The NavCent Air Coordination Group in Riyadh, essentially NavCent's representatives to JFACC, coordinated aircraft sortie plans, air-to-air tanking requests, combat air patrol requirements, air surveillance requests, and air-defense plans and intentions. Generally, they also fed into JFACC any NavCent comments and suggestions on procedures.

JFACC's right to exercise tactical control of NavCent and MarCent sorties worried many naval officers: JFACC might divert vital defensive assets at a crucial moment or otherwise misuse naval aircraft.[11] Actually, JFACC tactical control was a mechanism for redirecting sorties on short notice, a way to make the system more flexible.

Most naval officers did not initially appreciate the significance of JFACC. They did not understand the JFACC doctrine, what they were expected to do, or what they had the right to expect from USCinCCent and the JFACC. Not being familiar with the concept, they were ill prepared to help JFACC use naval aircraft as effectively as possible. They did not have any way to get training on the concept. Naval officers did not ignore JFACC deliberately; they just did not know what it was, had not been trained in it, and were far away from anyone who might have explained it.

Even reading the written material available on JFACC would not have helped the ComUSNavCent staff much, because there was not much JFACC doctrine. Doctrine suggested the joint force commander form a JFACC but gave little guidance on how a JFACC would actually work. The nearest thing to specific guidance on how actually to run things was a document that described a set of messages for requesting the air support requirements of each component and allocating the excess sorties—but JFACC did not follow that guidance.[12]

Air Tasking Order

To ensure unity of effort in the air, JFACC believed the forces needed centralized control of all sorties. The primary vehicle for devising the aircraft sortie schedule and executing the plan was the Air Tasking Order (ATO). During Desert Shield, the daily ATO was also used to deconflict air operations. An example shows why this was necessary.

On 10 August, before the ATO system became operative, eight *Independence* aircraft planned to fly to 28°30' north latitude to stimulate Iraqi air-defense systems and test the response of the Iraqi military to provocative actions by the United States. Due to problems with the KC-10 tankers, the aircraft could not reach their destinations. Before turning back, however, the lead F/A-18 detected a formation of unknown aircraft approaching. The pilot activated his master-arm switch (the first of a sequence of actions necessary to shoot). Soon the oncoming aircraft were identified as U.S. Air Force F-16s. There are two important points here. First, at this time aircrews had clearance to fire at aircraft beyond visual range. Shortly thereafter, aircrews were directed not to fire beyond visual range but to fire only if they had made a visual identification of their target. This reduced the chances for fratricide in the air, but it had subsequent consequences for the naval forces. Second, it's not good when the presence of friendly aircraft in the same airspace comes as a surprise. One purpose of the ATO was to avoid this type of surprise.

On 12 August, Lt. General Horner, in his role as USCinCCent Forward, ordered that all carrier air operations not in direct support of the carrier should be coordinated with USCentAF and the CentAF Tactical Air Coordination Center in Riyadh and placed on the daily ATO. He requested information on sorties and tanker requirements at least forty-eight hours in advance. His stated goal was to publish the daily ATO twenty-four hours before the effective date. If a sortie was declared to be in direct support of a carrier, it did not have to appear on the ATO and some battle groups frequently used this as a loophole. Generally, NavCent forces interpreted all overwater sorties as being in direct support. Another exception allowed flights over Oman to be flown without being put on the ATO.

The primary purpose of the ATO was to assign missions to each aircraft flying. A secondary but vital objective was to provide the information needed to avoid fratricide incidents. Having everyone know which aircraft will be flying where and when they will be there greatly decreases the likelihood of fratricide. Furthermore, in putting together the ATO, the JFACC would deconflict sorties to make sure that two or more coalition aircraft did not find themselves in the same place at the same time. The overall theme was that unity of effort could best be achieved through unity of command of all air sorties—a centralized air campaign run by JFACC.

The ATO was a gigantic military message—several hundred pages long during Desert Storm—sent out *every day* to everyone concerned with air sorties. It listed every sortie flying that day, the type of aircraft, its mission, call sign, IFF (Identification, Friend or Foe) codes, target complex, takeoff time, landing time, time over target, and refueling information. A section listed the special instructions (SPINS) covering the details of refueling tanker orbits and altitudes, search and rescue procedures, and communications plans. Weekly SPINS gave more detail.

Initially, the ATO assigned sorties takeoff times, the type and number of bombs to carry, and the amount of fuel to carry. To NavCent forces, this was micromanagement. Naval air wings strongly feel that it is their prerogative to decide the best weapon mix to achieve their assigned mission. The interactive CAFMS allowed the CentAF squadrons to input their recommended ordnance loads, so the final ATO would generally reflect their choices; the NavCent air wings, not having CAFMS, usually could not make such inputs. Thus, their bomb loads came as dictates from Riyadh and were deeply resented as Air Force interference in Navy tactical details. After a while, a compromise was reached: the ATO simply specified "best" ordnance loads for NavCent sorties.

During Desert Shield, the primary method for disseminating the daily ATO to ComUSNavCent ships was by hard-copy messages, typically transmitted by satellite. Because the communications channels were often clogged, even with a "Flash" precedence the ATO often failed to arrive electronically before the day's flights began.[13] Several other methods were tried in attempts to get the ATO to carriers more quickly. For example, Lt. Colonel Don Rupert, USAF, the Air Force liaison officer on the Seventh Fleet staff, tried to use a modem and a STU-III secure telephone to pass the ATO along commercial telephone lines. None of the alternatives worked satisfactorily.

To overcome these problems, during the planning phase of each ATO the NavCent liaison officers in JFACC would pass the preliminary plan to the carriers over the radio so the air wings could start their own planning. When the final ATO was promulgated, they would extract those portions relevant to the NavCent carriers (including information on sorties by aircraft from other services that might enter nearby airspace) and send only that part to the carriers, via hard-copy message.

During Desert Shield, much of NavCent regarded the requirement to place sorties on the daily ATO as a thorn in the Navy's side. NavCent forces had to get almost all overland flights on JFACC's daily schedule, the ATO (flights over water or over Oman being exempted). The Red Sea battle group had to place its training flights over Saudi Arabia on the ATO. The battle group on the North Arabian Sea side of the theater had a choice, and it generally chose not to put its flights on JFACC's schedule. Thus, over the many months of Desert Shield, the Red Sea battle groups were forced to become familiar with JFACC and the ATO, whereas the battle group in the North Arabian Sea avoided them as much as possible and succeeded pretty well. As a result, the latter battle group was less well prepared when it had to operate with JFACC and the ATO during Desert Storm.

Tomahawk

The Tomahawk cruise missile, which had never been used in combat, came in two major variants. First, there was the Tomahawk antiship missile (TASM), designed to be fired by one ship at another ship at distances greater than two hundred miles. Basically, the missile flew to a target area and used a radar seeker to search for a target. This variant was not used during Desert Storm; ComUSNavCent believed it made no sense for ships operating in the confined area of the Persian Gulf to carry such a long-range missile. To make room for the other, land-attack, variant of Tomahawk, on 14 September ComUSNavCent ordered all TASMs removed from NavCent ships.

The second type, the Tomahawk land-attack missile (TLAM), could be fired from ships and submarines at land targets more than six hundred miles away by programming it to fly to a particular point. The missile was extremely accurate and used two systems to navigate. First, as depicted in Figure 5–1, it used a series of previously loaded electronic maps of the ground under its flight path. The missile's radar determined the contour of the ground it was flying over; its computer compared this to the terrain contour maps in its memory to determine where it was and to alter its flight path accordingly. As it got nearer the target, it needed more accuracy than terrain contour matching (TERCOM) could provide, so it switched to digital scene-matching area correlation (DSMAC). The missile "looked" at the ground and compared what it was "seeing" with a stored digital image. After several such refinements of its location and flight path, the Tomahawk flew to the target and dived into it, with extraordinary accuracy.

People often question whether the second and subsequent missiles in a "stream" raid might have a problem finding the target due to smoke and debris from the impact of the first missile. The answer is that Tomahawk never looks at the target itself. The last DSMAC scene is several miles away from the target. This

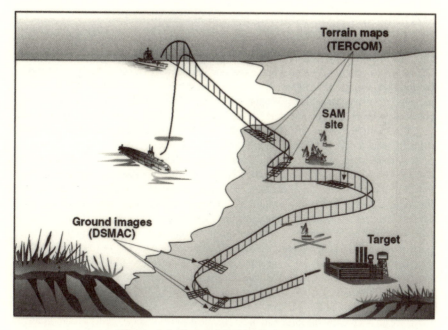

Figure 5–1. Tomahawk Missile Navigation

also ensures that the enemy cannot fool Tomahawk by camouflaging important targets.

The problem with the version of Tomahawk available during Desert Storm is that obtaining the data for the TERCOMs and DSMACs took time. Planning the mission route also took time. Up to the first of August, all the Tomahawk planning effort had gone into planning missions against the Soviet Union and other high-priority areas of the time. No missions had been planned against Iraq. On 30 July 1990, USCinCCent asked the Tomahawk mission planners to start preparing missions against Iraq.

By January of 1991, the mission planners at the cruise missile support activities connected with USCinCPac and USCinCLant had had a lot of practice and were quite proficient. They also had a library of TERCOMs and DSMACs with which to work. Between August 1990 and January 1991, however, there was a fair amount of confusion between the USCinCCent staff and the mission planners. These problems were exacerbated by the lack of familiarity with Tomahawk among the USCinCCent and JFACC personnel. For example, many of the early targets nominated were not appropriate for Tomahawk. Despite problems and changes in direction, in less than six months the mission planners prepared and distributed to NavCent forces an entire Tomahawk strike campaign.

NOTES

Sources for the intelligence included messages, the author's notes from briefings to the staff, and interviews with Mauz, Wright, and Wickersham. Primary sources for early air defense issues were CNA reports, messages, and interviews with Mauz, Marfiak, Dawson, and Johnson. Sources for early aspects of strike warfare included messages, CNA reports, and interviews with Mauz, Less, Wright, Johnson, and Wickersham. Other information on events came from books by Mandeles et al., Schwarzkopf, Mann, Gordon and Trainor, and the GWAPS survey. Books by Mann, Warden, and Winnefeld and Johnson provided some of the material for the Air Force views on strike and JFACC.

1. An exception, however, was the Fleet Marine Officer on the staff, Col. Frank Wickersham, who was far more optimistic. He knew the Marines who were guarding the coastal route and that they were confident they could stop the Iraqis. In August 1990 he told the author he knew the man in charge up there: "He does not know the meaning of the word retreat." Wickersham reluctantly conceded that they could be overwhelmed by numerically superior forces but said they would then "go to the ground" and harass the Iraqis' rear. Wickersham also said the amphibious force of Marines would land in the Iraqis' rear, across their supply lines (though the amphibious forces would not arrive until mid-September). Much later, Wickersham said he had based his optimism on visits to the area to be defended and to the commands.

2. DIA Washington DC 222044Z AUG 90.

3. We do not present the information on chemical and biological agents as authoritative, but to indicate the type of information given to the staff in August and September. This particular briefing actually took place on 2 October.

4. A few, such as Colonel John Warden, USAF, advocated ignoring close air support for the troops engaging the invading Iraqis and bombing only strategic targets in Iraq. That view never had a chance.

5. CTG 150.5 200800Z AUG 90, Personal for VAdm. Mauz from Lynch, Critical Support.

6. We are unable to judge how much of the change was due to their influence. Mauz later claimed that after Desert Storm, in a meeting at the Air War College, Glosson turned to him and publicly gave him credit for showing the Air Force how to roll back air defenses. Vice Admiral Wright, however, felt that CentAF felt SPEAR had not given them much that was new. He thought the plan changed but not necessarily in response to SPEAR. The author has heard Lt. Gen. Horner give the Navy credit for teaching how to defeat Iraq's air defenses.

7. So did the Navy, but its list of mistakes differed somewhat from the Air Force's.

8. We are indebted to Peter Perla's study, Perla et al., *The Navy and the JFACC,* for many insights throughout this book.

9. Except for land-based tanking.

10. Admiral Mauz distinguishes between tactical planning done by the aircrews on the carriers and overarching strike planning done in the Black Hole. He claims he knew the latter would be done in Riyadh.

11. Admiral Mauz says this did not worry him.

12. The extensive exchange of messages required by this procedure would almost certainly be impractical for a major operation like Desert Shield or Desert Storm.

13. From lowest to highest, message priorities are "Routine," "Priority," "Operational Immediate," and "Flash." Ordinarily, "Flash" is reserved for such messages as reporting contact with the enemy.

Chapter 6

Amphibious Forces

Marines had two roles in the early days of Desert Shield. First, Marines flown from the United States to Saudi Arabia were equipped with materiel from the Maritime Prepositioning Force. This enabled them to arrive quickly and to be able to fight soon after they arrived. Second, Marines in amphibious ships, when they arrived in theater, would provide the capability to make a "forced entry" into Saudi Arabia or Kuwait.

MARITIME PREPOSITIONING FORCE

On 8 August, the ships of Maritime Prepositioning Squadron 2 got under way from their anchorage in Diego Garcia.[1] These ships carried the equipment of the 7th Marine Expeditionary Brigade (7th MEB). Although troops can fly rapidly to any point in the world, they cannot do much without their heavy equipment—such as artillery, trucks, tanks, ammunition, and fuel.

The Maritime Prepositioning Squadron ships are floating warehouses where large quantities of equipment can be stored in climate-controlled conditions at several locations throughout the world. When a crisis threatens, an offload preparation party boards the ships and, while the ships sail to a friendly port near the crisis area, prepares the equipment for use. For a vehicle, this preparation involves mundane tasks like filling the radiator with water, putting fuel in the tank, filling the battery, charging it if necessary, and checking that the vehicle starts and runs. The first of the five ships of Maritime Prepositioning Squadron 2 arrived at al-Jubail, Saudi Arabia, on 14 August. Because these ships had gotten under way on such short notice, none had offload preparation parties on board. The ships' crews and the contractor personnel (on board to oversee the storage) prepared the equipment during the transit.

Meanwhile, the Marines of 7th MEB were flying from Camp Pendleton, California, and they arrived at al-Jubail about the same time as the ships. From 15 to 20 August 7th MEB "married up" with its equipment—that is, the equipment was distributed to the Marines. In concept, the logistics people arrive first, conduct the offload, sort items, and distribute the equipment as the combat forces arrive over a few days. That's not the way it happened. Because the Marines expected to go into combat shortly after they arrived in Saudi Arabia, they "front-loaded" the deployment with combat troops and only a few logistics people—a shooter-first policy. All the equipment came off the ships quickly and was given to the units as rapidly as possible.

Initially, the Army's 82nd Airborne Division occupied defensive positions on the approaches to al-Jubail. On 20 August, the 7th MEB Marines relieved it. As Marine AH-1W helicopters and AV-8B Harrier "jump jets" (fixed-wing aircraft capable of vertical takeoffs and landings) arrived in-theater, the helicopters went to the al-Jubail Naval Air Facility, and the jump jets went to King Abdul Aziz naval base just south of al-Jubail. On 22 August, the first F/A-18 fighter-bombers arrived at Sheikh Isa airfield in Bahrain.

Maritime Prepositioning Squadron 3 left its base in Guam on 8 August and sailed to al-Jubail. Marines of 1st MEB flew from their base in Hawaii and started marrying up with their equipment on the Maritime Prepositioning Squadron 3 ships on 26 August. Unlike 7th MEB, 1st MEB front-loaded its deployment with logistics personnel rather than combat personnel. Because Iraq had not attacked and 7th MEB was now moving to defensive positions, 1st MEB unloaded at a more manageable pace than had 7th MEB. On 2 September, Lt. Gen. Walt Boomer assumed operational control of all the MarCent forces and set up his headquarters at al-Jubail.

By early September the Marines had established a credible defense. Some MarCent ground forces had deployed to defensive positions. Marine F/A-18s flew combat air patrol over the northern Persian Gulf. Marine A-6s, AV-8Bs, and F/A-18s maintained strip alert for close air support missions if Iraq attacked. ComUSNavCent carriers were prepared to provide additional close air support. By mid-September, regimental-size task forces had moved to defensive positions to the north. If the Iraqis attacked along the coastal road, they still would greatly outnumber the Marine defenders, but Saddam had missed his chance to attack before the American defenses were in place.

AMPHIBIOUS TASK FORCE

Saddam Hussein has been quoted as saying later, "We made a vast mistake in not proceeding forthwith to invade Saudi Arabia."[2] If the Iraqis contemplated an invasion of Saudi Arabia in August or early September, they should have worried about an American amphibious landing in their rear. As Saudi Arabia contains few roads and one of them runs near the coast of the Persian Gulf, an amphibious landing could cut off the lines of communications of an invading force. One of the problems with conducting an amphibious assault during Desert Storm was the short coastline of Kuwait, which left few options for a landing site. During the early days of Desert Shield, however, the situation differed sharply. Had the Iraqis attacked south into Saudi Arabia in August or September as they threatened to do, they would have had to worry about the long Saudi coastline in their rear. They could not possibly have defended it all, and with their shaky logistics, they could not have stood even a temporary disruption of their supply lines. A landing anywhere in their rear along the coast would have been catastrophic for them. For the coalition, this prospect, combined with the intelligence assessments cited in chapter 5, made it urgent to get an amphibious capability into the theater as quickly as possible. Two separate groups of amphibious ships sailed: one from the East Coast of the United States, one from Subic Bay in the Philippines. Each started from nearly a quarter of the way around the world, and neither would arrive until early or mid-September.

Deployment of the Amphibious Task Force

At the Outset

On 9 August, 4th MEB, commanded by Maj. Gen. Harry Jenkins, was alerted for deployment. On the next day, Amphibious Group Two (PhibGru Two), commanded by Rear Adm. Bat LaPlante, was alerted. Presumably, the CJCS chose 4th MEB, even though 4th MEB lacked familiarity with the CentCom theater and problems, because it had already worked up for a NATO exercise and was more ready to deploy than 5th MEB on the West Coast.[3] Most of the thirteen amphibious ships of Amphibious Group Two had already been alerted to go on the NATO exercise.

On the other side of the world, the 13th Marine Expeditionary Unit (Special Operations Capable), 13th MEU(SOC), sailed west from Subic Bay in the Philippines embarked on the five amphibious ships of Amphibious Squadron Five. They would be accompanied by three logistics ships. The term "Special Operations Capable" appended to 13th MEU indicated that it had been certified as capable of performing a list of specific special-warfare tasks. These forces constituted Amphibious Ready Group (ARG) Alfa, on a regular deployment to the western Pacific. Because this was a standard deployment, the ships were ready to conduct an amphibious operation on short notice.

Marines of the 4th MEB boarded the PhibGru Two ships in Morehead City, North Carolina, and in Norfolk. The last of the PhibGru Two ships sailed east on 22 August. LaPlante had wanted all thirteen of his amphibious ships to sail as a group, because they had not practiced operating in such a large group for a long time. Some Navy Staff officers, however, worried that CNN was showing Air Force aircraft taking off to fly to the Persian Gulf and Army personnel leaving for the Gulf; they did not want CNN to show Navy ships loading but not going any-

Rear Admiral John "Bat" LaPlante, Commander, Amphibious Task Force, and Major General Harry Jenkins, Jr., Commander, Landing Force. Navy Photos.

where. On the other hand, the commander in chief of the Atlantic Command reportedly wanted the ships to sail one at a time, to maximize the CNN coverage. A compromise allowed the ships to sail in three groups. Unfortunately, this meant that during the transit LaPlante and Jenkins could not hold face-to-face meetings with some of their subordinates, and limited radio communications systems on board further degraded the opportunity to sort out problems with their subordinates.

Definition of Terms

Let's take a time-out to define a few terms used in amphibious warfare:

- Assault—an amphibious operation that involves *establishing* a force on a hostile or potentially hostile shore.
- Raid—an amphibious operation involving temporary occupation of an objective, followed by a *planned withdrawal.*
- Demonstration—an amphibious operation conducted for the purpose of *deceiving* the enemy by a show of force.
- Administrative landing—an *unopposed* landing.
- Administrative loading—a loading system that gives primary consideration to maximizing use of space without regard to tactical considerations; equipment and supplies must be unloaded and sorted before they can be used.
- Combat loading—arrangement of personnel and stowage of equipment and supplies that conforms to the anticipated tactical operation; each item is stowed so that it can be unloaded at the required time.[4]

"PERMA," a fundamental concept of amphibious doctrine, is a mnemonic for the sequence in which major events occur in an amphibious assault: planning, embarkation, rehearsal, movement, assault. First, doctrine calls for a higher authority to send the Commander, Amphibious Task Force (CATF) an initiating directive. The CATF is a Navy officer, Rear Admiral LaPlante in this case. Of equal status with CATF is a Marine officer, the Commander, Landing Force (CLF, pronounced "Cliff"), here Major General Jenkins. Doctrine strongly urges that the CATF and CLF both embark on the same ship. Based on the initiating directive, the CATF and CLF plan the operation. Among other things, the plan tells *what* to load on the ships and *how* to load them so that the items that are needed first will get unloaded first—combat loading, a vital planning element when a force must unload in the face of an enemy. Then the Amphibious Task Force rehearses the operation to find the flaws in the plan. After the rehearsal it revises the plan and re-embarks on the ships, loading them in accordance with the revisions. At this point, the amphibious force moves toward the amphibious objective area. The final stage culminates with the assault itself.

According to doctrine, during the planning CATF and CLF are coequals, but CATF is responsible for operations of the entire force and the overall operation; CLF reports to CATF upon embarkation and remains under his command. (Here the chain of command resulted in rank inversion: Jenkins wore two stars and LaPlante only one. This rank disparity is not uncommon and evidently caused no problems.) When the landing force establishes itself ashore, CLF becomes independent of CATF. That is how doctrine says things are supposed to be done. That is *not* how things were done.

The Real World

First, there was no initiating directive. Major General Jenkins viewed his instructions as being to get on the ships and go to the theater. At one time, he even thought he would be placed under the control of Lt. General Boomer, ComUS-MarCent. ComUSNavCent, still Rear Adm. (Sel.) Bob Sutton in Pearl Harbor when the deployment order was issued, did not know what the Amphibious Task Force would be required to do when it arrived in-theater. Jenkins and Rear Admiral LaPlante knew they had to be prepared to do many different things but had no specifics on any of the possibilities. Because of the urgency created by Iraq's threats to invade Saudi Arabia, the amphibious force could not wait until a set of plans was devised; the Marines therefore loaded everything they thought they might need, and they could not know in detail what would be needed first. This loading problem was exacerbated by the fact that a full MEB's equipment normally requires about twenty amphibious ships, but only thirteen were available.

LaPlante warned the commanding officers of his ships that they would face intense pressure to overload their ships; as the Marines did not know what they could afford to leave behind, they felt they had to bring everything. Despite

LaPlante's warning, his amphibious ships loaded in excess of capacity. Packing as much as possible on the available ships put the maximum combat power into the theater of operations as soon as possible, but the combat power would not be usable until the Marine equipment was restowed in the optimum way for a particular type of operation. If Iraq attacked, ComUSNavCent would need *immediate* combat power.

Administrative Versus Combat Loading

Rear Admiral LaPlante warned Commander, Second Fleet, (LaPlante's superior until he deployed) that the deployment order could be construed as requiring the Amphibious Task Force to arrive in theater assault capable but that the way the task force was being loaded, it might be capable only of an administrative offload, not an opposed landing.

If the ships were administratively loaded, upon its arrival in the Persian Gulf the Amphibious Task Force would have to produce a landing plan, selectively unload some equipment in a friendly port, and reload in accordance with the plan. This might take a week. Furthermore, it would be highly desirable for the amphibious force to conduct at least one rehearsal of the assault plan. Initially, Vice Adm. Hank Mauz and his staff did not understand the reasons for the lack of combat loading and the need to reconfigure. Perhaps unreasonably, Mauz wanted the Amphibious Task Force to be ready to conduct an assault soon after it sailed into the Persian Gulf. LaPlante's message to the commander of the Second Fleet warning that the Amphibious Task Force might have to reconfigure before making an assault had been readdressed to ComSeventhFlt by ComSecondFlt, but Mauz seems never to have seen it; perhaps it was lost or delayed in the overloaded communication system.[5]

On 22 August, Mauz received a message from LaPlante that hinted at the problem: "The way we are loaded imposes some limitations on immediate employment options."[6] LaPlante wrote that he and Major General Jenkins had made a deliberate decision to maximize the combat power embarked, even at the cost of some tactical flexibility (for instance, the ability to conduct an opposed assault immediately), and that as a result, though the Amphibious Task Force was not optimized for any one amphibious mission, it brought the potential for many. It would probably need a place to store some equipment ashore to gain the tactical flexibility it needed. To Mauz, the nature of these limitations was not clear. This time, the communications problem appeared to be a human failure to be sufficiently explicit. Mauz sent LaPlante a message asking him what tactical limitations his current loadout imposed. Evidently, Mauz did not realize their seriousness, because on 23 August he told Gen. Norman Schwarzkopf that eighteen ships (clearly referring to the thirteen PhibGru Two ships and five PhibRon 5 ships) were combat loaded and generally configured for amphibious assault operations.

On 28 August (perhaps before they received Mauz's latest request), LaPlante and Jenkins laid out their problems in detail. For example, two OV-10 fixed-wing observation aircraft that had been loaded on the helicopter carrier USS *Iwo Jima* (LPH 2) would have to be taken off by crane or helicopter. LaPlante said he had strongly opposed putting OV-10s on the *Iwo Jima* but had been overruled at the last minute by the commander in chief of the Atlantic Fleet.[7] LaPlante had heard that "in-theater personnel" insisted on the OV-10s and had accepted the consequent necessity of administrative load and offload. Unknown to LaPlante, Lt. General Boomer had asked that every effort be made to embark the OV-10s with 4th MEB, because he believed no other OV-10s were deploying and considered that capability very important.

LaPlante and Jenkins went on to inform Mauz that reconfiguration under way had eliminated the need to put gear ashore but they asked him to realize that "these ships are stuffed." The bottom line was,

We can operate loaded as we are—but we are much more cumbersome than we would like to be, and that will tend to slow us down. This was a conscious choice, you will recall—to bring as much of a MEB into theatre as possible in insufficient shipping. It is not an admin load, but neither is it wholly tactical; it is a compromise.[8]

Employment Options

To recapitulate, Vice Admiral Mauz would have eighteen amphibious ships in the theater by mid-September—thirteen Atlantic Fleet amphibious ships under Rear Admiral LaPlante with Major General Jenkins's 4th MEB Marines embarked, and five Pacific Fleet amphibious ships en route from Subic Bay with the 13th MEU(SOC) embarked. How would ComUSNavCent employ this force?

LaPlante and Jenkins expressed concern over potential sites for amphibious operations. Shoal water and mud flats extending far from shore in most places would limit naval gunfire and logistics support. Few locations would permit the amphibious ships to get close enough to shore to allow a quick buildup of combat power on the beach. They saw only two candidate areas along the Saudi coast, and they had not yet received beach survey data on those.

In his message on the concept of operations for the amphibious force, Vice Admiral Mauz recommended to General Schwarzkopf that he keep the amphibious forces afloat as an amphibious assault capability rather than send them ashore immediately to fight with MarCent. They could be offloaded to reinforce MarCent if that became necessary. He would organize the Amphibious Task Force into three amphibious assault groups that could be employed individually or as one large force. He intended to keep the groups in the North Arabian Sea, with one of them rotating into the southern Persian Gulf for "presence," operations, or port visits.

Mauz intended to have the amphibious force plan landings from southern Kuwait as far down the Saudi coast as al-Jubail. Mauz was upbeat, saying that if hostilities began the United States would quickly establish the total air and sea control needed for an amphibious operation. In an ominous and prescient comment, however, Mauz warned that mining could be a problem for amphibious operations, particularly near Kuwait.

While the amphibious force sailed toward the theater, Mauz ordered Major General Jenkins and Rear Admiral LaPlante to prepare specific plans for a variety of potential operations. To organize the tasking, the ComUSNavCent Operation Order divided the coastline from central Kuwait to central Saudi Arabia into three regions, numbered I through III from north to south. Planning for a landing in the central region was given the highest priority, the southern region the lowest priority. The order defined the regions and listed the types of operations the Amphibious Task Force was to be prepared to conduct in each. Also, because the amphibious force was the CinCCent theater reserve force, it might be tasked to reinforce MarCent forces ashore via an administrative landing.

As any amphibious plan would make sense only if it conformed to Lt. General Boomer's needs, Mauz gave Boomer a chance to comment on a draft of the plan. Boomer suggested adding a fourth area north of area I and changing the priorities for the regions to: north, far north, south, central. Unfortunately, though Boomer sent his suggestions with "Operational Immediate" precedence, Mauz did not receive the message for more than two days. It arrived just after his staff transmitted the final version of the order. Once again, limitations of the communication system had degraded planning.

On 4 September, on board the *Blue Ridge*, Colonel Frank Wickersham III, USMC, the Fleet Marine Officer on the ComUSNavCent staff, and Mauz briefed General Schwarzkopf, who had arrived in-theater about a week previously. First, Wickersham summarized the forces that were about to arrive in-theater:

- Twenty-one ships, including four large-deck aviation ships (the *Nassau*, *Iwo Jima*, USS *Guam* [LPH 9], and USS *Okinawa* [LPH 3]), with twenty fixed-wing and seventy-three rotary-wing aircraft embarked
- 10,200 Marines
- 180 tanks and armored vehicles
- Forty artillery pieces.

The "180 tanks and armored vehicles" shown on the briefing slide in fact included only seventeen tanks. Also, the more than ten thousand Marines were not all actual combat troops ("trigger pullers"). Many were support personnel.[9]

Wickersham then went over the employment options for the amphibious force in each of the three geographic areas (see Figure 6–1). Evidently reflecting Boomer's input, the definitions of the three regions were slightly different from those in the Operation Order.[10] Assuming defensive operations against an Iraqi penetration, potential amphibious operations included:

- Landing Area I (Mina Saud, Kuwait, just north of the Kuwait-Saudi border): raids and feints[11]

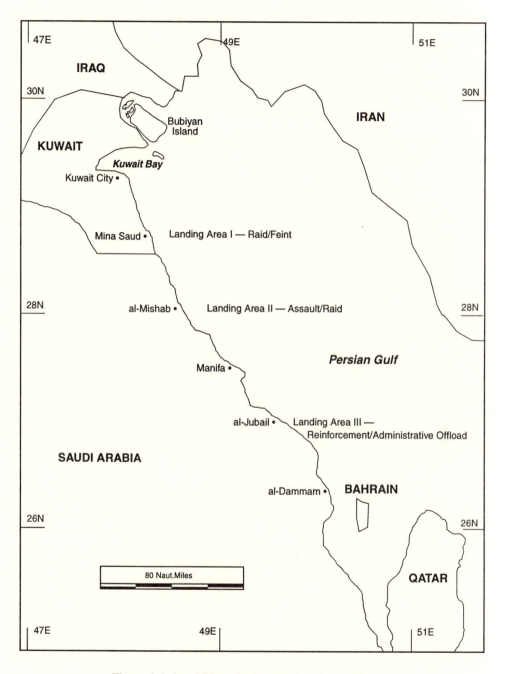

Figure 6–1. Amphibious Options Early in Desert Shield

- Landing Area II (near al-Mishab, Saudi Arabia): assaults and raids
- Landing Area III (al-Jubail, Saudi Arabia): administrative landing for reinforcement.

Wickersham noted that the northern area would have to be reviewed as an area for assault operations as force ratios became more favorable. He concluded by telling Schwarzkopf that any reconfiguration of the force would be completed by 28 September. According to Wickersham, Schwarzkopf heard the briefing without any notable comments. He seemed unconcerned about delay in providing an amphibious assault capability.

Meanwhile, LaPlante was not happy with what he had learned about the hydrography of the Persian Gulf:

West coast of PG is most difficult amphib challenge yet. . . . Show stopper here is the distance the mud flats extend from the coast . . . and these appear to exist nearly everywhere.[12] I have not yet seen an assault beach on the Saudi coast with which I am happy. If there do prove to be any, I'm sure at this point that they would be so few as to effectively eliminate surprise.[13]

Mauz thought this was good input—and he agreed.

Shortly before the amphibious force arrived in-theater, LaPlante sent Mauz plans for an amphibious assault (two options), a raid, and an administrative landing. The amphibious force had a problem with being asked to plan a feint; that tasking had sown confusion. LaPlante noted that joint doctrine for landing force operations did not discuss or define feints. He assumed a feint was a movement of portions of the Amphibious Task Force and supporting forces designed to reveal enemy capabilities and deceive the enemy as to one's own intentions. His staff had incorporated such maneuvers into its assault and raid plans. What Mauz had really wanted, however, was a plan for a demonstration separate from plans for raids and assaults.

To summarize, Mauz had asked for specific plans for four types of operations (assault, raid, feint, administrative offload) in three areas of interest (Boomer's fourth area had not been added to the tasking yet), with stated connections between the types of operations and the areas. In turn, LaPlante and Jenkins had provided generic plans for three types of operations (assault, raid, administrative offload) not tied to any specific area, because they did not have sufficient information to make specific plans for particular areas.

The amphibious forces arrived in the North Arabian Sea from 8 to 17 September. By mid-September the threat of an Iraqi invasion of Saudi Arabia had subsided somewhat. Intelligence deemed invasion less likely, because Iraq was setting up a defensive barrier in Kuwait. If Iraq did attack, the coalition was steadily improving its ability to resist the invasion. Because the Iraqis had not attacked during the previous month, Intelligence deemed them not very likely to do so now, when the odds were less in their favor. We do not know whether the threat of an amphibious assault played any role in Iraq's decision not to invade.

Iraq did not know the Amphibious Task Force was not combat loaded and might have thought that the Marines would be capable of assaulting a beach in force immediately upon arrival in the theater.

Communications Woes

Before his ships sailed, Rear Admiral LaPlante had sent a message to his commanding officers that stressed the need for clear communications:

There were only three battles of annihilation fought in the age of sail—all were fought by Lord Nelson. His success is attributed to the communication which existed between he and his subordinates. . . . Given our physical separation and the short-notice character of our operations to date, the importance of these communications cannot be overemphasized. It is not enough that my guidance be easily understood—it must also be nearly impossible to misunderstand.[14]

LaPlante was concerned about communications with his subordinates, but his warning applies also to communications with higher authority.

Communication problems—both equipment related and people related—affected early amphibious planning. As noted, because the Amphibious Task Force sailed in three groups Rear Admiral LaPlante and Major General Jenkins were unable to have face-to-face meetings with all of their subordinates. Equipment limitations hindered radio and message communications both with their subordinates and with their commander in the Persian Gulf. Vice Admiral Mauz probably did not receive the message from LaPlante warning of the need to reconfigure his ships. In a subsequent message, LaPlante did not clearly delineate the nature of his problems with overloaded ships whose loads needed to be reconfigured. Lt. General Boomer's input arrived too late to be included in Mauz's amphibious Operation Order. Mauz used nonstandard and ambiguous terminology in asking LaPlante to plan a feint and therefore did not get what he wanted.

Poor communications caused considerable friction between the Amphibious Task Force and ComUSNavCent staffs. Captain Gordon Holder, USN, the ComUSNavCent staff's only expert on the Navy side of amphibious warfare, might have smoothed over some of the rough spots; unfortunately, he was still tied up overseeing the Seventh Fleet port visit to Vladivostok. He would not rejoin the staff until late September.

Mauz could not wait until the Amphibious Task Force arrived in-theater to develop general plans for its employment. When Colonel Wickersham sent an informal message to Jenkins's Operations Officer to fill him in on some of the planning going on in the theater, it caused a "firestorm." Rear Admiral LaPlante viewed the message as saying in effect that the ComUSNavCent staff had selected the landing site for his assault and would tell him about the details later. He thought the CATF and CLF should select the assault beaches. LaPlante vigorously protested to Mauz, adding that Wickersham had proposed only a single rehearsal.

To LaPlante it seemed Wickersham was too far out ahead of the Amphibious Task Force and had not let it in on his thinking or provided feedback on the Amphibious Task Force's inputs. We believe much of the problem came from limited communications and the absence of liaison officers. Also, messages were delayed many days in transit and often did not arrive before another message went in the other direction, thus giving the appearance of ignoring inputs. As a result, misunderstandings plagued early relations between the Amphibious Task Force and ComUSNavCent.

Liaison officers can often compensate for a lack of good communications. An exchange of liaison officers would have allowed amphibious planning to take into account both the situation in the theater and the specific capabilities of the Amphibious Task Force. Also, face-to-face contact often elicits reasonable explanations that prevent misunderstandings from occurring and growing into major obstacles. On 24 August, while still en route to the theater, LaPlante asked Mauz to send him a liaison officer; instead, because the *Blue Ridge* had not yet arrived and Mauz had few staff officers with him, Mauz suggested the Amphibious Task Force send a liaison officer to him. LaPlante said he could not do that, because his staff was small and they had a lot of planning to do. Some on the ComUSNavCent staff considered this a faux pas; one-star admirals are not supposed to decline such requests from three-star admirals. This incident exacerbated the friction between the two staffs, especially concerning the issue of combat loading. (Mauz, however, claims that this apparent rebuff did not bother him—he had understood that LaPlante had a small staff.)

After reconsidering, LaPlante then sent his Chief of Staff to act as liaison to ComUSNavCent for several weeks. After the Amphibious Task Force arrived in-theater, staff officers from ComUSNavCent, USCinCCent, ComUSMarCent, PhibGru Two, and 4th MEB attended the first amphibious conference, aboard the *Blue Ridge* on 19 September. These and later face-to-face meetings ironed out many misunderstandings and, especially after Holder's arrival in Bahrain in late September, resulted in much smoother subsequent relations between the staffs.

With the benefit of hindsight, the biggest factor leading to misunderstandings was the failure of Mauz to convey, and of the Amphibious Task Force to perceive, the urgency of the situation. In August and early September, an amphibious assault several months down the road did not interest Mauz; an amphibious assault might be urgently needed as soon as the Amphibious Task Force arrived in-theater. On the other hand, given the lack of workups by the Amphibious Task Force, this may have been an impossibility. The Amphibious Task Force for its part failed to spell out clearly its limitations early in the evolution. The command in-theater should have been consulted before the Amphibious Task Force loading decisions were made, but no effective naval command with the overall picture and responsibility for all operations existed at the time. Mauz had not yet assumed command when key loading decisions were made. Lack of good communications and liaison exacerbated all of these problems.

FORCE MOVEMENTS AND RESTRICTIONS

At the same time Vice Admiral Mauz was developing amphibious plans, restrictions placed on operations by General Schwarzkopf were affecting the ability to execute those plans. As ComUSNavCent's briefing to General Schwarzkopf indicated, when force ratios grew more favorable, amphibious landings in Kuwait would be considered. However, Intelligence had already warned of possible Iraqi mining activity off Kuwait on 28 August; mining would greatly complicate any amphibious operation in the Persian Gulf. Mauz would have liked to have aircraft patrol the area off the Kuwaiti coast to detect any Iraqi mining of the Persian Gulf. Because mining international waters is a violation of international law, if NavCent forces could catch Iraq in the act of mining, they could sink or capture the minelayer (as the United States had done with the Iranian minelayer *Iran Ajr* in 1987).

Schwarzkopf, on the other hand, did not want to precipitate a war—probably for multiple reasons. First, he was not confident of being able to defend against an Iraqi attack until the heavy armored forces and all the support for the Air Force were in-theater. Second, he wanted to avoid bloodshed if possible. Furthermore, it was in the interests of the United States to maintain the moral high ground by not being too provocative. Setting operating limits, however, had serious consequences for naval operations in the Persian Gulf. One might reasonably ask whether the limits were consistent with showing the Iraqis that the United States was really serious about getting them out of Kuwait.

Initially, Schwarzkopf restricted NavCent forces from operating north of 27°00' north latitude in the Persian Gulf—about ninety nautical miles south of the Kuwaiti-Saudi border. On 3 September Mauz, with Schwarzkopf's permission, loosened the restriction to 27°30' north. The intention was for surface air-defense ships to stay near 27°00', but other ships could operate up to 27°30' to extend surface surveillance and to cover shipping into al-Jubail and Dammam. On 12 September, the limit was moved to 28°00' north, to provide presence, enhance surveillance coverage, promote mutual support and coordination with Saudi naval forces, and increase coverage for forces ashore. Saudi patrol boats were going all the way to the Kuwaiti border (about 28°32' north), and wanted the U.S. Navy to go farther north. Aircraft also had a limit, typically at 28°30' north. Depending on the situation, the exact limits changed from time to time throughout Desert Shield. What did not change, however, is that these limits were a persistent source of friction between ComUSNavCent and USCinCCent.

NOTES

The chronology of events in this chapter drew on CNA's reconstruction report, the Department of Defense's *Conduct of the Persian Gulf War*, and messages. The definition of terms used in amphibious warfare came from the DOD dictionary. Documentation of the misunderstandings between the amphibious task force and ComUSNavCent and amphibious employment options included messages (mostly "Personal For"), the author's observations, a concept paper written by Frank Wickersham, the slides and text Wickersham used to brief Schwarzkopf, and interviews with LaPlante, Jenkins, Mauz, and Wickersham.

1. General Alfred "Al" Gray, USMC, Commandant of the Marine Corps, says that in July 1990 he tried to persuade General Colin Powell, Chairman of the Joint Chiefs, to get the Maritime Prepositioning Force ships under way so they could serve as a deterrent to Iraq. Gray thought this idea never got the full discussion it deserved.

2. Khaled, *Desert Warrior,* 21.

3. 5th MEB would eventually deploy in December and arrive in-theater in January 1991.

4. Department of Defense, *Dictionary of Military and Associated Terms,* 5, 76. Vice Admiral LaPlante later pointed out that doctrine is not helpful in defining the difference. He defined tactical loading as allowing changes to the landing plan while en route to a landing. By that measure, the Amphibious Task Force was never tactically loaded, even during Desert Storm.

5. As the readdressed message was sent only "Priority," ComSeventhFlt did not receive it until 22 August. Mauz had already left the flagship to fly to Bahrain when this message was received at ComSeventhFlt. He still should have gotten a copy of the message on the *LaSalle,* but he might not have. Both copies of the message we located in the Center for Naval Analyses' archives were received on the *Blue Ridge.* In any case, a week later Mauz still did not know that the Amphibious Task Force was not combat loaded.

6. CTG 150.6 212136Z AUG 90, Personal for VAdm. Mauz from LaPlante, TF 150 Planning.

7. CinCLantFlt is the Navy component of the CinCLant, who was tasked to support USCinCCent. As such, he should not have been making what was, in essence, an operational decision.

8. TG 150.6 281550Z AUG 90, Personal for VAdm. Mauz info LGen. Boomer from Jenkins and LaPlante, Concept of Amphibious Operations.

9. The figure of ten thousand Marines did not include the 2,100 Marines of Regimental Landing Team 4 who would go ashore immediately to reinforce MarCent. These Marines could be reembarked for amphibious operations if necessary.

10. In particular, the region from Manifa to Damman, Saudi Arabia, had been an option for an amphibious assault in the Operation Order.

11. Note that "feint" is not a doctrinally defined term. Presumably, it meant "demonstration."

12. Colonel Wickersham has claimed that although this seemed a reasonable conclusion from the charts, exploitation of local lore and inspection of the sites revealed that many of these areas were usable—the mud flats lay over solid coral that could support vehicles.

13. CTG 150.6 041010Z SEP 90, Personal for VAdm. Mauz info MGen. Jenkins from RAdm. LaPlante, Desert Shield Planning Update.

14. CTF 22 151510Z AUG 90, Personal for Commanders and Commanding Officers from LaPlante, Desert Shield.

Part II

Preparations for Defensive War, 18 September– 8 November

This part of Volume I begins as the imminent threat of an Iraqi invasion of Saudi Arabia diminishes, and it ends with the announcement that force levels would be increased to allow an offensive option to drive Iraqi troops out of Kuwait. During this period operations generally became more systematic and routine, in contrast to the hectic early days of Desert Shield.

In chapter 7 we tie together the overall situation in mid-September and discuss the key decision on whether to sail a carrier into the Persian Gulf. Chapter 8 continues the story of the maritime interception operations as they evolved in a series of moves and countermoves. Coalition procedures changed in response to Iraq's increasing resistance to the sanctions. Chapter 9 concentrates on air operations, focusing on Vice Adm. Hank Mauz's efforts in planning, training, and rehearsing his forces for strike operations. In addition, we describe the continuing struggle of NavCent forces to maintain and refine their defenses against air attack. In chapter 10 we describe the planning, training, and rehearsing for amphibious operations, and also Gen. Norman Schwarzkopf's key decision about the number of amphibious ships to be retained in the theater.

Chapter 7

The Situation

In late September, the threat of an Iraqi invasion of Saudi Arabia was gradually subsiding, and the situation came close to being stabilized. Evidently, either Iraq had decided not to attack Saudi Arabia or had had no intention of doing so in the first place. It prepared defensive positions in Kuwait: barbed wire, antitank ditches, and other fortifications.

Also by late September, ArCent's 82nd Airborne Division had occupied defensive positions in the desert. MarCent forces, including 1st MEB, 7th MEB, Regimental Landing Team 2, and the 3rd Marine Air Wing, were also in position and fully operational. NavCent forces included two carrier battle groups, a battleship, an eighteen-ship Amphibious Task Force with ten thousand Marines embarked, and an assortment of other combatant and support ships. Most CentAF planes had arrived, and the ArCent's heavy divisions would arrive soon.

Alert times for carrier strikes—time within which they had to be able to respond to an order to launch a strike—had gradually lengthened since early August: from thirty minutes to sixty minutes to six hours on 13 August, to twelve hours in mid-September. Later in September, the alert time was relaxed again, to twenty-four hours.

By the end of September, Cdr. Wayne Perras, the ComUSNavCent Intelligence Officer, reported that the intelligence community as a whole believed it could provide five to seven days' warning before an Iraqi attack, but the USCinCCent staff, more conservative, said one could count on only thirty-six to forty-eight hours' warning.

Periodic intelligence reports warned of an increased likelihood of attack. For example, on 30 September, the USCinCCent staff estimated that the likelihood of an Iraqi attack or terrorism would increase somewhat on such holidays as the Prophet Mohammed's birthday on 1 October and Iraq's independence day on

3 October. Perras, however, described the Prophet's birthday as a day spent praying to decide what to do.

Intelligence constantly warned of the possibility of sneak attacks by the Iraqis.
The ComUSNavCent staff worried, for instance, that Iraq might equip seemingly
innocent civilian aircraft to fire Exocet missiles in a sneak attack on American
ships.

ROTATION OF FORCES

Rotation of naval forces to their home bases periodically caused friction
between the ComUSNavCent and USCinCCent. To set the stage, let us first discuss Gen. Norman Schwarzkopf's rotation policy, which was undoubtedly influenced by his Vietnam experience. In Vietnam, people served a one-year tour in the
country. For the most part, individuals rotated rather than units, so that a unit
would typically be manned by a mixture of newcomers, mid-tour people, and
short-timers, almost none of whom had been there longer than a year. Most
observers thought this was bad for unit cohesion and resulted in a lack of continuity.

Schwarzkopf's Desert Shield theater rotation policy assumed Desert Shield
would last for at least one year. It had the following features:

- Quality-of-life considerations were subordinate to preserving combat capability.
- Combat and combat support *units* operating in an austere and harsh environment
  would be rotated on a six-to-eight-month cycle.
- Support units not exposed to primitive living conditions and a harsh environment
  would rotate on a twelve-month cycle.
- Headquarters personnel would have a minimum twelve-month tour. Turnover would
  be phased to preclude block turnover of personnel, which might require some personnel to remain up to fifteen months.
- Certain key and essential commanders and staff might remain indefinitely.

Schwarzkopf considered operations at sea sufficiently harsh to qualify for the six-
to-eight-month rotation policy. Certain senior naval headquarters staffs—presumably those of ComUSNavCent, Middle East Force, and NavCent-Riyadh—would
remain in theater for twelve months or longer.

Because the Navy and Marine Corps operate differently than the other services,
they believe their rotation policy should be different from that of the Army and Air
Force. Navy and Marine Corps forces *regularly* deploy away from their home base
for six months at a time (more for some units)—six months without seeing homes
and families. As soon as they return from a deployment, they typically get one
month to recuperate, and then they start working up for the next deployment. The
Navy and Marine Corps feel that if Army or Air Force units deploy for a contingency (such as Desert Shield), once the contingency ends they return to their home
base and stay there until called for the next contingency. Navy and Marine units,

on the contrary, return to their regular deployment schedule when the contingency ends. Hence, the Navy is always thinking about the necessity to sustain forces over the long haul.

For the Navy and Marine Corps, a crisis or war deployment, like Desert Storm, is not much different from a peacetime deployment—as a deployment. For the Army and the Air Force, a deployment of any type is a unique event. The Navy's worldwide policy, designed to prevent morale breakdowns, wholesale resignations of officers, and plunges in enlisted reenlistment rate, requires that deployments not exceed six months and that turnaround time between deployments be at least twice as long as a unit's deployment. The usual Navy policy of six-month (homeport to homeport) deployments resulted in ships spending only four months or less in the CentCom theater, due to transit times. Thus, the Navy's policy conflicted with Schwarzkopf's policy of rotating combat units only after they had spent six to eight months in the CentCom theater. The Navy's emphasis on limiting the length of deployments caused friction with Schwarzkopf on a number of occasions. One conspicuous case involved the ComUSNavCent flagship and staff.

ComUSNavCent Staff and Flagship

Originally, despite Vice Adm. Hank Mauz's arguments to retain the *Blue Ridge,* Adm. Hunt Hardisty, Commander in Chief of the Pacific Command, had planned for the commander of Third Fleet, his staff, and his flagship, the USS *Coronado* (AGF 11), to relieve ComSeventhFlt, his staff, and his flagship, the *Blue Ridge*, after a few months. Later, the date moved to mid-January. This turnover would allow the *Blue Ridge* and the ComSeventhFlt staff to return to their homeport of Yokosuka, Japan, before the Navy's six-month deadline expired.[1] After the Third Fleet commander's tour, if the crisis continued, other numbered fleet commanders would take their turns. Eventually, the Navy might assign an admiral as a permanent ComUSNavCent. General Schwarzkopf, of course, wanted permanence from the start.

In early October, Hardisty decided that the *Blue Ridge* and her crew would return to Yokosuka in accordance with the six-month policy but that the ComSeventhFlt staff would remain indefinitely as the ComUSNavCent staff. The *Coronado* would deploy to the CentCom theater in January, but without the Third Fleet staff embarked. The *Coronado*, a different type of ship than the *Blue Ridge*, however, had much less space for offices and berthing. As an additional twenty-four officers and a number of enlisted personnel would soon augment the ComUSNavCent staff, living and working conditions would be extremely tight on the *Coronado*. Mauz sent Commander Charles "Barry" Beckman, USN, the Command-and-Control Officer on the ComUSNavCent staff, to Pearl Harbor to look over the *Coronado* to see what could be done. The answer involved putting trailers in the *Coronado*'s well deck for additional offices and berthing. Even then, both office space and berthing would be quite squeezed. This issue hung over the staff like a dark cloud for many months and was not finally resolved until after Desert Storm.

Red Sea Battle Groups

Between September 1990 and January 1991, the *Saratoga* and USS *John F Kennedy* (CV 67) battle groups periodically rotated between the Red Sea and the Mediterranean Sea. This exposed both battle groups to the CentCom procedures, plans, and environment, while still providing a near-constant presence in the Mediterranean Sea and opportunities for port visits for the crews. While in the Mediterranean Sea a battle group was under Commander, Sixth Fleet, and the European Command rather than ComUSNavCent and USCinCCent. For many years, U.S. policy had required at least one carrier battle group in the Mediterranean Sea at all times to prevent trouble or, if deterrence failed, to react to it. In 1990, the most likely source of trouble was Libya. If both carrier battle groups left the Mediterranean Sea, a vacuum would result that Libya might exploit in some way. In addition, rotating battle groups to the Mediterranean would allow training exercises. At this time, no port in the Red Sea would accommodate a carrier, and only Hurghada, Egypt, would take smaller ships. Spending months at sea without ever visiting a port is hard duty.[2]

The *Saratoga* and *Kennedy* each spent about a month at a time in the Red Sea during Desert Shield. The carrier battle group in the Red Sea was designated Task Group 150.5 (Carrier Battle Group Red Sea), and the battle group in the Mediterranean would be NavCent Task Group 150.9 (Carrier Battle Group Mediterranean). Each time the battle groups turned over, they would operate together in the Red Sea for a few days. Vice Admiral Mauz tried to arrange dual-carrier strike training during these turnover periods.

North Arabian Sea Battle Group

Other forces rotated to and from their home ports. The USS *Midway* (CV 41) battle group, homeported in Yokosuka, Japan, relieved the *Independence* battle group, homeported on the West Coast of the United States, in early November. Just as the Aegis cruiser *Antietam* had been taken from the *Independence* battle group to operate inside the Persian Gulf, ComUSNavCent detached another Aegis cruiser, the USS *Bunker Hill* (CG 52) commanded by Captain Thomas Marfiak, USN, from the *Midway* battle group to provide air defense inside the Persian Gulf. The *Midway* battle group, commanded by Rear Admiral Daniel "Dan" March, USN, was normally assigned to Seventh Fleet full-time as Task Force 70.

March had more experience than the average battle group commander, having previously commanded the USS *Carl Vinson* (CVN 70) battle group. As commander of Task Force 70, March commanded Seventh Fleet's battle force when multiple carriers operated together.[3] He had conducted both exercises and real-world operations in Seventh Fleet. A few years earlier, as a captain, March served as the CinCPacFlt Operations Officer under then–Rear Admiral Mauz. Thus, both Mauz and the ComUSNavCent staff were familiar with March and his staff.

Amphibious Task Force

The U.S. Navy did not have enough amphibious ships to sustain eighteen ships on station in the CentCom theater indefinitely and still maintain a reasonable deployment schedule for the people and ships. Other areas of the globe also had a call on amphibious assets. For instance, Operation Sharp Edge had several amphibious ships standing off the coast of Liberia at this time for a possible evacuation of noncombatants. Also, the amphibious ready group now in the North Arabian Sea would normally have been in the western Pacific. Its absence left a power vacuum there. Thus, to set up a sustainable rotation, the Navy needed to reduce the steady-state number of ships in the Central Command and also send home as soon as possible any amphibious ships not needed in the near future.

In mid-September, the thirteen ships of Amphibious Group Two, with the Marines of 4th MEB embarked, had just arrived in the North Arabian Sea on a short-notice deployment for Desert Shield. Thus, this force could stay in-theater until mid-January and still return to the United States before its six months were up. Keeping thousands of Marines packed like sardines in the amphibious ships for more than six months with little or no liberty was not a good alternative. The long-range schedule envisioned a group of Pacific Fleet amphibious ships, with 5th MEB embarked, relieving the Atlantic Fleet amphibious ships in January. But who would replace the Pacific Fleet amphibious ships when their six-month deployment was up? The inexorable tax exacted by long transit times meant that the Atlantic Fleet amphibious ships would have almost no refit time and could not realistically return to the CentCom theater so soon. Thus, before very long, the number of amphibious ships in the theater would have to be reduced.

As Amphibious Ready Group Alfa, comprising 13th MEU(SOC) and PhibRon 5, also now in the North Arabian Sea, had been on a regular deployment to the western Pacific when it was ordered to Desert Shield, it was due to return to the United States in November. Because the coalition was then in a "long-haul sanctions enforcement" mode, Vice Admiral Mauz wanted to send Amphibious Ready Group Alfa out of the theater on schedule. As we shall see in chapter 10, General Schwarzkopf did not.

FORCE MOVEMENTS

General Schwarzkopf's restrictions on how far north ComUSNavCent forces could move remained in effect: north latitude 28°00' for ships and 28°30' for aircraft, except that aircraft could conduct intercepts north of 28°30' (approximately the Saudi-Kuwaiti border) if required. Occasionally, exceptions were made.

Wisconsin Moves North

In late September, Vice Admiral Mauz ordered a mission to probe the Iraqi defenses. The battleship *Wisconsin*, accompanied by the Aegis cruiser *Antietam*, would move into the northern Persian Gulf, up to 28°45' north latitude for one hour. This position was about forty-five miles farther north than the usual limit on ships (latitude 28°00'). The *Antietam* and Marine Corps F/A-18 fighter aircraft would provide defense against air attack. This probe would see how long it took the Iraqis to detect and react to the ships. It would also be interesting to see what form that reaction took. Other objectives included demonstrating U.S. resolve to operate in international waters of the northern Persian Gulf and familiarizing the *Wisconsin* with the approaches to potential areas from which the battleship could provide naval gunfire support into Kuwait. Because Lt. Gen. Chuck Horner, ComUSCentAF, had scheduled an all-theater ordnance-loading exercise for the same day as the *Wisconsin* probe, Vice Admiral Mauz delayed the operation for one day. Otherwise, he could not have determined whether the Iraqis reacted to *Wisconsin*'s probe or to the ordnance-loading exercise.

On the morning of 27 September, the *Wisconsin* and *Antietam* sailed north. The *Wisconsin* planned to fly its Pioneer remotely piloted vehicle (RPV) ahead to search the intended track. This RPV, a small robot aircraft, could be launched, controlled, and recovered from battleships. It contains such sensors as television cameras, transmitting pictures back to the ship by a radio link. An RPV could be used for reconnaissance and to spot the fall of battleship gunfire. Just before midnight on 26 September, only a few hours before the *Wisconsin* started north, General Schwarzkopf ordered Mauz not to fly the RPV north of 28°00' north latitude, in accordance with Schwarzkopf's standing guidance. Two hours later, Schwarzkopf's staff directed that the RPV not be flown at all that day, presumably because it believed even an RPV might be too provocative.

After all the planning and all the delays, the probe itself took place without incident. NavCent forces detected no Iraqi reaction to the *Wisconsin*. One inference was that the Iraqis were not able to get good information on activity in the Persian Gulf.

Independence in the Persian Gulf

On 22 September, even before the *Wisconsin* had made her uneventful excursion north, Vice Admiral Mauz decided to send the *Independence* into the Persian Gulf for two days around the first of October.[4] This broke with the practice of the previous fifteen years. No U.S. Navy aircraft carrier had sailed in the Persian Gulf since the *Constellation* operated there in 1974. Furthermore, in 1974 Iran had been friendly to the United States. In 1990, however, Iran was quite antagonistic and could try to strike a blow. The mindset against operating carriers in the Persian Gulf was strong. For example, when the *Independence* battle group arrived in the North Arabian Sea on 6 August, the tasking message to the battle group directed

USS *Wisconsin*. On 27 September this battleship sailed into the northern Persian Gulf to probe Iraqi defenses. Navy Photo.

it to operate in the North Arabian Sea, Gulf of Oman, and Strait of Hormuz, with no mention of the Persian Gulf.[5] Also, recall that in August Mauz had designated this battle group as the North Arabian Sea Battle Group.

Carriers had not operated in the Persian Gulf for many years for several reasons. To conduct flight operations, aircraft carriers need sea room, because launching and landing aircraft often involves steaming into the wind for thirty minutes or more at a time. The lighter the wind, the faster the carrier has to steam to get the required minimum wind speed across the deck. At certain times of the year, winds in the Persian Gulf are often quite light. In the absence of natural wind, the carrier might have to steam at thirty knots to launch some heavily loaded aircraft. Thus, it might travel fifteen miles or more in a straight line into the wind. Furthermore, the wind does not always blow from a convenient direction.

The Persian Gulf is typically a bit more than a hundred miles wide, but the navigable area is significantly smaller, because of obstacles such as small islands, shoal water, oil platforms, and abandoned wellheads. Running a ship aground usually does not impress either one's friends or one's enemies (or one's commander). During Desert Storm, Rear Adm. Dan March, commander of the *Midway* battle group, once reported that the *Midway* had come within less than a mile of an uncharted abandoned wellhead just beneath the surface.

With the restricted navigable areas in the Persian Gulf reducing a carrier's freedom, a potential attacker need not search a huge area of ocean to obtain targeting data on a carrier. This deprives a battle group of a prime defensive advantage—mobility—and forces it to rely more heavily on defensive weapons.

With Iran potentially hostile, the warning times for attack in the Persian Gulf became frighteningly short. Iran controls the entire northeast side of the Persian Gulf. Attack aircraft can fly low over the mountains of Iran and avoid detection until they reach the Persian Gulf. They can then fire a missile at a ship in the middle of the Persian Gulf almost immediately. In addition, Iran had Silkworm antiship missiles covering the Strait of Hormuz, and Iranian aircraft flew regular reconnaissance patrols that looked out over the Persian Gulf. Thus, for the previous decade U.S. Navy carriers had chosen to support operations in the Persian Gulf from the North Arabian Sea.

In view of all these problems, why did Mauz decide to bring the *Independence* into the Persian Gulf? At the time, he gave four reasons:

- If hostilities started, operating inside the Persian Gulf would halve the distance to potential targets.
- The excursion would give the carrier battle group familiarity with potential operating areas for possible use in the event of hostilities. The carrier could become comfortable with the confined operating area, wind conditions for flight operations, and other environmental factors.
- It would visibly demonstrate carrier battle group capabilities to friendly countries in the region and to friendly navies involved in maritime interception operations.
- The excursion would send a message to Iraq that would add to its problems.

One reason for believing operations in confined waters might be feasible was that the Navy had conducted a series of pertinent experiments for a number of years. Although many systems and tactics the Navy prepared for use in a global war with the Soviet Union were not well suited for littoral operations (operations near land), in this case the Navy had developed and practiced exactly the right tactic.

First, in the mid 1980s, Second Fleet had experimented with operating carriers in Norwegian fiords so they could attack targets in the Soviet Union while the carriers stayed in a "safe haven." Mauz himself, with the *America* battle group, had operated in Vestfjord on the Norwegian coast. Commander, Sixth Fleet, had looked at using the Aegean islands in the eastern Mediterranean Sea in the same way. In the Pacific Ocean in the late 1980s, while Mauz was Deputy Chief of Staff for Operations and Plans at CinCPacFlt, Vice Admiral Diego "Duke" Hernandez, USN, at Third Fleet had developed the concept of using the Aleutian Island chain as a series of havens, or near-land operating areas (NLOAs), to use as stepping stones to approach the Soviet Union.[6] Third Fleet had tested the concept in a sequence of exercises that showed that operating in NLOAs, though not a panacea, was a useful option. Two of the battle group commanders in the Third Fleet part of PacEx-89 had been Rear Adm. Jerry Unruh, embarked on the *Constellation,* and Rear Adm. Dan March, embarked on the *Carl Vinson.* Interestingly, Unruh had operated willingly in confined areas, but March had shown reluctance to operate *Vinson* in NLOAs. About this time, Mauz, now in the western Pacific as commander of the Seventh Fleet, also started experimenting with NLOAs. During PacEx-89, he had had a carrier operating in an NLOA called the Hook of Hokkaido.

All these experiments had given the Navy a lot of experience operating in confined areas. Some of the problems in the Persian Gulf differed significantly: no surrounding mountains meant no radar shadowing, but also no worries about aircraft flying into a mountain shortly after launching from a carrier. The problem of having to adjust the deck cycle of flight operations remained, but the Navy had learned how to overcome it.

Mauz worried about the reaction of Unruh (now commanding the *Independence* battle group) and the aviators in his battle group to bringing the *Independence* into the Persian Gulf. Mauz flew out to the *Independence* to broach the idea. To Mauz's pleasant surprise, the reaction of Unruh and his aviators was "hot damn." They even pulled out charts they had already worked up showing the portions of the Gulf in which they could fly.

Iran remained a big question mark. Asking General Schwarzkopf if he had any objections, Mauz told the CinC he intended to keep a weather eye cocked toward Iran while the *Independence* was in the Persian Gulf. Mauz did not want to advertise this operation in advance; he wanted to get the *Independence* through the Strait of Hormuz before Iran knew what was happening. Mauz would announce the operation only after the *Independence* entered the Gulf. Schwarzkopf ran

Mauz's proposal to send the *Independence* into the Gulf past Gen. Colin Powell, who liked the idea. Schwarzkopf told Mauz to do it.

On 26 September, Mauz sent his proposed public affairs statement for the operation to Schwarzkopf for approval but for release not earlier than 1 October. On the same day, Mauz's staff learned that American television networks were already broadcasting that the *Independence* would go into the Persian Gulf—before most of the staff knew of the decision. The *New York Times*, in a story datelined Washington, 25 September, reported the *Independence* would enter the Persian Gulf and (incorrectly) that Schwarzkopf had requested the move. According to Mauz, Schwarzkopf was just as angry as Mauz's staff about the leak.

Mauz had had valid tactical reasons for not advertising the *Independence's* transit in advance; someone higher in the chain of command probably thought he saw an advantage in doing so. Whether the operation should have been announced in advance is not the issue. The problem is that higher authority evidently decided to leak the information without consulting Mauz.

One subsequent newspaper story quoted naval analysts as questioning the repositioning because it would subject the ship to missiles in tight quarters. Another story, which termed the move a gamble, quoted experienced naval officers as stating flatly that the carrier could not conduct flight operations in the obstructed waters of the Gulf on the tight schedules such operations require.

Despite the news leak and dismissing the doubts of the critics, Mauz sent the *Independence* into the Persian Gulf on 2 October. He says he never thought of postponing the operation. During the transit through the Strait of Hormuz, the *Independence* steamed within range of Iranian Silkworm missiles. Two SH-3H helicopters loaded with flares and chaff stayed aloft. On deck in a five-minute alert status were an EA-6B electronic jammer, an S-3A with chaff, and an A-6E with two electronic warfare pods. Had the Iranian Silkworm site become active, these aircraft would have jammed and laid a continuous layer of chaff until the carrier got out of range of the missiles. In addition, the cruiser USS *Jouett* (CG 29) and frigate USS *Taylor* (FFG 50) stayed close to the *Independence* to defend against any missiles launched toward the carrier. These arrangements were not considered extraordinary; staffs make such preparations routinely for any operation that might expose the force to danger from a potential enemy. While the *Independence* was in the Gulf her aircraft were restricted to stay south of 27°30' north latitude to avoid being overly provocative, even though U.S. aircraft routinely flew to 28°30' north at that time. The operation went smoothly.

Schwarzkopf and Mauz even visited the *Independence* while she sailed in the Persian Gulf. Schwarzkopf gave a speech to the crew on the hangar deck. Everyone not on duty was there—thousands of sailors. At everything Schwarzkopf said, the crew cheered wildly. Mauz thought Schwarzkopf got a great uplift from this—he had tears in his eyes. He told Mauz he knew the Army had problems out there in the desert, but now he knew the Navy had no morale problems and he could count on it. The two flag officers then went to the *Wisconsin*, where Schwarzkopf got the same kind of reaction. (Afterwards the battle group assessed that the Iranians failed to locate the *Independence* until she was about to leave the Persian Gulf on 4 October.)[7]

Midway in the Persian Gulf

When the *Midway* arrived to relieve the *Independence* in early November, Mauz wanted the *Midway* to become familiar with operating in the Persian Gulf right away. He sent her into the Gulf from 5 to 8 November, with two full days of flight operations. This time the inbound transit was overt. The battle group was in Readiness Condition II (heightened readiness, but not the highest), and while within range of Iranian Silkworm missiles the *Midway* kept the Aegis cruiser USS *Mobile Bay* (CG 53) and the guided-missile destroyer USS *Nicholas* (FFG 47) nearby for protection. A package of aircraft that could jam and decoy any missiles stayed on five-minute alert as long as the *Midway* was within range of the Silkworms. In addition, as a special precaution, the letter of instruction ordered one helicopter to search for mines ahead of the formation. While operating in the central Persian Gulf, the *Midway* conducted "NLOA-type flight operations." That is, it tried to stay in a relatively small area while conducting flight operations.

PERSONNEL

Augmentation of ComUSNavCent Staff

Approximately twenty-four active-duty officers and reservists augmented the ComUSNavCent staff in late October and early November. The reservists came from ComSeventhFlt 111—the reserve unit based in Dallas that regularly supported the ComSeventhFlt staff. They typically did their annual two weeks of active duty by augmenting the staff whenever Seventh Fleet had a major exercise. The reservists stood some of the watches to relieve the regular staff of the burden.[8]

The reservists came from all walks of life. Captain John Engstrom, USNR, especially well respected by the staff, later became commanding officer of the reserve unit. The staff trusted him enough to make him a battle watch captain even at the most crucial periods, such as the start of Desert Storm. While Engstrom stood watch in the Persian Gulf, his wife ran their rice farm. (Unfortunately, business was bad. About a quarter of all American rice exports went to Iraq; when economic sanctions closed this market, the rice farmers suffered.) Commander Michael "Mike" Harbin, USNR, was writing a book on the history of religions. He continued his writing during his spare time over the next several months. His travels in the region as the ComUSNavCent Political-Military Officer provided a major foundation for his book.[9]

End-Strength Ceiling

Originally, General Schwarzkopf told the National Command Authority that slightly more than two hundred thousand people would be deployed for Desert Shield. Now, the projected number had grown considerably, and pressure from Washington mounted to send people home, in keeping with letting the sanctions work and defending Saudi Arabia. On 6 October Schwarzkopf imposed a ceiling of 250,000 people for Desert Shield forces. As the planned flow of forces into the theater would take the personnel level to 258,000 people, eight thousand needed to be trimmed from the planned levels. He asked his subordinates to tell him how they planned to cut their forces. (For future reference, note that Schwarzkopf here demanded a 3.1 percent reduction overall. If he spread this reduction evenly over all components, the NavCent share would be 1,100 people.)

Vice Admiral Mauz objected to Schwarzkopf's inclusion of the more than ten thousand afloat Marines in MarCent's total rather than in NavCent's figures, as Vice Admiral Mauz had operational control of those forces until they were established ashore. Nevertheless, Mauz gave Schwarzkopf a plan for reducing his personnel level from 35,797 to 30,637 (excluding Marines afloat), a reduction of 5,160 personnel—but not until the middle of January 1991. A key part of this plan required slashing the number of amphibious ships from eighteen to nine, thus reducing NavCent's personnel count by the crews of half the amphibious ships. This became the subject of another, concurrent dispute between Schwarzkopf and Mauz, which we discuss in chapter 10.

Mauz had sent what he thought was a polite message to Schwarzkopf; so he was quite surprised when Schwarzkopf called him, madder than hell. (According to Mauz, this was the only time Schwarzkopf ever raised his voice with him.) Mauz thought Schwarzkopf acted as though this was the first time he had heard of this issue. He speculated that Schwarzkopf's staff, notoriously reluctant to tell him bad news, had not briefed him on the inconsistencies in what he was asking Mauz to do—reduce people without reducing ships.

Schwarzkopf followed his verbal lambasting with a written reply to Mauz that was unusually brusque for an exchange between flag officers:

I have imposed my own ceilings; yours is 31,500.

We must . . . not wait until January as you propose.

Your plan assumes the outchop of the amphibious ships associated with 4th MEB. This is a separate issue impacting on our overall combat capability. We will review amphibious options in the next few days and let you know how to factor this into your plan.[10]

From Mauz's point of view, Schwarzkopf was ordering him to take larger cuts than any other component but not allowing him to reduce the number of amphibious ships.

In response, Mauz described Schwarzkopf's reply as "an unexpected blow" that "places me in a catch-22 position." He pointed out that Schwarzkopf had proposed that ComUSNavCent absorb 50 percent of the personnel reduction—four thousand out of eight thousand for all of USCinCCent's components—even though NavCent forces were the leanest force in the theater and constituted only 14 percent of all CentCom forces. "There appears to be a misunderstanding of naval forces and employments." If he could not carry out his planned reduction of amphibious forces, Mauz argued, then a four-thousand-person reduction equated to reducing six to twelve combatant and support ships. Mauz bluntly concluded, "I could not do that and still carry out my mission."[11]

Mauz also pointed out that a number of vitally needed naval units (such as Navy-dedicated combat search and rescue assets) designated for deployment could not be issued deployment orders until the personnel cap issue was resolved. After listing these units, Mauz admitted that his previous input had failed to include a destroyer tender with 1,200 people. (Somebody on his staff had simply overlooked it.) Mauz again argued for including the afloat Marines in NavCent personnel figures because they came under his operational control and were naval forces until placed ashore. He repeated his case for reducing the number of amphibious ships in-theater while the coalition was in the mode of letting the sanctions work and defending Saudi Arabia.

Mauz's plan adjusted his previous numbers for the various factors he had discussed. He assumed that the number of amphibious ships would be reduced in accordance with his proposal. Although he did not mention the timing, his planned end-strength reduction would not be achieved until mid January—contrary to Schwarzkopf's desires. Excluding the Marines afloat, he gave an end-strength of 32,900—1,400 more than Schwarzkopf's imposed ceiling.

Schwarzkopf's reply was unyielding: "Your task remains to plan toward the cap of 31,500."[12]

That was not the last word on the subject, however. A week later, Schwarzkopf raised NavCent's personnel ceiling to thirty-four thousand and made his decision to keep more amphibious ships in theater than Mauz wanted. Ironically, less than two weeks after that the pressure became, once again, to get as many forces as possible into the CentCom theater.

MORALE

Did the average sailor think events would culminate in war? Some anecdotal evidence comes from four best-selling T-shirts at the Administrative Support Unit in Bahrain:

1. "I'd fly 10,000 miles to smoke a camel," with a drawing of two jets making a run on an Iraqi whipping his terrified camel in an attempt to get away from Baghdad
2. "Coming soon to a country near you: GULF WAR III"
3. Copy of the Hard-Rock Cafe T-shirt with the caption "Kuwait City, Closed for Business"

4. Copy of Hard-Rock Cafe T-shirt with "Kuwait City, Closed for Business," and "Baghdad, Opening Soon!"

LOGISTICS

Military Sealift Command ships continued to deliver a stream of equipment and supplies to support the buildup ashore. Because the ships were controlled by the U.S. Transportation Command—a unified commander in the same command echelon as USCinCCent—ComUSNavCent played little role in this, though he provided the forces that controlled the seas and made it all possible. In particular, the sealift ships were one of the reasons for the requirement to provide air defense in the central Persian Gulf. Eighty-five percent of all dry cargo during all of Desert Shield and Storm moved by sea. If petroleum, oil, and lubricants are included, then 94 percent of all cargo moved by sea.[13]

Commander, Naval Logistics Support Force, CTG 150.3, under Rear Adm. (Sel.) Bob Sutton in Bahrain, was in charge of most of the logistics for ComUS-NavCent and was assigned responsibility for several tasks that did not seem to fit anywhere else. These assignments included:

- Naval cargo handling and port group operations
- Naval fleet hospitals ashore and hospital ships
- Defense of naval facilities ashore, including port security and harbor defense
- Explosive ordnance disposal
- Mobile diving and salvage unit operations
- Naval construction (SEABEEs)
- Naval Administrative Support Unit in Manama, Bahrain
- Military Sealift Command support.

Vice Admiral Mauz based his general guidelines for logistics support on the procedures developed during Operation Earnest Will starting in 1986. In large part, ships from the Pacific Fleet were supported by the Pacific Fleet logistics chain, and ships from the Atlantic Fleet, operating in the Red Sea, were supported by the Atlantic Fleet and Mediterranean logistics chain:

- The Seventh Fleet logistics command would coordinate resupply and sustainability for naval forces in the Persian Gulf and North Arabian Sea.
- The Sixth Fleet logistics command would coordinate resupply and sustainability for naval ships in the Red Sea, except that the Seventh Fleet logistics command would supply fuel to ships in the Red Sea.
- Middle East Force ships in the Persian Gulf would be sustained primarily by in-port replenishments and by logistics helicopters.
- Shuttle ships would sustain station ships with provisions, fleet freight, and nonairworthy cargo.
- Air transfer points would support major force concentrations, such as the carrier battle groups and the Amphibious Task Force.

Mauz adopted these procedures because they reflected operational arrangements that had worked in the past.

A variety of logistics ships supported the forces at sea: combat stores ships delivered food, including fresh fruits and vegetables; oilers and ammunition ships accompanied each battle group; repair tenders fixed equipment.

On 3 October, Captain Ross Hendricks, USN, the ComUSNavCent Logistics Officer, reported that an Australian tanker would refuel ships in the *Independence* battle group. Similarly, U.S. tankers refueled ships from other countries. Hendricks described this multinational operation as "fully integrated—we will figure out the cost in 1995."

Saudi Arabia agreed to pay for all fuel burned in the CentCom area of responsibility. In early November, Hendricks reported that NavCent ships had received "free oil" from the Saudis. Was it "free"? Later, the Saudis would load the physical commodity into a U.S. Navy tanker, and then everyone would agree it was free; right now, it was free in the sense that the Saudis gave a check to the U.S. Treasury to offset the cost of the fuel. Mauz wanted to have the Navy's tankers loaded with Saudi oil, rather than have Saudi Arabia send a check to Washington. The staff suspected that if the money went to Washington, most likely it would end up in the general treasury; the Navy would be charged for the fuel but not benefit from the reimbursement. Hendricks understood that when U.S. tankers refueled ships from other countries, the U.S. government billed those countries for the fuel at the rate of $1.04 per gallon. If so, this did not seem right; the allies might not find it humorous. If the United States was receiving free fuel, then it should not charge the allies and make a profit. ComUSNavCent protested to the Joint Staff that the United States would lose credibility with the allies. A member of the Joint Staff replied that the Comptroller of the Office of the Secretary of Defense required this arrangement but that the Joint Staff recognized the problem and was working to change the policy. Procedures were not established to transfer free fuel to the allies until March 1991. Approval was eventually received to transfer fuel without charge retroactive to August 1990, but the delay and confusion had caused resentment among the allies.

THE FIRST REPORT IS ALWAYS WRONG

No matter how much writers talk about the fog of war, it is difficult for the reader really to understand that a commander must not simply believe many of the first reports he receives. Our first example shows how circuitous communication routes and reluctance to share military secrets caused delays and misunderstandings that strained relations with allies.

Egyptian Troop Convoy

In mid-September, the Egyptian government requested air support for an Egyptian troop transport convoy that would be sailing from Alexandria to Yanbu, Saudi

Arabia, on the coast of the Red Sea. This request went first to the Saudis, who passed it to Schwarzkopf's staff, who in turn told Mauz's staff orally. They then relayed the information to the Red Sea Battle Group.

In his book, HRH General Khaled bin Sultan, Joint Forces Commander, describes his view of what ensued:

We established good communications on this subject and, the minute the Egyptians set sail, the Americans were informed so that they could escort the troopships to the point where our own navy could take over.

All seemed set. However, a day or so later I received a heated and somewhat panic-stricken call from Cairo. Some 24 hours out of port, the vessels carrying an Egyptian brigade had come under attack from two carrier-based American planes—the very aircraft which were supposed to protect them! Evidently unable to identify the ships, the American pilots had opened fire. They may only have fired warning shots, but these were close enough to cause considerable alarm: the Egyptians thought it was a real attack. I could hardly believe my ears. Where were the ships now? I learned they had turned tail and headed back to their home port in Egypt. Someone on the American side had goofed.

. . . Schwarzkopf could not believe the attack had happened, but he finally admitted it and apologized.[14]

Now for NavCent's view: the first message request, sent late on 21 September, had listed twenty-four ships and given a *three-day window* in which the ships would complete loading and sail from Alexandria, with no indication of when the ships might enter the Red Sea, or of radio frequencies on which the U.S. Navy could contact them. Not only was the message incomplete, it did not arrive at NavCent headquarters until 25 September, on a retransmission.[15] The ComUS-NavCent staff received the list of ships by telephone on 23 September.

Meanwhile, during the night of 21–22 September, the USCinCCent staff told the ComUSNavCent staff that the Egyptian troop convoy had reported two apparently separate incidents. The ComUSNavCent staff suspected the reports might be garbled. The first report from the USCinCCent staff told of helicopters attacking the convoy. Later, the USCinCCent staff reported that these were Egyptian helicopters providing a send-off to the convoy. Still later in the night, the USCinCCent staff relayed reports from the Egyptians that their ships were being bombed by aircraft. About that time, the *Kennedy* air wing was doing practice bombing, supposedly about seventy nautical miles away. Two possible explanations came to mind. First, at night, pyrotechnics look much closer than they are. Second, perhaps somebody's position was wrong.

In response to queries from the ComUSNavCent staff, the Red Sea Battle Group reported that two A-7s had flown to a clear area, circled to be sure the area was clear, dropped two smoke markers, and each made five dive-bombing runs on the smoke markers, dropping ten practice bombs. They saw no ships near the smoke markers but had noticed ships about thirty miles away.

The Office of Military Cooperation in Cairo sent a message to the Secretary of State—with information copies to the Secretary of Defense, the Joint Chiefs of Staff, and USCinCCent (but not ComUSNavCent)—giving the Egyptian side of the story. At the time of the incident, the troop convoy had not yet arrived in the Red Sea. Two Egyptian Navy escort ships in the Red Sea waiting for the convoy saw three unidentified planes pass nearby, drop inert ordnance, and depart. The Egyptian ships radioed for assistance. The Egyptians claimed that, apparently in response, American helicopters with searchlights were shadowing the convoy. The position of the Egyptian ships given in this incident was approximately thirty nautical miles from where the A-7s said they dropped the ordnance (in agreement with the story told by the A-7s that they dropped the practice bombs thirty miles from the nearest ships).

Whatever the "ground truth," the culprit was the lack of direct communications between the Egyptians and the Red Sea Battle Group.

Swimmers in the Water

Long reporting chains could cause problems even when everyone involved was from the same country. At 2200C on 4 November, the ComUSNavCent battle watch received a phone call from the ComUSMarCent Operations Officer. He reported that the Marine port security detail at al-Jubail had detected swimmers in the water near the cargo ship *Staff Sgt William R Button*. Suspecting saboteurs, they had rounded up the swimmers, who turned out to be a SEAL team. The briefing to Vice Admiral Mauz and the ComUSNavCent staff said the Marines "hauled them out of the water and almost shot them." Because someone could in fact get shot, it is a major blunder not to inform the local port security organization before putting swimmers in the water in a port nervous about sabotage. If the story were true, someone should have been in very serious trouble.

But the story wasn't true. SEALs were on board the *Button* in al-Jubail for a meeting to plan an upcoming helicopter-insertion exercise to support maritime interception operations. They walked around the ship to familiarize themselves with the location of hatches and general layout of the ship. A Marine sentry on the pier saw unidentified people walking around the ship, so he talked to the SEAL leader, got the story, and sent word up the chain of command to MarCent head-quarters. After going through several levels of the chain of command, however, the story became rather badly garbled. The essential element of the story was wrong: no one had ever been in the water.

NOTES

The description of the situation at this time came from the author's notes of briefings given to the ComUSNavCent staff. Sources for the rotation of forces were messages and interviews with Mauz. Sources for force movements included messages, logs, CNA reports, and interviews with Mauz, Bernie Smith, Less, and Johnson. The Washington perspective relied on articles by Healy, Scarborough, and the *New York Times*. Sources for personnel issues included messages and interviews with Mauz. For logistics, sources included messages, the CNA reconstruction report, and the book by Matthews and Holt. For the stories in "the first report is always wrong," sources included Khaled's book, messages, ComUSNavCent Battle Watch Captain Events Log, and the author's observations.

1. A crew swap for the *Blue Ridge* was considered at one time but was rejected. Technically, the *Blue Ridge* was forward deployed to Yokosuka, not homeported there.

2. On the other hand, the *Independence* and her battle group never made a port visit from August until mid-November, after they had been relieved and left the CentCom area. Admiral Mauz notes that hard duty and long times at sea do not equate to bad morale, provided a ship's company has a clear mission and purpose. He says that some of the highest morale he ever saw was aboard ships at sea more than six months.

3. One aircraft carrier plus its escorts constitutes a carrier battle group. Combining battle groups creates a carrier battle force.

4. Back in Washington, the Navy Staff put together point papers on the subject. Rear Admiral Anthony "Tony" Less, USN, talked to the person who had been the commanding officer of the *Constellation* when she sailed in the Persian Gulf. According to Less, Admiral Frank Kelso, the Chief of Naval Operations, had made a decision that aircraft carriers could operate in the Persian Gulf. We believe that the idea, and the ultimate decision, to operate the *Independence* inside the Persian Gulf came from Vice Admiral Mauz. Although the Navy Staff could advise Mauz, it was not in the operational chain of command.

5. CTG 800.1 061915Z AUG 90, BG Delta NAS Ops. Note that this tasking came before Mauz and the Seventh Fleet staff arrived.

6. Vice Admiral Diego "Duke" Hernandez, commander of Third Fleet, did not like the term "safe havens," or the connotations of the term "haven" itself. He thought that although these areas provided some defensive advantages, they by no means ensured safety. He directed his Center for Naval Analyses representative (the author) to come up with an alternative term; the best the analyst could do was "near-land operating area," or NLOA (pronounced "en-low-ah" by some and "no-la" by others).

7. The ComUSNavCent Chief of Staff, Capt. Bernie Smith, did not like the way the coalition tipped its hand in putting a carrier in the Persian Gulf. He wanted to bring in a carrier by surprise and keep it there.

8. In early and mid-September, the staff formed four battle watch teams of four officers each. Each watch was six hours long, which would make each officer's watch start at the same time every day. To equalize the burden of the night shift, the watch was "dogged" every Wednesday. This meant that two watches were shortened to only three hours each so that everyone's duty shifted six hours every week. On the 19th of September the watch teams were reduced to only three officers each, reflecting the perception of the reduced threat of Iraqi attack. Six watch teams were then formed, standing three six-hour watches and two three-hour watches each day. The net result was that each person's duty time slipped by one notch a day, and occasionally each had a day without a watch. Of course, all the officers also had their normal "day job" (actually twelve hours plus per day). The heavy workload, shifting sleep cycle, and lack of sleep inevitably took a heavy toll on the staff. The arrival of augmentees to the ComUSNavCent staff allowed it to form seven battle watch teams of five officers each. The number of officers on each watch team was increased

temporarily to be sure that the augmentees got the maximum amount of indoctrination as rapidly as possible.

9. The book was published in 1994. Michael A. Harbin, *To Serve Other Gods: An Evangelical History of Religion* (Lanham, Md.: University Press of America, 1994.)

10. USCinCCent 091500Z OCT 90, Personal for VAdm. Mauz from General Schwarzkopf.

11. ComUSNavCent 130827Z OCT 90, Personal for General Schwarzkopf info LtGen. Boomer from Mauz, End-Strength Ceiling.

12. USCinCCent 221400Z OCT 90, Personal for VAdm. Mauz from General Schwarzkopf, End-Strength Ceiling.

13. Of dry cargo moved by strategic lift during all of Desert Shield and Storm through 10 March 1991, 544,000 tons moved by air; 3,048,000 tons (85 percent) moved by sea. If petroleum, oil, and lubricants are included in the totals, then 544,000 tons moved by air and 9,151,000 tons (94 percent) moved by sea. Matthews and Holt, *So Many, So Much, So Far, So Fast,* 13. Cohen, *Gulf War Air Power Survey, Volume V,* Part I, Table 20, 76, citing the same sources as Matthews and Holt, gives slightly larger numbers for the amount of dry cargo moved by sea.

14. Khaled, *Desert Warrior,* 224–25.

15. Because this message was sent with precedence "Priority," it was not received by ComUSNavCent until 252252Z, on a retransmission.

Chapter 8

Tightening the Noose

Between 18 September and 8 November 1990, the economic sanctions imposed on Iraq began to solidify on two fronts—first with additional UN Security Council resolutions against Iraq and second with improved naval enforcement procedures. These actions closed loopholes and tightened the economic noose around Iraq.

Given the enormity of the task of forcing Saddam Hussein out of Kuwait, the United States needed to convince Iraq that it would enforce sanctions established through UN Resolutions 661, 665, and 670, and that other countries would support the U.S.-led effort. Saddam Hussein, on the other hand, wanted to make the Americans look like the bad guys. He counted on the U.S. public to experience Vietnam flashbacks, on Arab countries not to support outside interference in Arab quarrels, and on Moslem countries not to support infidels, thus leading to the demise of the coalition. NavCent forces, by enforcing the sanctions, would play a key role in sustaining the coalition. The additional resolutions, combined with the refined techniques of intercepting suspect merchant vessels, contributed to the long-term stability of the coalition.

Throughout this period, the previous tentative signs of Iraqi cooperation, as seen in chapter 4, subsided, and Iraqi resistance to sanction enforcement seemed to increase. Whether acting as individuals or collectively under orders from the Iraqi leadership, the masters of Iraqi ships pushed for a confrontation. For the United States to disable a merchant ship would surely fuel the Iraqi propaganda machine.

INTELLIGENCE

To allow advance planning and coordination, NavCent forces needed early information concerning a merchant ship's identity, destination, cargo, location, course, and speed. A P-3 maritime patrol aircraft operating from Masira, Oman, provided early warning and often vital data once a suspect ship was under way. Intelligence organizations, in turn, often alerted the P-3s about suspect ships. Some of this intelligence came from such mundane sources as public information on ship movements, and some from classified sources. Intelligence also gave NavCent forces background information concerning Iraq (and its companies). One way information was passed was through a Joint Intelligence Liaison Element (JILE) that deployed to ComUSNavCent on the *Blue Ridge*. The JILE worked with a variety of intelligence organizations outside the theater and passed information, including on subjects other than interception operations, to the ComUSNavCent staff.

On the same day as the UN Security Council passed Resolution 670 (the third resolution on sanctions), 25 September 1990, the JILE staff briefed Vice Adm. Hank Mauz, ComUSNavCent, on the overall effectiveness of sanctions against Iraq and characterized the operation as one of the most successful embargoes ever. JILE estimated that Iraq was exporting fewer than fifty thousand barrels of crude oil per day, versus 2.6 million barrels per day previously. This small amount of exported oil went via truck to Jordan. Iraq evidently did not receive payment for this oil; it was payment of Iraq's debt to Jordan. JILE estimated that Iraq was importing only about $0.1 billion ($100 million) worth of goods per month compared to $1.1 billion per month before the sanctions.

Iraq's material reserves were generally slim. Intelligence estimated that Iraq's industrial sector had a six to twenty-four-month supply of most spare parts, less in some areas, and only a three to four-month stock of rubber tires. JILE estimated that Iraq had four or five months of food reserves, excluding the May harvest, and Iraq faced two harsh realities about the May harvest: it imported its seeds and depended on one million Egyptian workers to harvest the crops. Intelligence also reckoned that Iraq had reserves of about one billion dollars in foreign currency and gold to pay for imports—enough to pay for only about one month's typical imports. JILE judged that Iraq had stolen "only" five hundred million dollars in gold and hard currency from Kuwait. Furthermore, JILE thought the Iraqis would have trouble selling gold on the world market and would have to take a reduced price if they tried.

Iraq had a few prospects for bypassing the sanctions. Intelligence indicated that about two hundred companies had approached Iraq about circumventing the embargo. JILE judged that Iraq needed 125,000 tons of food each month. Theoretically, it could have met half its food needs by air (aircraft still flew into Baghdad at this time), but most analysts believed it unlikely that Iraq would actually import significant amounts of food by air. JILE also said Iran remained a big question mark, with the greatest potential for breaking the embargo. Iran was following a policy of "calculated ambiguity," but so far JILE had detected no significant sign of Iran breaking the embargo. JILE concluded that Saddam Hussein viewed the sanctions as a siege—a test of wills—and thought he could outlast the UN's will to enforce them. He probably figured he would have to endure the sanctions for six to twelve months. JILE's bottom-line judgment stated that sanctions would *not* force Iraq out of Kuwait. Mauz agreed.

As the bureaucratic and international policies of the UN began to tighten, so too did the operational end of those policies—albeit not as smoothly as the political rhetoric. On the policy end were the speeches and votes at the UN; the operational end involved physically stopping and inspecting the ships. This was a learning process for the U.S. and allied navies as well as for the Iraqis. As the coalition ships carried out their missions, the Iraqis were essentially taking notes—the information on procedures and the sequence of escalation enabled the Iraqis to test U.S. resolve by knowing what to do and when to do it. Coalition forces would then counter with different procedures and shorter escalation times. This repeated move-countermove game was part of the nature of the coalition's maritime interception operations with Iraqi ships, as illustrated below.

MARITIME INTERCEPTION OPERATIONS

During the false start to maritime interception operations, warning shots had failed to stop the *Khanaqin* and *Baba Gurgur*. After the UN authorized the use of force, the *Al Fao* stopped subsequent to warning shots being fired. It seemed likely, however, that warning shots, if not backed up by disabling at least one ship, were not likely to work much longer. As described below, warning shots were not consistently effective—they stopped one Iraqi ship in late September then failed to stop the next ship.

Tadmur: Warning Shots Succeed

The frigate *Elmer Montgomery* first tracked the *Tadmur*, a 3,627-dwt Iraqi tanker, on 27 September 1990 in the northern Red Sea outbound from Aqaba, Jordan, en route to Basra, Iraq (see Figure 8–1). The *Elmer Montgomery* invited the Spanish frigate *Cazadora* (F 35) to participate in the interception. The *Tadmur*'s master refused to stop, claiming he was carrying only ballast and not prohibited cargo. Later he claimed that the ship's owners had ordered him not to stop in the Red Sea. In all, the master refused to stop five times; the *Elmer Montgomery* issued two final verbal warnings. Eventually, the master stated he would stop only if forced to do so, and the *Elmer Montgomery* responded by firing .50-caliber warning shots across the *Tadmur*'s bow. After the warning shots, the *Tadmur* agreed to stop.

The lead boarding party consisted of sailors from the *Elmer Montgomery* and the U.S. Coast Guard Law Enforcement Detachment (USCG LEDet). The *Cazadora* provided her own boarding party. Once the parties were on board, the master cooperated, but he was angry over the visit and search. He made statements about the United States killing Iraqi babies and asked whether he and the crew were being taken hostage. The *Tadmur* was cleared to proceed once confirmed to be in

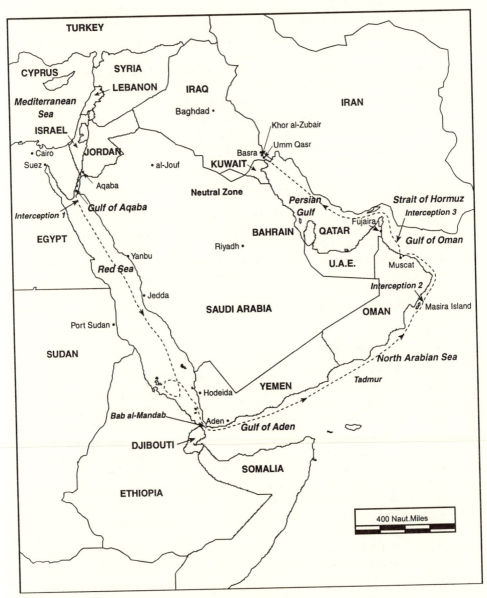

Figure 8–1. *Tadmur*

ballast with the paperwork in order. Although it took repeated verbal warnings and warning shots, this intercept was successful. Warning shots had stopped the ship.

Iraq might have used the *Tadmur* as a test case to learn the maritime interception operations procedures in hopes of evading them in the future. Because the master did not possess an up-to-date crew list, he had to collect passports to generate one, thus revealing that four of the crew were Iraqi government officials. One of these officials asked detailed questions about the procedures: for example, about the weapons of the boarding party, the type of air cover and machine guns, and other countries represented in the Red Sea.

Al Wasitti: Warning Shots Fail

The decision to use disabling fire continued to pose the most serious dilemma facing the Maritime Interception Force. First, even though the UN had endorsed the use of force, shooting at unarmed civilian ships would not be good for the coalition's image. Second, in the words of Vice Admiral Mauz, if the United States disabled a ship, it essentially "bought the ship." The United States would be obligated by the law of the sea to render assistance to a disabled ship. Further complicating the issue was the possibility of environmental hazards from a leaking oil tanker and, most importantly, the possibility of human loss. Finding a port to which to take a leaking tanker would be difficult, if not impossible. The *Khanaqin* interception had demonstrated to Iraq the U.S. reluctance to risk killing civilians. If warning shots failed to convince a ship to stop (as with the *Khanaqin*), what would happen? It seemed that disabling a ship, with all the accompanying risks, was the inevitable outcome—but then the British found an alternative solution.

The British frigate HMS *Battleaxe* (F 89) first tracked the Iraqi cargo ship *Al Wasitti* (8,300 dwt) on 7 October in the Gulf of Oman heading toward the Strait of Hormuz. As the on-scene commander, the British commanding officer began planning the interception and invited the *Reasoner* and *Adelaide* (both frigates) to assist in the boarding. For the first time, the plan called for a helicopter to insert six Royal Marines onto the main deck. The *Battleaxe*'s rules of engagement allowed her to do the boarding only outside Omani waters, which required the *Adelaide* to position herself to prevent the *Al Wasitti* from entering them.

With the plans and multinational forces in place, the *Battleaxe* began the interception on 8 October 1990. The *Al Wasitti* refused to answer repeated calls on the bridge-to-bridge radio. The *Battleaxe* responded by firing 20 mm warning shots across the *Al Wasitti*'s bow. Again the *Al Wasitti* did not respond. The *Adelaide* fired the next round of warning shots—76 mm, with no effect. The *Reasoner* fired two five-inch rounds across the *Al Wasitti*'s bow. She still did not respond. Meanwhile, the United States started the process of going up the chain of command for disabling-fire authority.

The launching of a boat was used as a feint to distract the *Al Wasitti*, and the *Adelaide* launched her helicopter as a decoy for the actual insertion team. Minutes before the frigate HMS *London* (F 95) launched two helicopters with the team, crew members of the *Al Wasitti* were sighted opening valves and dumping water over the sides of the ship. In addition, the crew turned on all of the main-deck fire stations. The entire main deck was now wet. Fortunately, this did not adversely affect the insertion team. It took only two minutes for the Royal Marines to rappel onto the deck and secure the bridge. So far, the first helicopter insertion was a success.

The Iraqis might have dumped water over the sides to prevent a boarding from small boats. Wetting the deck, however, seems more like a countermeasure to prevent a helicopter insertion, or at least make one difficult. But as the coalition had not conducted a helicopter insertion before, how could the Iraqis have known what was coming?

The Royal Marines met with no resistance from the crew and easily secured the ship, but they did not actually control it. To slow the ship, the master claimed he needed to change the fuel oil used in the engine. This presented a problem that highlighted a rules of engagement (ROE) conflict among the multinational force and a deficiency in American equipment. The *Reasoner*'s motor whaleboat could not travel fast enough to catch up to the *Al Wasitti,* and the British ROE did not allow them to stop a ship forcibly without reason. To solve this problem, the *Battleaxe*'s RHIB (rigid-hull inflatable boat) transferred the *Reasoner* boarding party. Once the U.S. team was on deck, the master's attitude changed. He became belligerent and now refused to allow his ship to be searched and stated, "We are now at war." The *Reasoner*'s boarding team, consisting of four sailors and a USCG LEDet team of four, began the search and found the *Al Wasitti* to be empty. Declared a cleared vessel, the *Al Wasitti* continued her course to Iraq.

That evening, after the boarding party left the *Al Wasitti,* Vice Admiral Mauz received information that it might be carrying nuclear-related material. Reportedly, this had been briefed to the Joint Chiefs of Staff, along with the information that the search that day had been cursory. Mauz had to decide whether to reboard the *Al Wasitti.* The ComUSNavCent Intelligence Officer had no evidence to support either statement, but did not hold key references concerning either evidence about the nuclear material or the thoroughness of the search. If the sensitive material was small, it could have been hidden anywhere on ship, but then it could also have been flown to Iraq instead. In June 1990 the *Al Wasitti* had picked up material for the Iraq Atomic Energy Commission from the United Kingdom, but it had been to Iraq since then. Mauz finally decided that the intelligence was too weak to warrant reboarding the *Al Wasitti.*

Again the Iraqis had demonstrated their resistance to the maritime interception operations. This time the coalition responded with three different countries firing warning shots for the first and only time in a single interception. To do so, each had to receive authority from its own chain of command regardless of the other nations' decisions. Despite the fact that the *Al Wasitti* never changed her course or altered her speed, she ultimately lost.

Valuable lessons were learned with the *Al Wasitti* interception. On the positive side, the British successfully demonstrated an alternative to disabling fire. On the negative side, U.S. participants realized that RHIBs, because of their better durability, speed, and seakeeping abilities, were more effective than standard U.S. Navy motor whaleboats for these operations.

Helicopter insertions (or vertical insertions, as they came to be known) became a de facto change in procedures, because they offered a solution to the problems associated with disabling fire while still effectively enforcing the UN sanctions. Vertical insertions provided an intermediate step between warning shots and disabling fire. Disabling fire remained an alternative, however, if the Iraqis did anything to make vertical insertions seem dangerous.

Why had NavCent forces not initiated vertical insertions earlier? In the Red Sea, SEALs had practiced insertions from SH-3s, but this program had experienced a setback when an SH-3 went into the water. Time was lost while awaiting waivers to allow operations in which SH-3s would carry large numbers of SEALs. As we shall see later, NavCent forces in the Red Sea eventually employed this capability.

Tadmur: Reinterception

After coalition forces declared a ship cleared and allowed her to proceed, NavCent forces would continue surveillance to ensure that ships made no additional port calls or took on any cargo. NavCent forces and allied ships received regular update messages that contained lists of merchant ships and their location. These messages covered all the waterways and ports in the patrol regions. Thus, the NavCent forces continued to track the *Tadmur* loosely after she had been boarded and released on 27 September. Subsequently, an intelligence update reported suspicious loitering by the *Tadmur* in the southern Red Sea and Gulf of Aden area. A P-3 maritime patrol aircraft sighted the *Tadmur* on 6 October 1990 in the North Arabian Sea. ComUSNavCent decided to reintercept the *Tadmur*. Because coalition forces intercepted the *Tadmur* and the *Al Wasitti* on the same day and only two hundred nautical miles apart, they delayed boarding the *Tadmur* until the completion of the *Al Wasitti* boarding.

The British frigate HMS *Brazen* (F 91), as the on-scene commander, began this second interception with calls on the bridge-to-bridge radio. The guided-missile destroyer *Goldsborough,* with a USCG LEDet embarked, and the Australian guided-missile frigate *Darwin* came on-scene to support the interception and provide additional boarding parties. The *Tadmur*'s master freely offered information that he was in ballast and traveling from Aqaba, Jordan, to Basra, Iraq, but, as before, refused to consent to a boarding. In addition, he refused to muster his crew. However, when the *Brazen* stressed they would board and search his ship despite his obstinacy and that his actions only endangered his crew, the master mustered them. The *Darwin* helped persuade him by conducting a close-aboard, high-speed pass on the *Tadmur*'s port side. Uninvited guests were about to drop in on the *Tad-mur.*

After the crew had gathered topside, Royal Marines rappelled onto the *Tad-mur*'s deck and secured the ship for the *Goldsborough* and *Darwin* boarding parties. The boarding parties found four government officials (as they had the first time), seven tons of flour and rice, and fifty gallons of cooking oil. The bags of rice were labeled "from USA to Jordan." The master reported the cargo had been loaded in Aqaba on 26 September and was for the crew and their families. This contradicted the report of the first boarding, when the USCG LEDet had reported the *Tadmur* to be empty. The items were stored in the staterooms and the centerline tank, the top area beneath the main deck. In addition to the cargo, two newly welded plates aroused the British team's suspicions, for the ship's records did not show any recent work done on the *Tadmur.* The master explained these were cover plates to water tanks, and he offered to open them to confirm they did indeed cover water tanks. The British declared the cargo to be prohibited and in violation of the UN sanctions. They offered the *Tadmur* diversion options that included Muscat, Oman. The master refused and offered instead to jettison cargo. The British rejected this option. The *Goldsborough* and *Darwin* detached, and the *Brazen* escorted the *Tadmur* to Muscat.

Where the cargo came from is unclear. Perhaps while the *Tadmur* loitered near Aden, she transferred cargo from another ship. Or perhaps the very small quantity of cargo had been overlooked or thought to be trivial during the first intercept on 27 September.

Tadmur: Diversion

The second *Tadmur* interception lasted more than four days from beginning to end. Differing ROE between the United States, Australia, and the United Kingdom, and diplomatic complications of diverting the *Tadmur* to Oman caused the delay. The problem of differing ROE and procedures came into play, with the on-scene commander being the British and the lead boarding officer being a USCG LEDet. They had different rules for various situations.

The ROE covering diversion ports differed among the coalition members. The United Kingdom had such authority in its ROE, but the Australians and Americans had to obtain it. Oman took over twenty hours to agree to accept the *Tadmur* and another twenty-nine hours of negotiations to berth the ship. This put a great strain on the boarding party, which had to deal with a nervous and potentially hostile crew. Despite the British ambassador's argument that it was a tremendous amount of effort for a "pathetic pile of stuff," the British government insisted that Oman impound the *Tadmur* for violating the sanctions. "Impound" was considered to be stronger than "detain," suggesting the transfer of ownership.

With regard to the tactical level of this interception, the operation had occurred without incident. Even with different ROE, the multinational force had worked together in a professional manner. The problem occurred after the interception at the political and diplomatic level between the British and the Omani governments. Complicating the situation further, neither the U.S. nor the Australian team, due to political sensitivities, could participate in bringing the *Tadmur* into port, and given Oman's previous refusal to accept the *Zanoobia*, entering Muscat would be sensitive.

The original agreement between the British and the Omanis over the *Tadmur* entering Muscat evidently lacked clarity. Once in port, the British expected the Omanis to conduct their own search of the *Tadmur* and to impound both the cargo and the ship. Evidently, this was a British cabinet-level view. The Omanis did not agree. They maintained the British should remain in charge of the *Tadmur;* once the cargo was offloaded, she was to anchor away from port or in international waters. The Omanis had no intention of impounding an Iraqi ship. On 12 October, the *Tadmur* sailed, on Omani authority.

Regardless of whether the Omani and British governments failed to understand their agreement or whether one government changed its mind, the *Tadmur* was now en route to Basra. On 12 October, the *Brazen*, assisted by the *Adelaide* and *Reasoner*, intercepted and boarded the *Tadmur* again. They offloaded the cargo, minus that needed for the crew to reach port, to the *Brazen*. The master and the crew on the *Tadmur* cooperated, and she was released the same day. The *Brazen* returned to Muscat to unload the impounded cargo. As the boarding party departed, the *Tadmur*'s master reportedly said he hoped the allies were better coordinated if the shooting started!

MARITIME INTERCEPTION FORCE CONFERENCES

The changes at the tactical level, like the vertical insertion, are important for two reasons. First, they were consistent with UN resolutions in closing the loopholes to put more pressure on Iraq; second, they demonstrated the compatibility of the different navies involved, which is relevant because all the countries involved had different ROE. The *Tadmur* and *Al Wasitti* interceptions both provide good examples of multinational efforts with successful conclusions. To counter potential problems of communication and coordination, as highlighted with the *Tadmur* and *Al Wasitti* interceptions, the allied navies held Maritime Interception Force conferences and monthly meetings, beginning 9 September in Bahrain. Subsequent conferences were held on the *LaSalle* in Abu Dhabi, UAE; on the Canadian auxiliary oiler-replenishment ship HMCS *Protecteur* in Bahrain on 12 December 1990; and on the Australian replenishment tanker HMAS *Success* (OR 304) in Dubai, UAE, on 9 January 1991.

The conferences typically addressed a variety of issues, including such topics as scheduling patrol assignments, defining patrol sectors, and coordinating procedures for ship-to-ship and air traffic control communications. Once the differences were understood by all, they became a source of strength. In addition to the periodic conferences, similar but smaller meetings were also held, along with informal luncheons, exchanges, and briefings. In the Red Sea, contacts between the Greek, French, Spanish, and U.S. participants increased mutual understanding and helped standardize procedures.

At the time of the first conference, France was the president (a rotational position) of the Western European Union (WEU). The French would not agree to anything without approval from Paris. The French navy representative attended, but a French foreign office representative stood by his side and did all the talking. The French wanted to carve out a piece of the maritime interception operations to be led by the WEU. Unlike the other countries, they would not agree in advance to do whatever the United States proposed, but would cooperate. (They shared ship schedules, used similar procedures, and joined in multinational interceptions, but would not do anything that might make it appear the French were under U.S. command.) Except for the Italians, other allied navies rebuffed this move by the French.

Generally, the various allies, each anxious to make positive contributions to the UN effort, worked well together. NATO and bilateral structures allowed easy integration of communications. Years of U.S. Navy exercises and training with these allies allowed for a unified approach to procedures, tactics, logistics, and intelligence sharing. Shortly after the second Maritime Interception Force conference, another significant, lesson-learning intercept took place—one of particular importance to the U.S. Marines.

HELICOPTER INSERTIONS BECOME ROUTINE

Given the increased Iraqi resistance and the British experiences with the *Tadmur* and *Al Wasitti* boardings, vertical insertions were valuable because they allowed a ship to be boarded either with or without the cooperation of the master or the crew. The threat of disabling fire remained, but vertical insertions added another option before the use of that force. In addition, disabling fire was a "Washington" decision, thus requiring much more time for approval. Vice Admiral Mauz quickly saw the advantages and decided to use the technique at the next opportunity. With that in mind, the next step was to train the SEALs and MEU(SOC) in using minimum force in securing a ship—something that goes against much of their training.

The typical vertical insertions followed this sequence. SEALs or a MEU(SOC) team would rappel down from a helicopter onto a ship and then secure it (bridge and engineering spaces) for a boarding party. A LEDet from the U.S. Coast Guard usually led the boarding party. Typically, it used a small boat to transfer to the suspect vessel. Because of their drug interdiction experience, USCG LEDets knew how to secure ships using minimum force and how to search for contraband. USCG LEDets also played an important role in briefing SEALs and MEU(SOC) teams on their procedures.

Al Mutanabbi: First U.S. Helicopter Insertion

Early in October, the *Al Mutanabbi,* a large (130,241-dwt) Iraqi tanker, departed Aden, Yemen. The initial information on the *Al Mutanabbi* indicated she was empty and en route to Umm Qasr, Iraq. Intelligence indicated that the *Al Mutanabbi* would maneuver to avoid inspection, that is, stay in territorial waters. Despite the fact that the maritime interception operations had the cooperation of the coastal states involved, coalition ships still needed clearance to enter their territorial waters.

On 11 October 1990, a P-3 maritime patrol aircraft spotted the *Al Mutanabbi* in the North Arabian Sea headed for the Gulf of Oman with an estimated date of arrival in the vicinity of Masira Island of 13 October. The frigate *Brewton* steamed to that area to intercept the *Al Mutanabbi*. Because of the early warning information, coalition forces planned a rehearsal for 12 October, with the actual interception planned for 13 October. The *Brewton* and a 13th MEU(SOC) team from the amphibious ship USS *Ogden* (LPD 5), part of the Amphibious Task Force, conducted the rehearsal. The scenario went through all the steps of the initial inquiries, the warning shots, the insertion, securing the ship for inspection, and the USCG LEDet boarding to conduct the search.

After the rehearsal, the participating parties were briefed on the lessons learned, anticipated events and plans, and their assignments. Having all participants at the briefing allowed the on-scene commander to determine the ROE of other countries and plan accordingly—an improvement over earlier boarding plans and missions. In this case, the Australians and British had authorization up to warning shots. When the *Al Mutanabbi* arrived in the vicinity of Masira Island, the U.S. and coalition forces stood ready.

Before the initial inquiry, the *Brewton* launched a helicopter for video-recorded reconnaissance of the *Al Mutanabbi*. The helicopter then proceeded to the *Ogden* to let the MEU(SOC) review the videotape. This facilitated the boarding by giving the insertion team a current picture and allowing its members to determine the best place to rappel down onto the deck.

As expected, the master stalled, saying he could not stop the ship without the owner's approval; if it were up to him he would stop, but he did not own the ship, and it would take two to three hours to contact the owner. The master added that he was proud to be an Iraqi and that he was only doing his job. The *Brewton* gave the *Al Mutanabbi* fifteen minutes to stop and allow for a visit and search. The *Al Mutanabbi* replied: "Okay, but it will take me thirty minutes to stop." The *Brewton* replied that he now had fourteen minutes left.[1]

The verbal warnings did not coerce the *Al Mutanabbi* into stopping. The escalation of force outlined in the Operation Order called for warning shots next. Instead of warning shots, however, the *Brewton* instructed the *Darwin* to conduct close-in maneuvers to demonstrate the allied resolve to stop the *Al Mutanabbi*. Capt. Bernie Smith, the ComUSNavCent Chief of Staff, acting for Vice Admiral Mauz who was out of the area, authorized warning shots, but after *Darwin*'s aggressive close-in maneuver towing a spar, the *Al Mutanabbi* began to slow. The ComUSNavCent staff warned the *Brewton* they had intelligence that sixty people were on board the *Al Mutanabbi;* the master claimed fifty-two people were on board. The boarding teams and helicopter-insertion teams never knew what to expect when boarding a ship, and contradictory information like this always raised the tension level. (The additional eight people were later accounted for and described as guests.)

At the time, the ComUSNavCent staff believed, based on previous events, that the Australian spar maneuver deceived Iraqis into thinking it was a disabling device. Later it learned that when in sight of the bridge, the Australians would fire off a small charge attached to the spar. When the Australian ship disappeared under the bow of the ship where it could not be seen from the bridge, its crew would throw "thunder charges" overboard that would explode; the Iraqis would see effects of the explosions but not be able to tell that charges had been thrown over the side. The Iraqis evidently thought the spar was a disabling device or that the Australians were dropping mines into the water. Because of the nature of combined operations, in some ways the on-scene commander seemed to have great flexibility in the way he accomplished his mission.

As it had been done in the rehearsal, the MEU(SOC) team executed the insertion as the *Al Mutanabbi* slowed. The purpose was to show force and intimidate crew members. A CH-46 helicopter with the insertion team embarked and a UH-1N helicopter gunship providing cover launched from the *Ogden*, controlled by the *Brewton*'s air controller. The coordination worked well, and the insertion was successful. The crew offered no resistance and quickly brought the *Al Mutanabbi* to a stop.

Once the MEU(SOC) team secured the topside deck and engineering spaces, the USCG LEDet-led boarding party from the *Brewton* and the party from the *Darwin* boarded and began to search. They found the *Al Mutanabbi* empty, with clean ballast. The search teams also discovered a substantial amount of food on board for the crew and visitors, but not enough to be considered cargo. Declared a cleared vessel, the *Al Mutanabbi* continued her journey to Iraq.

Despite the obstinacy and the delay tactics by the master, this interception represented a significant milestone in U.S. maritime interception operations—the first U.S. vertical insertion. Because of early intelligence reports on the *Al Mutanabbi*, continued surveillance, thorough planning, and the rehearsal, the boarding and search had gone smoothly.

When the *Al Mutanabbi* had agreed to slow and said she needed thirty minutes to stop, the ComUSNavCent battle watch received a report of a Mach-1 air contact over Kuwait headed out over the Gulf. Nothing more came of this, but it raised the tension level. There was a feeling that some time when ComUSNavCent was preoccupied with a boarding in the North Arabian Sea or northern Red Sea, Iraq would strike ships in the Persian Gulf. ComUSNavCent often raised the alert level during tense boardings. Similarly, during the *Khanaqin* affair in August, Gen. Norman Schwarzkopf had ordered Vice Admiral Mauz to raise the alert status.

By mid October, two months into the maritime interception operations, the United States and the allies were winning the move-countermove game with Iraq. The USCG LEDets provided expertise on how to search a ship and properly read manifests, while the Marines and Navy SEALs demonstrated how to take over a ship without disabling it. In addition, the coalition was holding together well, and the allied navies demonstrated their ability to work together successfully during the *Tadmur*, *Al Wasitti*, and *Al Mutanabbi* interceptions. But as always, even with the success of the vertical insertions, disabling fire remained a viable threat for any noncooperative ship suspected of violating the sanctions.

Al Bahar Al Arabi: Iraqi Resistance Persists

The destroyer USS *O'Brien* (DD 975), while operating in the central Persian Gulf, encountered the Iraqi ship the *Al Bahar Al Arabi*, a small (6,953-dwt) fish refrigeration ship traveling from Basra, Iraq, to Aden, Yemen.[2] Countries participating in this intercept included the United States, Italy, and Australia.

The *O'Brien* first sighted the *Al Bahar Al Arabi* on 20 October 1990. Because the *O'Brien*'s visual classification of the *Al Bahar Al Arabi* did not correspond to her self-declared description, Rear Adm. Bill Fogarty (ComMidEastFor) directed the *O'Brien* to intercept and search her. The ship's master agreed to slow and allowed the U.S. team to board. A helicopter from the *O'Brien* flew over the *Al Bahar Al Arabi* for inspection purposes, as well as to provide air cover for the boarding party. The master had no crew manifest and seemed uncertain of the number of crew members, but he offered that there were thirty-five. Eventually, the boarding party accounted for thirty-one crew members, which the master then confirmed to be the correct number. The crew consisted of Iraqis, Egyptians, Indians, and Nigerians.

The boarding party found lumber and pipes and declared the cargo to be prohibited. The master explained that the wood was to be used to stabilize future cargo and the pipes were for ship repairs—the stated reason for the voyage to Aden. This did not satisfy the inspection team. They offered the master the option of returning to his port of origin (Basra) or diverting to Bahrain. Saying he feared being arrested in Bahrain, the master opted to return to Iraq. At this point, the boarding party disembarked.

Six minutes after stating his preference to return to Iraq, the master changed his mind and reported he intended to maintain course and sped toward Aden while dumping the cargo overboard. We do not know why the master changed his mind, but a representative from the owner's company was on board and could have influenced the decision. The *O'Brien* reported seeing the crew dumping the material overboard.

The *O'Brien*, while trailing, continued to issue radio warnings to stop. The *Al Bahar Al Arabi* refused to respond and did not stop. The master now sounded quite bellicose; they could come and kill him, but he would not stop. Vice Admiral Mauz wanted to get this ship into port. He was suspicious of the crew, because the master had not had a crew list. In addition, Mauz worried that the *Al Bahar Al Arabi* might in some way be associated with terrorists. This might explain why the master feared being arrested if he diverted to Bahrain. A second concern centered around the possibility that the *Al Bahar Al Arabi* might be headed for Aden to assist in repairing other Iraqi ships.

The *O'Brien* fired .50-caliber, 25 mm, and five-inch warning shots across the *Al Bahar Al Arabi*'s bow, with no effect. Because of the location of the *Al Bahar Al Arabi*, Rear Admiral Fogarty then directed the *O'Brien* to break off and return to her station in the central Persian Gulf. The Italian frigate *Libeccio* (F 572) picked up trailing the *Al Bahar Al Arabi* and escorted her through the Strait of Hormuz, where the *Reasoner* joined the *Libeccio* to continue surveillance of the *Al Bahar Al Arabi*.

Several options to reintercept the *Al Bahar al Arabi* were considered. Mauz decided to let the Australians on the *Adelaide* do it. This would allow the United States to observe their capability while remaining close if additional forces were needed (specifically a 13th MEU[SOC] team embarked on the *Ogden*). The *Al Bahar Al Arabi* would be boarded again and diverted on 22 October, with the Australians designated as on-scene commander for the multinational force. Possibilities for diversion ports included Muscat in Oman and Fujaira in the UAE. The latter was chosen, and the United States took the initiative to make arrangements.

During the morning of 21 October, the plans for boarding the *Al Bahar Al Arabi* were finalized and briefed to the participants. The plan called for the *Ogden's* Marines to be on standby in case the Australians ran into trouble, but that the *Ogden* would not be used otherwise. Mauz was told that the members of the Australian fast-rope team were not special warfare forces but simply ship's crew that had been practicing for about six weeks, and this worried him. The *Libeccio* continued surveillance of the *Al Bahar Al Arabi* until the *Reasoner* took over on 22 October. In early morning, once all participants were in position, the interception would begin. The *Reasoner* had authority for warning shots, at the on-scene commander's (Australian) direction. In addition, before the beginning of the interception, General Schwarzkopf gave Mauz authority to use disabling fire if necessary. (We do not fully understand why disabling fire was authorized for the *Al Bahar Al Arabi* but not for other Iraqi ships that tried to avoid being boarded during this period. Our best estimate is that it had to do with the possibility of a connection with terrorists.)

Instead of warning shots, the *Adelaide* and *Reasoner* maneuvered around the *Al Bahar Al Arabi*. The *Adelaide* conducted "aggressive high-speed" maneuvers in front of the *Al Bahar Al Arabi* while issuing radio warnings to stop and warning that a device towed by the *Adelaide* (the spar) would be used next if she did not stop. The *Reasoner* shouldered the *Al Bahar Al Arabi* to prevent her from turning away from the *Adelaide*.

The *Adelaide* team was inserted by helicopter, but instead of using the fast-rope technique it used a wire and boarded in tandem. This technique is similar to vertical insertions used by the British and the United States, except that it is slower. Once the Australian teams secured the ship, the U.S. team from the *Reasoner* boarded by motor whaleboat. Although the *Al Bahar Al Arabi* carried prohibited cargo, the Australians deemed the material to be on the "low end" of the contraband list and did not consider it of substantial size. Ultimately, the *Adelaide* as on-scene commander cleared the *Al Bahar Al Arabi* to proceed. Overall, the intercept went smoothly and can be considered a success. That does not mean, however, it was without fault.

We can draw a parallel between the *Al Bahar Al Arabi* and *Tadmur*. First, both carried prohibited cargo, although in small amounts. Second, each was boarded more than once. The coalition diverted the *Tadmur* and removed her cargo eventually, and the indications are that the United States intended to apply the same principles to the *Al Bahar Al Arabi*. But because on-scene commanders from different countries ran the two boardings, the *Al Bahar Al Arabi* was allowed to proceed. This incident illustrated a potential weakness in the multinational maritime interception operations. One says "no," the other says "yes" to allowing ships to proceed to their destination.

Amuriyah: Iraqi Resistance Increases

The *Amuriyah*, a 157,000-dwt Iraqi tanker en route from Aden, Yemen, to Basra, Iraq, was first tracked by a P-3 aircraft after she left Aden on 24 October heading north along the Yemeni and Omani coasts. Though apparently empty, she had to be intercepted.

As with the *Al Bahar Al Arabi*, the early information on the *Amuriyah*'s movements allowed the multinational forces to assemble forces and plan for the interception. The United States brought the *Reasoner* with an embarked USCG LEDet and the *Ogden* with embarked MEU(SOC) and SEAL teams, and the carrier air wing (CVW-14) from the *Independence* provided SuCAP (surface combat air patrol). Coalition assets included the *Darwin*, tasked to provide a search team and to perform its aggressive tactical maneuvers with a spar, and the *Brazen* in a support role standing by. Planning and rehearsals took place while the ships were en route to rendezvous with the *Amuriyah*. All participants discussed a spectrum of scenarios up to hostility and the use of minimum force as necessary.

On 28 October the plan went into action. The *Reasoner* launched a helicopter to conduct reconnaissance of the *Amuriyah*. The *Reasoner* quickly went through the verbal requests for information and verbal warnings to stop. When the *Amuriyah*'s master did not respond, the *Darwin* began her aggressive maneuvers. At the same time, two *Amuriyah* crew members used a water cannon on the deck. Perhaps having learned about helicopter insertions from the previous interceptions, they wet the deck in an apparent attempt to complicate the helicopter insertion and possibly prevent it altogether.

The *Amuriyah*'s master finally acknowledged the radio calls with a refusal to stop until he received word from the owner. As the *Darwin* conducted her second maneuver against the *Amuriyah*, the master continued his obstinacy, stating that he was clearly in ballast and that he did not trust the United States. He had no intention of stopping.

To increase the pressure on the *Amuriyah* to stop, the *Darwin* began her third maneuver against the *Amuriyah* and this time used a spar. The *Reasoner* shouldered the *Amuriyah* to prevent her from turning away, evidently with limited effectiveness. Still, the *Amuriyah* showed no signs of slowing. The *Darwin* made a second run with her spar. This time the *Amuriyah* responded by turning slightly to avoid the spar; one minute later the *Amuriyah* turned hard to port. By now the ships were approaching Omani territorial waters. The *Reasoner* received permission to continue the intercept into Omani territorial waters, up to three miles. The *Amuriyah* stated it would take two to three hours to contact the owner. The *Reasoner* responded that it now had fifteen minutes to show signs of slowing.

The efforts to stop the *Amuriyah* escalated to warning shots. The *Darwin* fired two hundred .50-caliber rounds, and the *Reasoner* fired two five-inch rounds three hundred yards ahead of the *Amuriyah*. In addition, an F/A-18 and an F-14 from the *Independence* made eight subsonic, low-level passes—during which the crew of the *Amuriyah* cheered. The master, when warned of the impending helicopter insertion, stated his refusal to accept a boarding party.

As soon as the low-level passes by the aircraft ended, the MEU(SOC) team boarded on a dry part of the deck, while a UH-1 gunship from the *Ogden* provided cover. Once on the *Amuriyah*'s bridge, the Marines ordered the master to stop the ship or they would do so from the engineering room. Although the master said he would stop the ship, he showed no signs of doing so. What finally convinced the master to stop the ship was Marines tracing the fuel lines in the engineering room so as to stop the main engine by fuel starvation, which could damage the engine. In the darkened engineering spaces, a U.S. Marine encountered an ax-wielding Iraqi. The Marine, showing tremendous restraint, physically restrained and disarmed him.

The *Amuriyah* began to slow, but the master remained very uncooperative and now refused to muster the crew. Therefore, the back-up SEAL team boarded the *Amuriyah* via helicopter and helped control the crew. With a second security team on board, the master became less belligerent, and all thirty-seven crew members were accounted for. Once the *Amuriyah* slowed, the *Reasoner* search team, consisting of a USCG LEDet and *Reasoner* personnel, boarded. The Australian Navy search team boarded by separate boat.

While being questioned in his cabin about the nationalities of the crew, the master once again became belligerent and had to be forcibly removed to the bridge. The passports for the crew were not found in the master's cabin or in his safe. The boarding party checked them individually by escorting each crew member to get his passport. Thus far, they had discovered no cargo. They had, however, found three crates of tea in the master's cabin. The tea was reported to have been bought by the master and the chief engineer in Aden for their personal use. The search team did not dispute this, but they believed that the tea may have come from the *Zanoobia's* illegal cargo (a thousand tons of tea), and therefore the search team was ordered to search the vessel very carefully. The search lasted over three hours before the *Amuriyah* was declared a cleared vessel.

The *Amuriyah* interception was significant for a couple of reasons. First, because of the uncooperative nature of *Amuriyah's* master, it was the first to require both a MEU(SOC) and SEAL team. Second, it entailed considerable resistance, both passive and active, by the Iraqis. The passive resistance included not answering bridge-to-bridge communications, not mustering the crew, and refusing to stop the ship after agreeing to do so. Neither the master nor the crew showed any signs of fear. As mentioned above, when the fighters conducted their subsonic passes, the crew cheered.

Active resistance included uncooperative behavior by the master and crew members that required the MEU(SOC) to restrain them, and the use of water cannons—producing a potentially precarious situation for the Marines fast-roping onto the deck, had the Iraqis used the water cannons effectively. Further active resistance measures included the master's trying to take the crew pay list from the USCG LEDet officer; a crew member refusing to leave a water cannon until he had to be physically removed; and, of course, the ax-wielding Iraqi. Chapter 5 of Volume II describes how, three months later, the *Amuriyah* would have a final, shining moment in the sights of NavCent forces.

During this period, the multinational Maritime Interception Force denied Iraq the economic benefit of its shipping yet avoided the uncertain consequences that would ensue if it disabled an unarmed civilian ship. The vertical insertions offered a solution to the qualms about disabling when intimidation and warning shots failed. In some situations, warning shots proved to be effective, as did the Australian spar and high-speed maneuvers. Regardless of differing ROE, the allied navies worked together professionally. The Maritime Interception Force conferences aided in this process by providing a forum to solve coordination and communication difficulties. Ships carrying prohibited cargo into the Persian Gulf en route to Iraq or Kuwait had not gotten past the allied navies. The noose was tightening around Iraq.

NOTES

The author's notes of briefings given to the ComUSNavCent staff were the source for the intelligence section. The accounts of the interceptions came primarily from messages (especially the after-action reports), and the author's observations of events at the ComUSNavCent command center, and logs. The CNA reconstruction report was used for a few details. The British report by Agnew et al. was especially helpful for events in which the British participated. Information on the maritime interception force conferences came in part from the book by Miller and Hobson.

1. USS *Brewton* 142210Z OCT 90, *Al Mutanabbi* After Action Report/Lessons Learned.

2. *Lloyd's Maritime Directory* does not list the *Al Bahar Al Arabi* but does list the *Al Sahil Al Arabi*. The Navy Operational Intelligence Center's *Iraq: Merchant Marine Identification Guide* lists both ship names.

Chapter 9

Air Plans and Operations

As the situation became less hectic in September, plans for a strike campaign changed emphasis and began to mature. Major problems faced by ComUSNav-Cent included getting Tomahawk cruise missiles integrated into the strike plans, determining how much ordnance would be needed, and rehearsing the strike plans. One preparation for a coalition bombing campaign was a series of probes, termed Desert Triangle operations, of the Iraqi air defenses. Iraqi aircraft in turn probed the coalition's air defenses. These sorties, culminating in what we term "Iraqi Triangle" operations, highlighted some difficult air defense challenges faced by NavCent forces.

STRIKE PLANNING

As the threat of an Iraqi invasion faded during September, emphasis gradually shifted to the offensive strike plan. Nevertheless, the JFACC (Joint Force Air Component Commander) planners continued to revise the defensive plan (known as the D-Day Air Tasking Order), which covered the first twenty-four hours of air strikes if Iraq invaded Saudi Arabia. As of 19 September, the plan scheduled NavCent aircraft for interdiction sorties rather than close air support—that is, deep strikes as opposed to attacks against enemy forces actually in contact with friendly forces. Because this reactive plan would be executed only if Iraq attacked, and therefore on short notice, plans included aircraft from only one Red Sea carrier (the *Saratoga* or *Kennedy*), as the other carrier would likely be in the Mediterranean. The assignment of targets to the air wing of the North Arabian Sea carrier, *Independence*, focused on reducing the threat to ships in the Persian Gulf from Iraqi forces in Iraq and Kuwait: Ras al-Qulaya Silkworm site, Ras al-Qulaya naval base, ground control intercept sites, Shaiba airfield, and Umm Qasr naval base.

Targets assigned to the Red Sea battle group included Tallil airfield, a ground control intercept site, and Jaliba airfield.

NavCent personnel would serve as mission commanders for all these strikes. Though NavCent could provide most of the aircraft, these strikes also included British GR-1s, Air Force EF-111s and F-16s, and Marine Corps F/A-18s and EA-6Bs. In addition, NavCent aircraft would provide SEAD (suppression of enemy air defenses) support for a U.S. Air Force (USAF) B-52 strike. Navy strike leaders would set times on target for the CentAF and coalition aircraft participating in these strikes. Because the *Kennedy* carried A-7s instead of F/A-18s like the *Saratoga*, and the two types of aircraft had different capabilities, the strike leaders took care to devise plans that either air wing could execute.

In October, representatives of the Red Sea battle group met with participants from the U.S. Air Force and British Royal Air Force and agreed on tactics, aim-points, and ingress and egress procedures for integrated strikes. By early November, the plans had needed only minor revisions.

Years later, Vice Adm. Hank Mauz expressed the opinion that by October the Navy was more or less a full partner in the strike planning process, though not in numbers of people involved. Of twenty-nine officers in the Black Hole (the JFACC strike planning cell) at the end of September 1990, only two were from the Navy—Commanders Maurice E. "Fast Eddie" Smith, USN, and Donald "Duck" McSwain, USN, who represented the Red Sea and North Arabian Sea battle groups, respectively.[1] These two commanders had incredible influence and responsibility for relatively junior officers, but there were only two of them, and when they needed more "horsepower" they had to call in Rear Adm. Tim Wright, who was NavCent-Riyadh, head of Mauz's liaison group in Riyadh. Eventually, Wright brought in Captain Lyle "Ho Chi" Bien, USN, a former air wing commander, to be there all the time to answer questions on the spot. Still, no Navy person held significant decision-making authority on the JFACC staff.

TOMAHAWK

If the Tomahawk land-attack missile were to be used, it would be for the first time in combat. Articles in the press expressed doubt that Tomahawk would work as advertised. In a relatively muted criticism published in the *Air Force Times,* Fred Reed stated that he suspected the Navy had exaggerated the effectiveness of Tomahawk.[2] Another writer stridently proclaimed Tomahawk "technically incapable of the required accuracy" and a "high-tech toy"; he flatly asserted that "ample evidence is available to show that this missile won't work as advertised" and that the missile's digital scene-matching area correlation (DSMAC) algorithm had never been rigorously tested.[3] Michael Getler in the *Washington Post* correctly pointed out that the United States had many high-tech weapons that had never been tested in combat. He gave a number of examples of sophisticated weapon systems that did not work as expected when used in combat for the first time. He concluded there was a nagging history of initial missteps.[4]

Vice Admiral Mauz recalled having to "sell" Tomahawk just about every week. He thought the major resistance came from Washington, rather than from Gen. Norman Schwarzkopf, Lt. Gen. Chuck Horner, or Brig. Gen. Buster Glosson. Mauz invited Horner to the *Blue Ridge,* where Commander Eugene "Geno" Nielsen, USN, ComUSNavCent's Tomahawk expert, showed Horner how Tomahawk would work.

Mauz heard secondhand that the resistance came from Gen. Colin Powell. Rear Adm. Tim Wright was told that when Glosson briefed Powell on the strike plan, Powell had pulled out a study he had been given before leaving Washington showing that Tomahawk was not reliable, and indicated he wanted it pulled out of the strike plan.[5]

Powell was skeptical initially. He was shown the same video again and again with the same Tomahawk missile hitting the same wall. He asked a lot of questions about the system and visited the Cruise Missile Support Activity in Norfolk. He wanted to know how the missile worked when it was not fired at China Lake, where there had been several years to work on the same terrain contour matching scenes. Finally, he reached a reasonable comfort level. (Powell later did not recall giving any instructions about taking Tomahawk out of the plan and thought he would not have told strike planners to do so. He recognized, however, that sometimes if the CJCS "scratched his nose," that might be interpreted as an order or desire.)

Despite the doubters, Mauz won the argument and got Tomahawk included in the attack plan. The Navy believes it persuaded Powell and others by showing a plot superimposed on a baseball diamond of the scattering of test Tomahawk shots about the aimpoint (see Figure 9–1). This plot showed that if the aimpoint were the pitcher's mound, all the test shots would have fallen in the infield. Thus, there was no need to worry about Tomahawk missiles landing in nearby neighborhoods. Powell later recalled that the baseball diagram increased his confidence level but was not decisive. In chapter 16 of Volume II, we shall see how actual results compared with this prediction.

After Tomahawk had been included in the attack plans, the cruise missile support activities discovered an error in some of the missions already planned.[6] Those missions had to be pulled temporarily from the attack plan until planners could devise new ones for those targets. In a message to senior Navy admirals in Norfolk and Pearl Harbor, Mauz urged greater quality control on Tomahawk mission planning. He noted that every time he had to back Tomahawks out of the plan because of mission planning snags, he had to "sell" the weapon all over again.

The general concern about performance in the first combat use of any weapon system was valid. The Navy had tested the Tomahawk missile to show that it could fly and hit a target accurately if properly programmed. But would the entire system (target and aimpoint selection, route planning, missile programming, and missile flight performance) work under the stress of real-world conditions? Desert Storm would be a tough test. Mission planners at the cruise missile support activities faced the major challenge of obtaining good enough imagery to plan targets

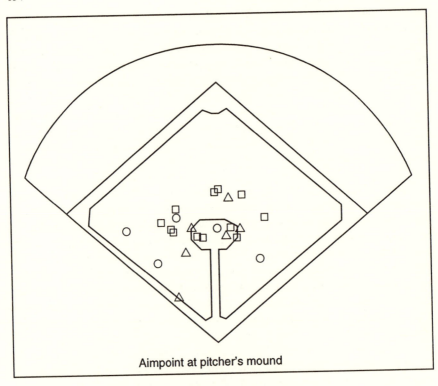

Aimpoint at pitcher's mound

Figure 9–1. Tomahawk Missile Accuracy

and routes. Then they had to plan a large number of missions in a short time and devise the code to load into the missiles.

Additional concerns went beyond the internal workings of the missile and its programming, to the manner in which JFACC would use it. Some problems arose from unfamiliarity with the technical details of using the weapon system; other problems were more operational in nature. Although Tomahawk could be used in several roles (for instance, precision strikes in heavily defended areas, making a political statement), prior to Desert Shield the Navy emphasized having the missiles support strikes by manned aircraft so that they would be a force multiplier. A few cruise missiles would take out enemy defenses to allow reusable aircraft and precious aircrews to get through with less risk. Now, in part because JFACC did not trust Tomahawk, and in part because (for the then-current version) the time at which a missile would reach the target could not be accurately predicted (it can be for later versions), the missiles would not be used in close coordination with manned aircraft strikes. Up to mid-September, all targets nominated for Tomahawk by JFACC were independent of tactical manned aircraft strikes. In later plans, though some Tomahawks would be aimed at Iraq's defenses in the early hours, most would be aimed at various fixed targets not directly connected with manned aircraft strikes.

NavCent strike planners on the *Blue Ridge* initially did not have all the information they needed. For example, in planning large strikes using several ships, NavCent planners needed to know such things as the maximum number of missile-mission combinations that each ship could plan and execute. Ships used several different launch and fire-control systems, and no single document listed all the necessary information.

Closely sequenced launches of multiple missiles from several ships had never been practiced. Mauz recognized the challenge in ensuring that such a complex weapon system worked right the first time in combat. Therefore, starting in October he ordered an extensive exercise program to test Tomahawk command, control, and execution from alert order through missile alignment and built-in test-equipment checks. This exercise series, Nemean Lion, started on a small scale and built up to more complex events.

Because Tomahawk once fired cannot be recalled or destroyed, Mauz ordered extensive safeguards to ensure that no inadvertent launches occurred during these exercises. After each exercise the ComUSNavCent staff solicited lessons learned, digested them, and altered the procedures to solve any problems. These exercises revealed a number of problems that could have delayed or even prevented Tomahawk launch had they been the real thing. For example, the strike planners found that mission plans from the Atlantic and Pacific Fleet cruise missile support activities differed in format and composition.

As another example, after Nemean Lion I the battleship *Wisconsin* reported that she had used one launch position for six missions, then moved to another launch position for the remaining eleven missions. Ten of those eleven missions could have been launched from either location; if the permissible launch area for one mission could be moved, a single launch point could accommodate all seventeen missions. The *Wisconsin* also noted that knowing the launch positions of other Tomahawk-firing platforms would help her avoid having her missiles fly over the other ships. As the planners identified and solved these problems, they grew increasingly confident they could successfully execute a large missile strike on the first try.

ORDNANCE REQUIREMENTS

In mid-September, Vice Admiral Mauz became concerned about whether the Red Sea battle groups had sufficient ordnance. Whereas the *Independence* battle group in the North Arabian Sea was accompanied by two ammunition ships, the USS *Flint* (AE 32) and USS *Kilauea* (T-AE 26), each of the two battle groups that would operate in the Red Sea in the event of hostilities had only one ammunition ship, with less capacity than either of the two ships supporting the *Independence*. Seemingly, they each had less than one-half the ordnance that the North Arabian Sea carrier did. Mauz asked ComSixthFlt to provide more ordnance for the two battle groups from the Mediterranean, but ComSixthFlt thought the Red Sea battle groups already had enough. Not satisfied, Mauz asked the civilian Center for Naval Analyses operations analyst on his staff (the author of this book) to look into ordnance requirements.

Estimating ordnance requirements presents more difficulties than one would think. One must predict in detail how that most unpredictable of human endeavors—war—will unfold. The straightforward way to estimate requirements would be to count the number of targets of each type that need to be damaged or destroyed, estimate the number of weapons required to achieve the required degree of damage to each target, then add them all up. That method would not work here. First, Mauz's staff didn't know the overall number of each type of target (Intelligence continually discovered more), or how many of each type JFACC would assign to NavCent. Second, NavCent forces had to prepare both for close air support of ground troops in contact with the enemy and for strategic strikes against leadership, economic, chemical, and other targets deep in Iraq. Third, NavCent forces did not know which type of weapon would prove effective against each kind of target. For example, the use of laser-guided bombs (LGBs) against tanks and other vehicles was not yet anticipated. Fourth, large uncertainties in the effectiveness of weapons existed. The history of air warfare indicated that aircraft often needed a tremendous number of bombs to destroy most targets. One hoped that modern guided weapons and extremely accurate bombers dropping unguided weapons would produce a quantum leap in effectiveness, but one could not bet everything on this unproven hope. Most of these uncertainties could be accommodated using appropriate approximations and safety margins. The primary problem, however, was that Mauz did not know which targets JFACC would assign to his forces.

Therefore, the operations analyst estimated the requirements for a "level-of-effort" campaign, rather than the requirements for destroying a specified set of targets. The calculation would estimate the quantity of ordnance needed to sustain operations for twenty days. He got around the uncertainty in Mauz's tasking by considering two scenarios, one all strategic strike and the other all close air support after the first day. The analyst calculated the requirements for each type of ordnance for each scenario. The larger of each type of ordnance needed for either of the two scenarios was set as the overall requirement.

This method was fairly good for "dumb" (unguided) weapons, such as the Mk-80 series, and for cluster weapons like the Mk-20 Rockeye and CBU-59 APAM (antipersonnel, antimateriel).[7] For "smart" (guided) weapons, the analyst and the NavCent strike planner assumed that NavCent aircraft would use some LGBs in the first three days but that after the effectiveness of the Iraqi defenses had been degraded, aircraft would shift to low-level delivery of unguided Mk-80 weapons.

If standoff weapons were needed, the aircraft would fire Walleye missiles (a glide bomb guided by a video data link between the bomb and the aircraft). Because of these assumptions, the analyst and strike planner did not see a need for a huge number of LGBs.

Still harder to estimate was the need for antiradiation missiles (ARMs). These missiles home on enemy radar emissions and explode at the antennas. NavCent forces intended to use a lot of ARMs the first day to neutralize or destroy Iraq's air-defense system. One hoped the need would then decline, but how fast depended on the Iraqi radar operating tactics, the effectiveness of ARMs in destroying radars, and the number of spare antennas the Iraqis possessed. The rate at which the use of ARMs would decline was strictly an educated guess.

Later, when General Schwarzkopf ordered each component to have a thirty-day ordnance supply on hand instead of the previous twenty-day supply, this methodology was extended in a straightforward manner. Still later, when Schwarzkopf wanted a sixty-day supply, the methodology was again extended, but this time the planners eliminated the scenario that called for all close air support after the first day. Instead, they used a second scenario in which NavCent aircraft conducted mostly strategic strikes for the first three days, then about half close air support thereafter. During Desert Storm, NavCent forces had enough level-of-effort weapons (relatively inexpensive dumb bombs) for their own use and enough excess weapons to give some to CentAF and MarCent forces.

As alluded to above, in a joint operation a component commander does not know the share of a particular type of target his forces will have to counter—not even after the war has begun. At one point, Schwarzkopf sent a message complaining that his subordinates had arranged for sixteen thousand Hellfire missiles to be sent to the CentCom theater. As Hellfire was designed to kill a tank with one shot, this should be enough to destroy every tank in the Iraqi inventory four times over. He could have added, but did not, that weapons other than Hellfire could also kill tanks.

STRIKE REHEARSALS

The Navy conducted a series of rehearsals of the strike plans to train the people, verify planning factors such as fuel consumption, and find any glitches. Ideally, rehearsals replicate the actual aircraft numbers, flight distances, flight altitudes and speeds, ordnance loads, timing, rendezvous, and every other detail of the actual mission, except that the aircraft drop the ordnance on a training range rather than on the actual target.

Vice Admiral Mauz kept pushing for a full-scale rehearsal with CentAF aircraft and simultaneous times on target to test every aspect of the plan. Because he knew that multiservice, multinational operations rarely, if ever, go smoothly the first time, Mauz wanted interaction with CentAF tankers, AWACS aircraft, and fighters; coalition aircraft; and the entire command-and-control process. He never got what he wanted during this period of Desert Shield. Nevertheless, NavCent aircraft, especially those in the Red Sea, interacted with CentAF tankers and learned valuable lessons that would make the actual Desert Storm operations much smoother, even though these were not the desired full-scale rehearsals. In pushing for full-scale, multiservice, multinational strike rehearsals, Mauz seems to have taken the lead. He believed that CentAF always was reluctant to stage integrated rehearsals.

Mauz's firm belief in the value of practicing strikes realistically went back at least to the April 1986 Libyan strike, codenamed El Dorado Canyon, when he had commanded the *America* battle group and had also been the Sixth Fleet Battle Force commander in charge of two carrier groups. Initially, that operation had been planned as an all-Navy strike. Two carriers had conducted a series of realistic strike rehearsals duplicating the altitude and airspeed along a strike route of the same length as the actual operation, with the planned amounts of fuel and weapons. Mauz thought these rehearsals had been of immense value in avoiding potential problems and had been a major factor in the Navy's loss of zero aircraft in the operation. In contrast, when Air Force aircraft were added to the strike, Mauz recalls that the Air Force had not had time to practice its strikes. As a result, Mauz averred, only when the Air Force aircraft flew over the target had they learned that the assigned combination of bomb loads, airspeed, and altitude required them to be in afterburner, leaving a long fiery trail across the sky, highly visible to the enemy. The Air Force had lost one aircraft. Although we have not verified the afterburner aspect of this story, its influence on Mauz's desire for realistic rehearsals is clear.

Adequate CentAF support for air-to-air refueling constantly worried NavCent throughout Desert Shield and Desert Storm. With multiple air-to-air refuelings, one can extend an aircraft's range until the limiting factor is the endurance of the human beings inside the aircraft. Navy carriers have some tanker aircraft, but they carry much less fuel than the large Air Force tankers. Thus, long-range strikes by large numbers of aircraft require land-based tankers. Many years ago, the Navy had fought to have its own force of land-based tankers. It lost. The Air Force controls essentially all land-based tankers. Primary land-based tankers in use in 1990 included the KC-135 (derived from the Boeing 707) and the KC-10 (derived from the DC-10).[8] To win the earlier battle, the Air Force had agreed to support the Navy as required, but demand for tankers always seemed to exceed the supply. NavCent strike efforts depended critically on the availability of CentAF tankers. Most NavCent officers believed JFACC planners did not give NavCent its fair share of the tanking. CentAF officers had a different view. Reportedly, they wanted NavCent's aircraft carriers in the North Arabian Sea to move closer to the targets, into the Persian Gulf, and they wanted NavCent forces to use fewer support aircraft for each strike. Both actions would mean consuming less fuel and therefore reduce NavCent tanking requirements.

Air-to-air refueling. A Navy A-6 refuels an EA-6B. Navy Photo.

It may seem amazing to the layman, but the U.S. Navy and most of the allies use a different air-to-air refueling system than the U.S. Air Force. The Navy uses a probe on the receiving aircraft that is inserted into a basket trailed behind the tanker aircraft; the Air Force uses a boom on the tanker and a receptacle on the receiver aircraft. Not surprisingly, the two systems are incompatible. At one time, tankers had to be refitted with different hoses to accommodate Navy aircraft. By the time of Desert Shield, however, tankers could be equipped to accommodate both Air Force and Navy systems on the same sortie. The Navy and the Air Force also use different procedures for making the connections. In the Navy, the tanker aircraft holds the basket steady while the receiver aircraft flies the probe into the basket. In the Air Force, the receiver aircraft holds steady while the boom operator on the tanker "flies" (maneuvers) the boom into the receiver aircraft's receptacle. Prior to Desert Shield, Navy aircraft periodically practiced refueling from Air Force land-based tankers. These training periods were infrequent, however, and not every pilot had recent experience doing so. In addition to solving the physical and procedural problems of linking up with the tankers, NavCent and CentAF also needed to work out coordination and communication problems. Thus, the Com-USNavCent staff considered it imperative to practice tanking large NavCent strike packages.

18–20 September

When the aircraft carrier *Kennedy* arrived in the Red Sea (from the United States) to relieve the *Saratoga*, the ComUSNavCent staff arranged for both carriers' air wings to conduct the first large-package strike training on 18–20 September. (By a large-package strike, we mean one involving the full mix of bombers, electronic jammers, HARM (High-speed Anti-radiation Missile) shooters, command-and-control aircraft, tankers, and fighters, totalling at least a dozen aircraft and often many more.) The lessons-learned message from the *Saratoga*'s Carrier Air Wing 17 cited several positive aspects of the exercise and noted that all players had experienced an "exponential increase" in the confidence level of fuel-consumption estimates and the tanking, launch, and recovery of large packages of aircraft.

The lessons-learned message also noted a number of problems. Most reflected a preference for doing things the Navy way and resentment at being forced to do them the Air Force way. For one thing, Carrier Air Wing 17 wanted the Air Tasking Order at least eight hours prior to the launch time. Also, it wanted the strike leader, rather than the Air Tasking Order, to assign specific aircraft to specific tankers. The message contained the first of many complaints about the revolving light and the fuselage flood lights on the tankers. As was common in these evolutions, the Navy pilots wanted the tankers to lock the boom in position and not try to "help" the aircraft into the basket as is done with Air Force aircraft. Finally, Navy pilots preferred KC-10 tankers rather than the KC-135s, because they found it much easier to take fuel from a KC-10. The bottom line was that most of the aircraft would have made it to the target but that there had been rough spots along the way.

6–7 October

The *Kennedy* and Carrier Air Wing 3 conducted the next large-package strike training, on 6–7 October. The intent was to conduct three large strike events over a thirty-hour period. Each event would replicate the real strike plans with regard to tanker tracks, distance, air speeds, and altitudes. The culminating phase of the simulated attack would occur at the Tabuk target complex in western Saudi Arabia.

The routes flown included the actual tanker tracks, a flight that replicated the actual distance to the target, and a return to the carrier via the tankers. Almost all aircraft carried the actual planned ordnance loads; a few carried representative "drag counts" instead. ("Drag counts" are a measure of the air resistance caused by carrying bombs, missiles, drop tanks, electronic pods, and so on.) Fuel-consumption rates are estimated based on the total drag count; maneuverability is also a function of it. Replicating the correct drag count would be important, for example, in evaluating the feasibility of tanking speeds and altitudes.

The lessons-learned message from Rear Admiral Riley Mixson, USN, commander of the *Kennedy* battle group, praised the Air Force tankers and concluded that the overall execution had been excellent. Mixson reported that most problems experienced by the *Kennedy* and her air wing during the first strike rehearsal had been corrected. He also noted that some fuel-consumption figures had been revised based on the rehearsal. Finally, however, he believed that assigning eight A-6s to a single tanker was unworkable. Either the aircraft should be redistributed among the tankers, another KC-135 tanker should be added, or the A-6s would have to carry one fewer bomb each so they could add a drop tank of fuel.

24–25 October

When the *Saratoga* entered the Red Sea in late October to relieve the *Kennedy*, the ComUSNavCent staff again took advantage of the opportunity to schedule a dual-carrier large-package strike exercise. This experience would include three large-package strikes over a thirty-hour period. Vice Admiral Mauz directed both battle groups to make this rehearsal as realistic as possible, including participation by the joint and combined forces expected for the actual strike operations. He set the objective and made it clear he considered this an important evolution.

Rear Adm. Nick Gee, commander of the *Saratoga* battle group, tried to arrange integration with Air Force AWACS, combat search and rescue, and other aircraft so as to exercise joint command-and-control procedures. Gee also requested Air Force F-15 fighters to provide opposition to the strike. We have conflicting reports about the extent of CentAF participation in this rehearsal, but it seems clear that it fell far short of what Mauz wanted.

Gee's lessons-learned message praised the overall mission execution and flexibility of the Air Force tankers as excellent but noted problems with tankers straying too far from their designated orbit points and with the boom operator "helping" the boom. Whereas one lesson of the early October rehearsal had been that eight A-6s per tanker were too many, Gee said that four aircraft per tanker were too few. (During Desert Storm, eight A-6s per tanker were deemed acceptable if A-6 tankers acted as "hose multipliers," that is, if A-6s configured as tankers rather than bombers took fuel from the Air Force tanker and then distributed the fuel to other aircraft in the strike.)

Mauz thought NavCent forces had learned a great deal from working with the Air Force tankers, but he still wanted realistic practice with all CentAF aircraft. When Mauz sent his lessons learned to ComUSCentAF, he hit hard on getting more Air Force participation. He recommended that future rehearsals include: realistic, representative multiservice participation, including AWACS, in full-scale exercises; multiple realistic targets; multiservice strikes on the same target; combat search and rescue; and air opposition to strike groups. Mauz also recommended standardizing KC-135 interservice procedures and made some specific suggestions. He ended by asking ComUSCentAF to take the lead in organizing a major strike exercise involving the Air Force, Marine Corps, and *Midway* aircraft during the last week of November.

DESERT TRIANGLE

On 29 October, CentAF began daily "Desert Triangle" operations, which called for flying various aggressive profiles toward the Iraqi and Kuwaiti borders to assess Iraqi reaction to air threats. Four F-16s flew at high speed to within fifteen miles of the border, then climbed and flew parallel to the border. Other profiles involved flying high over Saudi Arabia until close to the Kuwaiti border, then diving as the aircraft approached the border, and turning to parallel the border as close as ten miles away. The objectives were to:

- Stimulate Iraq's air defenses so the Americans could assess the defensive response
- Observe Iraqi reactions
- Keep Iraq's air force flying, making it use up spare parts.

After a few days, Navy and Marine Corps aircraft joined these operations. Desert Triangle operations by the Red Sea battle group on 2 and 3 November included four F-14 "pulse aircraft," four F-14 combat air patrol aircraft, two E-2Cs, two EA-6B jammers, two S-3B electronic intelligence support aircraft, an AWACS mission control aircraft, and KC-135 tanker support. The pulse aircraft would fly a triangular pattern, descending and accelerating as they approached the Iraqi border. These Desert Triangle operations complemented the strike rehearsals. In the absence of the joint strike rehearsals that Vice Admiral Mauz wanted but never really got, Desert Triangle operations filled a gap. They helped NavCent forces learn to operate with CentAF aircraft and their command-and-control procedures.

In its postexercise report for the events of 2 and 3 November, the battle group reported a number of problems in coordinating with CentAF, mostly having to do with NavCent and CentAF aircraft not being on the same radio frequency or using different codes to encrypt voice communications. The report argued that different control systems for NavCent and CentAF aircraft caused uncertainties and heightened the potential for fratricide incidents. One proposal was to have the AWACS control all fighter aircraft, including the Navy's.

As the Desert Triangle operations and various strike rehearsals continued, problems gradually got solved; the Red Sea battle group's postexercise report on 3 December concluded that connectivity problems in initial Desert Triangles appeared to have been solved.

As stated above, one objective of Desert Triangle was to observe the Iraqi reactions. Three days after the initial Air Force Desert Triangle operations, on the morning of 1 November, the intelligence briefer at the ComUSNavCent morning staff meeting reported no observed Iraqi reaction at all. In a separate report just a minute later, the same briefer told of a large number of Iraqi flights over land and water on the previous day. He described these flights as being in a chain, in which each headed for the border then turned away. One violated the Saudi border by about eight miles. This event was characterized as an Iraqi version of Desert Triangle. It also marked the first time in eight days that Iraqi aircraft had flown over the Persian Gulf. Perhaps the Iraqis had reacted to Desert Triangle after all.

AIR DEFENSE

NavCent forces in the Persian Gulf depended critically on the warning provided by AWACS. But were they getting the data they needed, and was this line of defense always in place? After exploring these two questions, we then describe how the "Iraqi Triangle" operations brought those problems to the forefront.

On 15 October, during a ComUSNavCent staff discussion of air-defense problems, someone mentioned that there was no radar coverage when the AWACS plane went off station to refuel. Two AWACS aircraft sorties a day each covered the eastern orbit for twelve hours. Each refueled once during its on-station time. The ComUSNavCent staff believed that the Air Force was too predictable, that Iraq could predict the refueling times and mount a surprise attack. The United States had fed Iraq AWACS data during the Iran-Iraq War, and the ComUSNavCent staff believed this familiarity would help Iraq understand and exploit this AWACS behavior. The staff asked its Center for Naval Analyses operations analyst (the author) to determine whether the AWACS tanking periods were predictable and, if so, whether Iraq could exploit that fact. Later, the staff amended the tasking to include determining whether Iraq actually exploited the predictability in timing its flights over the Persian Gulf.

The operations analyst looked at the scheduled refueling times for the eastern AWACS (the one that would cover the Persian Gulf) from 15 October to 7 November. Although the ATO schedule tried to introduce some variation into the AWACS schedule by directing the aircraft to randomize their refueling times within a block of time, the time windows allowed for refueling were short, and the start times of the windows were not really random. For the night AWACS one could pick a one-hour block within which there was better than a three-out-of-four chance that the AWACS would be refueling at some point; for the day AWACS, one could pick a one-hour block that would give a two-out-of-three chance. The analyst concluded that the pattern of AWACS refueling was sufficiently predictable that Iraq could exploit it to get an edge, especially at night, though it would not guarantee not being detected. As a result, Vice Admiral Mauz again asked Lt. General Horner to reduce the predictability of the AWACS, with the result that subsequent AWACS refueling times were made more random.

The operations analyst, after looking at the predictability of AWACS refueling times, addressed the question of whether Iraq was actually exploiting that predictability. To help him do this, ComUSNavCent intelligence personnel provided data on Iraqi flights over the Persian Gulf during the period in question. The analyst plotted on the same graph the times when the aircraft first went over water and the AWACS refueling times. Most Iraqi overwater flights occurred during the day and clearly did not exploit the refueling times for the AWACS aircraft. However, the only two Iraqi flights that went over water during the night occurred at the predictable AWACS refueling time. Although this suggested the possibility that Iraq had exploited the more regular pattern at night, two events hardly constituted evidence. The analyst's report concluded that whether Iraq was exploiting the regularity was less important than whether they could do so.

After a week during which the coalition detected no Iraqi aircraft over the Persian Gulf, and only one over-water flight during the week before that, Iraqi aircraft made at least two flights on 31 October. The next day, Mauz wanted to know whether the AWACS had held contact on the Iraqi aircraft and had transmitted the information to NavCent ships. The commanding officer of the cruiser *England* (Mauz's old ship) had told Mauz that the AWACS aircraft did not report tracks over the Persian Gulf because according to the technical operating directive it was not in their Track Production Area (which excluded most overwater zones). The ComUSNavCent Operations Officer, Capt. Bunky Johnson, thought they had changed that. Mauz was uncomfortable relying on secondhand information and wanted to know the real story.

Up to the end of October, the two air-defense cruisers in the Persian Gulf were the *Antietam* (detached from the *Independence* battle group) and the *England*. The commanding officer of the *Antietam* was the antiair warfare commander in the Gulf. When the *Midway* battle group arrived to relieve the *Independence* battle group, the cruiser *Bunker Hill* detached from the battle group. She and another cruiser, the USS *Worden* (CG 18), relieved the two cruisers in the Persian Gulf. Mauz designated the *Bunker Hill*'s commanding officer, Captain Tom Marfiak, as the antiair warfare commander in the Persian Gulf. While the *Antietam* and *Bunker Hill* conducted their turnover from 30 October to 1 November, the *England* served as the antiair warfare commander in the Gulf.

The commanding officer of the *England* followed up his conversation with Mauz with a message on 5 November that raised some alarming issues. He claimed that although the data link with the AWACS appeared to be functioning well, it was not. After 7 October, AWACS had ceased reporting tracks over the Gulf on a regular basis. Some AWACS flights did report the tracks, but the practice was not consistent. Thus, according to the *England*'s message, NavCent's air-defense ships in the Persian Gulf thought they were getting something they often did not get. Mauz thought this was a useful message, though it contained a few discrepancies due to a limited viewpoint. About this time, Mauz directed Capt. Bunky Johnson to investigate bringing E-2Cs into Bahrain to surveil the northern Persian Gulf. This was done by using an E-2 detachment from the USS *Theodore Roosevelt* (CVN 71).

IRAQI TRIANGLE

Possibly (as noted) in reaction to the U.S. Desert Triangle operations, on the first five days of November, two to five Iraqi flights over the Persian Gulf were detected each day, which caused increasing concern. Exercise Imminent Thunder, a mid-November amphibious exercise in the Persian Gulf ordered by General Schwarzkopf, made the situation even more critical, because initial plans had ships operating relatively close to the Kuwaiti border. All the air-defense players in the Persian Gulf were concerned about the aggressive behavior of the Iraqis and the lack of warning time for ships in the northern Persian Gulf.

Rear Adm. Bill Fogarty, ComMidEastFor, tasked with oversight of air defense in the Persian Gulf at this time, formalized his concern in a message to Vice Admiral Mauz. Fogarty said fourteen sorties had been detected in the first five days of November. (Actually, reviewing data from various sources, ComUSNav-Cent Intelligence eventually counted twenty sorties.) Fogarty enumerated the various sources of early warning for low-flying aircraft and gave the typical time delays inherent in each type of report. He estimated that air-defense ships in the central Gulf would have only three to seven minutes' warning before an Iraqi aircraft could reach launch range for Exocet antiship missiles. He noted that such positioning of his ships was necessary to provide air defense for the resupply and medical support ships transiting to al-Jubail and Dammam and to protect friendly and U.S. ships in the central Persian Gulf. The upcoming amphibious exercise made the problems even more urgent.

Fogarty wanted two things. First, he wanted an AWACS aircraft dedicated to NavCent support; if that was not possible, he recommended that the eastern AWACS orbit be moved farther east to provide continuous detection of low-flyers over the entire northern Persian Gulf. Second, Fogarty wanted the ROE changed to establish a "line of death" at latitude 28°30' north (roughly the latitude of the border between Kuwait and Saudi Arabia); if an Iraqi aircraft went south of that line and headed for a U.S. or friendly ship, it could be considered hostile and engaged. Fogarty got neither of his requests. About this time, in fact, Mauz decided that Fogarty's air picture on the *LaSalle* was not as good as that on the *Blue Ridge*, in part due to equipment differences, in part due to staff expertise. Therefore, Mauz shifted oversight responsibility for air defense in the Persian Gulf to his own staff on the *Blue Ridge*.

On Tuesday, 6 November, all hell broke loose. At least twenty-five Iraqi aircraft flew over the Persian Gulf. It started with one aircraft about 0530C and another about three hours later. Then at least six Iraqi aircraft came out.

That morning, "Knite 36-2," a USMC F/A-18, was flying combat air patrol (CAP) in the Whiskey-1 station in the northern Persian Gulf. At 0858C, the controlling ship, the *Worden*, gave him a vector to intercept three groups of suspected Iraqi aircraft heading south at high speed. The *Worden* initially told Knite 36-2 to stay south of 28°30' north latitude, but it waived that restriction when the lead Iraqi aircraft came within fifty-five nautical miles. Knite 36-2 obtained good radar contact on two Iraqi aircraft at forty-six miles and detected what he evaluated as jamming. The "bogies" turned west at about sixteen nautical miles and flew over Kuwait The closest point of approach to Knite 36-2 was about ten miles. This had come extremely close to a shooting incident.

A few minutes later, another six Iraqi aircraft flew over the Persian Gulf, then four more about 1015C, and another six at 1500C. Many flew provocative profiles. Several times flights of Iraqi aircraft flew down the Gulf in a stream toward the American ships until they were uncomfortably close to Exocet missile launch range, then turned west at seemingly the last minute and flew over Kuwait.

The displays in the ComUSNavCent command center on the *Blue Ridge* showed a stream of red (hostile) aircraft symbols heading for the blue (friendly) ships in the northern Persian Gulf, then turning away. It seemed clear that Iraq was trying to send a message: we have the capability to attack you and the will to stand up to you. In retrospect, perhaps it was all a bluff; if so, it was an excellent one. Although the ComUSNavCent staff had long believed the situation would eventually erupt in hostilities, it knew that many previous crises had been defused short of fighting. Watching the events that day, the author was struck by the overwhelming feeling that this time was different from all the other crises; this time, war was inevitable—Iraq would not back down.

Major General Royal Moore, USMC, the commanding general of 3rd Marine Air Wing, later complained that self-defense considerations should have dictated that the controlling ship (the *Worden*) give Knite 36-2 clearance to fire when the bogie reached a certain distance. Moore thought the *Worden* had ordered Knite 36-2 not to fire; the *Worden* claimed the pilot never asked for permission to fire. (The reader should realize that the ROE always allowed the pilot to fire if an aircraft exhibited hostile intent.)

Moore felt that keeping the CAP station south of 28°30' north latitude severely limited the aircraft's ability to detect low-level, high-speed threat aircraft. (CAP aircraft had permission to intercept bogies north of 28°30' if the situation dictated.) He believed his aircraft needed ROE to meet the threat without giving away the critical advantage, especially in view of the provocative flights of the previous few days. Moore was emphatic: "I would rather explain why one of my pilots shot down an Iraqi aircraft than why a Marine was lost for failing to fire first."[9]

On 7 November, another thirteen Iraqi aircraft were detected over the Persian Gulf. Six came down to north latitude 28°42' (only twelve nautical miles north of the limit on the CAP station) before turning away. The ComUSNavCent staff believed that Iraq had figured out how far north the American CAP aircraft could go. After a lull around the Moslem Sabbath (which is on Friday) Iraqi air activity resumed, with one or two overwater flights a day from 10 to 12 November, then six flights a day on four occasions from the 14 to 22 November. These events were ominous enough for routine, day-to-day operations. But there was a further complication—General Schwarzkopf had ordered an amphibious exercise for mid-

November, with a landing near al-Mishab in northern Saudi Arabia, only about twenty nautical miles south of the Kuwaiti border. We discuss this exercise—Imminent Thunder—in chapter 13.

NOTES

Sources for strike planning included messages and interviews with Mauz, Wright, Powell, and Arthur. Other views of Tomahawk came from articles by Reid, Arnett, and Getler. Details of the calculations of ordnance requirements came from an internal memorandum the author wrote in September 1990. For the strike rehearsals, the primary sources were the planning and after-action messages. Additional sources included the CNA reconstruction reports and interviews with Mauz and Johnson. Information on El Dorado Canyon came from interviews with Mauz and an article by Tanik. Sources for the discussion of air defense included messages, interviews with Mauz, and internal memoranda written by the author in November and December 1990.

1. For the period from August 1990 through January 1991, Mandeles et al. list forty-eight officers as Black Hole strategic air planners. McSwain and Smith were the only two Navy officers.

2. Fred Reed, "Worth Watching if the Shooting Starts," *Air Force Times,* 5 November 1990.

3. Eric H. Arnett, "Surgery with a Tomahawk," *Bulletin of the Atomic Scientists,* November 1990.

4. Michael Getler, "Are U.S. Forces Really Ready for War?" *Washington Post,* 14 October 1990.

5. Wright was not present when Glosson briefed Powell.

6. At the time of Desert Shield and Storm, the two cruise missile support activities planned the Tomahawk missions. The two cruise missile support activities were in Hawaii under USCinCPac and in Norfolk under USCinCLant.

7. The Mk-82 is a five-hundred-pound bomb; the Mk-83, a thousand-pound bomb; and the Mk-84, a two-thousand-pound bomb.

8. The USMC has some propeller-driven KC-130s, primarily for use with its tactical aircraft.

9. CG 3rd MAW 071943Z NOV 90, Personal for Lt.Gen. Boomer info RAdm. Fogarty from Maj.Gen. Moore, CAP Aircraft, as quoted in ComUSMarCent 080620Z NOV 90, Personal for VAdm. Mauz from LtGen. Boomer, CAP Aircraft.

Chapter 10

Amphibious Exercises

In mid-September an eighteen-ship Amphibious Task Force sailed in the North Arabian Sea under the command of Rear Adm. Bat LaPlante, with Maj. Gen. Harry Jenkins commanding the landing force of ten thousand Marines. The task force soon began a two-pronged effort to prepare for combat action. It conducted a series of amphibious exercises—five by the end of January 1991, four "Sea Soldier" exercises plus Imminent Thunder. The second prong was planning for actual operations. Initially, the Amphibious Task Force made generic plans for landings if Iraq invaded Saudi Arabia. In the absence of a specific landing plan, the first Sea Soldier exercise was general training rather than a rehearsal of a specific operation. Then the Amphibious Task Force started planning for an assault at Ras al-Qulaya in southern Kuwait. Sea Soldier II was a rehearsal for that specific landing.

SEA SOLDIER I (CAMEL SAND)

Exercise Camel Sand, later renamed Sea Soldier I, took place off Oman from 29 September to 5 October 1990. The objectives were to familiarize troops with desert conditions, allow reconfiguration of loads among the amphibious ships, and practice generic landing plans. The general concept was an assault to defend Saudi Arabia by landing behind advancing Iraqi forces to cut their lines of communications. Because the Amphibious Task Force did not have a specific landing plan, the planning and training could not address peculiarities of a particular landing site or details of a landing plan. Therefore, the task force practiced several alternative landing sequences.

The initial schedule for Sea Soldier I contained a series of events of gradually increasing complexity, culminating in a full-scale surface and air assault on 5 October. Earlier exercise events would move up to six thousand Marines ashore for weapon firing practice, familiarize them with the desert environment, and exercise small-unit tactics.

Because any shells that did not explode would present a long-term hazard to the local populace, Oman would not allow the Marines to fire artillery or mortars or to drop bombs. Thus, the Marines could not calibrate their artillery, nor could they practice close air support using live weapons.[1]

In the 29–30 September simulated raid that was part of the Sea Soldier I buildup, the surf and swell from the southwest monsoon precluded surface operations. Surf prohibited beaching operations by all assault craft except LCUs (landing craft, utility), which itself could not be launched safely from ships because of the sea swell. Nevertheless, Rear Admiral LaPlante described the air assault part of the raid as successful beyond expectations. He declared it had been the first air assault in his memory using four helicopter carriers—and perhaps the first one ever. Each of the three waves had contained twenty-four to twenty-six helicopters. He concluded on an upbeat note: "Given the size of the [Amphibious Task Force], the lack of predeployment work-ups, the unfavorable sea conditions, and the general [amphibious warfare] experience level out here, I am tremendously encouraged by today's ops."[2]

The next day, surf conditions improved enough to allow launching fifty-five AAVs (assault amphibious vehicles). LaPlante assessed the boat operations as "not so good," due to the moderate gradient of the ocean's bottom, the surf and swell, and trafficability problems on the beach caused by soft, deep sand. The surf and a strong current prevented use of causeways. LaPlante declared that the extremely shallow gradient in the Persian Gulf would prohibit the use of causeways there also. He concluded in a message to Vice Adm. Hank Mauz that

this week's ops tend to confirm discussions with you and your staff—that hydrographic conditions here drive the problem, and beyond large or small raid type ops (limited duration) or insertion using prepared facilities there are few options for traditional employment of amphibious forces. We need to expand our thinking to less conventional operations such as port/airport seizure, heavy raids, and so forth.[3]

Although the amphibious force considered Sea Soldier I as a generic rehearsal, the ComUSNavCent staff regarded it instead as amphibious *training*. The difference: until you have an objective and a plan, you cannot have a rehearsal. Once you have a plan you can load the ships accordingly, execute the plan, and see how it goes. Nevertheless, the Amphibious Task Force received valuable training on conducting amphibious operations in the region.

AMPHIBIOUS PLANS

As related in chapter 6, by the time the Amphibious Task Force arrived in the North Arabian Sea in mid-September it had devised generic plans for amphibious assaults, raids, and administrative offloads at a variety of locations along the

Kuwaiti and Saudi Arabian coastlines. These general plans did not have all the details worked out. One could not complete detailed plans without knowing specific locations, which depended on how far Iraq's invasion of Saudi Arabia proceeded.

Overview

By the end of September the amphibious force had devised ten general employment options for the 4th Marine Expeditionary Brigade (4th MEB) and 13th Marine Expeditionary Unit (13th MEU) (Special Operations Capable), operating either separately or together. As of 30 September Major General Jenkins considered the landing plans for three of the options essentially complete, with plans for other options under development. Jenkins stated a goal of conducting exercises involving all ten options.

During September and early October it gradually became clear that Iraq would not invade Saudi Arabia. The emphasis of the amphibious plans changed from defensive (defend Saudi Arabia by landing behind the Iraqis if they invaded) to offensive (eject the Iraqis from Kuwait by landing in Kuwait), which restricted possible landing options. Previously, the amphibious force had not had the luxury of picking a specific spot for a landing, because it would have depended on how rapidly the Iraqis advanced into Saudi Arabia. Now, the amphibious force could develop plans for an amphibious landing at a specific location in Kuwait. This was an advantage; unfortunately, a specific location also brought disadvantages.

The initial lack of detailed charts of potential landing areas presented one problem. In the end, the British gave the NavCent forces a set of 1985 charts of the Kuwaiti coastline supplied by a British company.

The buildup of Iraqi defenses in Kuwait presented a greater problem for an offensive operation. In early October the Defense Intelligence Agency (DIA) concluded that Iraqi forces in Kuwait were concerned about an amphibious assault. The DIA summarized Iraqi preparations:

- Four infantry divisions in defensive positions along the coast
- Beach minefields
- Barbed-wire barriers
- Field artillery sited to support coastal defense
- Forward observation sites on the offshore islands of Maradim and Qaruh
- Preparations for four coastal Silkworm antiship missile sites
- Flights over the extreme northern Persian Gulf that seemed to practice and threaten antishipping attacks
- Regular naval patrols off the Kuwaiti coast
- Pipes leading into coastal waters to pump petroleum into the water so it could be ignited, forming a barrier against an assault force
- Five loaded tankers anchored off Kuwait that could dump petroleum to be ignited, or simply to create a massive oil spill off potential landing beaches.

In addition, evidence suggested Iraq might have begun to lay mines in the water off Kuwait. For example, Iraqi patrol boats returning to Ras al-Qulaya seemed to follow particular, set routes when returning to port. Restrictions by Gen. Norman Schwarzkopf on where NavCent forces could go to observe such activity greatly hindered collection of this intelligence.

Ras al-Qulaya

ComUSMarCent claimed that seizing a port in Kuwait was an absolute necessity for its campaign plan. In early October, Vice Admiral Mauz, ComUSNavCent, tasked the Amphibious Task Force to plan a landing in southern Kuwait in the fifteen-nautical-mile stretch between Mina Saud and Mina Abd Allah (see Figure 10–1), which was north of the previously defined amphibious operation area I (see chapter 6). The Amphibious Task Force judged this area to have hydrography more favorable to amphibious operations than that of any of the previously considered areas. Regrettably, this area contained the Ras al-Qulaya naval base, one of the most heavily defended areas on the entire Kuwaiti coastline. This base lay about thirty miles south of Kuwait City. The Iraqis had already constructed trenches, fences, concrete walls, numerous bunkers, over 250 fighting positions, and revetments for armored vehicles, artillery, and supplies.

Deep-water mines posed a serious problem. Intelligence found indications that Iraq might have deployed mines in Kuwait harbor and off Ras al-Qulaya. Rear Admiral LaPlante assumed that naval mining had already occurred and that although the Iraqis had not yet mined the channel, they would do so it if losing the base seemed imminent. He noted that Iraq possessed a variety of foreign-made and locally produced moored and bottom mines, both influence and contact. Based on the ineffective employment of mines in the Iran-Iraq War, however, Iraqi expertise in mine warfare was considered rudimentary.

Despite the challenges, Rear Admiral LaPlante told Vice Admiral Mauz that his planners were off and running, happy to be working on a specific plan. Once they built a plan to seize Ras al-Qulaya, they intended to tailor a scenario to rehearse it during the next training period (Sea Soldier II), at Ras Madraka, Oman.

About two weeks after the tasking, Mauz's staff summarized for him the Amphibious Task Force's initial plans. The Marines would seize the port and within two or three days link up with MarCent's forces. The requirement to link up with the assault force would somewhat restrict MarCent's options. Intelligence estimated Iraq had 17,500 troops within ten miles and 41,000 within twenty miles (though some were in the front lines facing Saudi Arabia and would not be available to contest a landing). The Iraqis also had 500 tanks, 240 artillery pieces, and 250 armored vehicles within twenty miles. The plan called for about nine thousand Marines to land with only seventeen tanks. To get an acceptable force ratio, the ComUSNavCent staff thought, they would need deception to make the Iraqis move away.

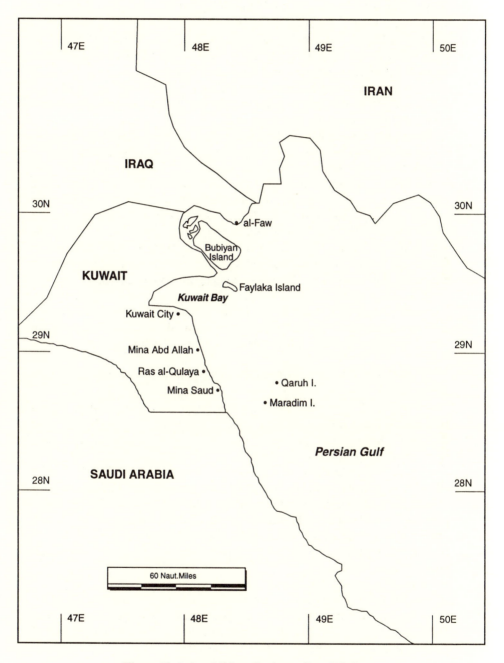

Figure 10–1. Amphibious Options—Ras al-Qulaya

Although the deep-water mines posed a serious problem, shallow-water mines were considered a "show stopper." The staff asked their resident SEAL, Commander Ed Bowen, USN, about the capabilities of SEALs to search for shallow-water mines buried on the bottom. Bowen estimated the area that one SEAL team could search in one night. He added that looking for buried mines was just about the most dangerous thing one could ask a person to do: the procedure involved poking one's arm around in the mud and feeling for them. The divers would quit as soon as they found a single mine, because the chances of finding two mines without blowing oneself up were quite small.

Though Ras al-Qulaya seemed to be the best of a poor set of options, Mauz was not happy. If the Marines seized it, the port could support a post-assault logistics offload, though this operation would be marginal for the larger ships. Unfortunately, Ras al-Qulaya lay only twenty miles north of the border and about twelve miles behind the Iraqi defensive line. An alternative would be to land MarCent supplies at al-Mishab in northern Saudi Arabia, about twenty-five miles below the Kuwaiti border, then truck them north. Seizing Ras al-Qulaya would reduce the land supply line by about forty-five miles, which might not be worth the effort. To shorten the supply line substantially one needed to seize a port well behind the Iraqi lines. Mauz wanted to know the rate at which supplies could be moved through the port of Ras al-Qulaya; he sarcastically guessed that the port could support fewer people than would be put ashore to seize it. Mauz said he wanted a briefing that included why the target was important, the threat, prerequisites (air sorties, naval gunfire, time, mine countermeasures), a landing plan, and assumptions.

On 26 October, Mauz's staff briefed him again on the amphibious force's revised plan for Ras al-Qulaya. The plan now had LCACs (landing craft, air cushion—a hovercraft) going into the beach first. The mine countermeasure experts estimated that they would need three days for exploratory sweeps. If they found nothing, the landing could proceed; if they found mines, they would need thirty days to clear them. This was a problem.

As MarCent's attack was to support Gen. Norman Schwarzkopf's primary offensive thrust in the west, MarCent could not drive the overall timing. Similarly, because the amphibious landing in turn was a supporting attack for MarCent's advance, it could not drive MarCent's timing. Thus, the timing of the primary ArCent attack would set the timing of the amphibious landing. If an amphibious landing was important, it would have to proceed when the progress of the higher-priority attacks dictated.

With the guidance then in effect, however, if mines were found the landing would have to be delayed until a path through them was cleared; one would not know whether a landing was possible until the night before the scheduled landing. Therefore, Lt. Gen. Walt Boomer, ComUSMarCent, could not plan his overall ground campaign to depend critically on the landing.

On the one hand, if Boomer declared an amphibious landing vital to his plans, then Mauz would be willing to accept more risk. If the landing were not vital to the ground campaign, Mauz was not willing to run those risks.

Mauz still preferred a raid (that is, go in and then get out) and seemed reluctant to endorse the assault. Although he would have liked to conduct an amphibious landing, he thought geography and other factors did not meet the needs of a landing. Also, in response to some wild claims being made, he said he was not convinced the Amphibious Task Force was really tying up several Iraqi divisions by threatening an amphibious landing. Mauz's reluctance to endorse an assault (seen by many Marines as essential for the survival of the Marine Corps in the upcoming budget wars) undoubtedly adversely affected his relations with some Marines.

About late October or early November, Marines from the Marine Corps Combat Development Command in Quantico, Virginia, briefed Mauz to propose an assault at al-Faw, the Iraqi peninsula far up in the northern Persian Gulf, next to Iranian territory. This option, too, had disadvantages. Mauz thought the Marines had no plan for what they could accomplish if they did manage to land there. LaPlante thought an opposed landing at al-Faw would be very difficult, because it put the amphibious ships in an untenable position with respect to shallow water and narrow channels. The proximity of Iranian territory posed another problem.

SIZE OF THE AMPHIBIOUS TASK FORCE

During the early days of Desert Shield, when the Iraqis might have contemplated invading Saudi Arabia, the counter-threat of an amphibious landing along their exposed flank on the Persian Gulf should have been a significant deterrent. As the U.S. ground and air forces arrived in-theater, however, the situation changed significantly. The invasion threat subsided. The Iraqis started building defenses in Kuwait. If Iraq did not invade Saudi Arabia, the only water flank Iraq would have to worry about was a relatively short stretch of the Kuwaiti coast. Iraq could concentrate its defenses at the few sites suitable for a potential amphibious assault.

Usually, military commanders continually demand more forces. Vice Admiral Mauz, in early October, looking at the fading threat of an Iraqi invasion of Saudi Arabia and at the employment options for amphibious forces in Kuwait, concluded that it made no sense to keep all the amphibious force he had. Desert Shield seemed to be in a long-term sanctions-enforcement mode. Under those conditions, he needed only a few amphibious ships. In a message to General Schwarzkopf, Vice Admiral Mauz argued, with remarkable prescience:

Paucity of suitable landing sites and extremely limited operating space due to hydrographic conditions lead to conclusion that we should not depend on conventional surface assault as primary means of executing CinCCent amphibious options. Hydrographic surveys show narrow assault beaches which preclude rapid movement of combat power ashore by conventional surface assault craft over several beaches. Additionally, mine clearance operations (or at least the process of confirming presence/absence of mines) could significantly delay or eliminate surface assault option. If opposed by [air] and [surface] threat, defense of a large amphibious task force in northern Persian Gulf presents significant problems, so expect ATF [Amphibious Task Force] would not move into northern Gulf until some time after hostilities. Ability to provide NGFS [naval gunfire support] is also limited by hydrography, with only 16 inch guns able to reach all potential targets prior to artillery movement ashore.[4]

Mauz wanted to retain the flexibility that came from the capability for a large assault, but he believed such an operation was a long shot. He thought that the main use for the amphibious force would be raids, noncombatant evacuation operations, and reinforcement. Therefore, he recommended the eighteen-ship Amphibious Task Force be eventually reduced to nine ships. Because USCinCCent was still in the mode of letting sanctions work and defending Saudi Arabia, Mauz wanted to allow the five Pacific Fleet amphibious ships (Amphibious Ready Group Alfa) to leave on schedule in early November, so they could return to their homeports within six months of deploying. He also wanted to allow the thirteen Atlantic Fleet amphibious ships to leave on schedule in mid-January, when nine amphibious ships from the Pacific Fleet would relieve them. Mauz believed the nine relieving Pacific Fleet amphibious ships could adequately maintain the threat of an amphibious landing. He pointed out that this plan allowed the amphibious forces to maintain their six-month deployment cycles and reduced naval personnel in the theater by nearly four thousand. (See chapter 7 for a discussion of the dispute over personnel numbers.) Mauz told Schwarzkopf that his proposal would provide about seven thousand Marines afloat in a useful configuration—and "that ain't bad."[5]

Major General Burton "Burt" Moore, USAF, Schwarzkopf's Operations Officer, replied that the USCinCCent staff was developing a coordinated position and would make a recommendation to Schwarzkopf on the level of amphibious forces needed. He acknowledged Mauz's concerns but argued:

We believe that a viable amphibious force does impact Iraqi planning (4–5 divisions guarding the coast) and could influence defensive and/or offensive operations. The issue is how big a force do we need, and how should it be configured to meet CinC requirements for both the short and long term.[6]

Moore recommended a thirteen-ship Amphibious Task Force with about seven thousand Marines embarked (the same number of Marines afloat as in Mauz's plan but four more ships). He argued that these numbers fit the landing area limitations. He wanted the amphibious force to be credible enough to fix a large number of Iraqi forces. The thirteen ships would provide a viable force for deception, deterrence, feints, or assaults.[7] Moore also listed a specific mix of ship types and the tactical configuration of the embarked troops but felt that the proper ship mix was best left to ComUSNavCent.

Moore acknowledged Mauz's concerns but said that Lt. General Boomer viewed MEB-size amphibious landings as an achievable objective that would act as a combat multiplier for ground and air efforts ashore. Marine air power could make up for the limitations on naval gunfire support. Moore planned to brief Schwarzkopf as soon as he received Mauz's inputs.

The ComUSNavCent staff prepared a briefing that described how they intended to use a nine-ship amphibious force at Ras al-Qulaya. They believed the nine-ship plan had the same combat power as the previous eighteen-ship plan, the difference being that the Marines would have fewer days of supplies. Mauz went to Riyadh and presented the briefing to Schwarzkopf on 29 October. In his thirty-minute briefing Mauz used the Ras al-Qulaya assault as an illustration of what could be done. He told Schwarzkopf about needing three days of exploratory mine countermeasures (assuming no mines were found). Mines made the assault "chancy." He also noted that the landing might end up being in MarCent's rear, given the short distance from the border and the time needed to look for mines. Mauz argued that the Ras al-Qulaya assault was the most demanding of the reasonably feasible amphibious options but it could be executed by a properly configured nine-ship amphibious force.

The odds were against Mauz: the USCinCCent staff position proposed maintaining thirteen amphibious ships; Boomer supported thirteen ships; rumors abounded that the Commandant of the Marine Corps, General Alfred "Al" Gray, USMC, had also lobbied for more amphibious ships. (He had so argued to the other Joint Chiefs. Gray's argument for additional amphibious ships was grounded in the view that amphibious forces constituted the decisive, strategic reserve.) Schwarzkopf decided thirteen ships were better than nine ships. He conceded that Mauz could reduce the amphibious force from eighteen to thirteen ships by allowing the five Pacific Fleet amphibious ships, Amphibious Ready Group Alfa, to leave the theater early in November as scheduled.

SEA SOLDIER II

As the list of potential landing sites narrowed, the amphibious exercises evolved from generic training landings to rehearsals against a specific landing site. The Amphibious Task Force conducted Sea Soldier II from 30 October through 8 November off the coast of Oman west of Ras Madraka, to rehearse an amphibious assault at Ras al-Qulaya. The Amphibious Task Force staff superimposed the reefs, shoals, oil fields, structures, roads, and airfields in the Ras al-Qulaya area on their charts and maps of the exercise area to replicate the constraints on planning and force movements. They also overlaid on them the real-world Iraqi order of battle.

After SEALs conducted reconnaissance, the main assault occurred, consisting of an over-the-horizon launch of eight LCACs from twenty-five nautical miles off the beach and eight LCUs launched from twelve miles. Despite offshore fog, this wave landed on the center of the beach, only thirty seconds late. The sight of the landing craft emerging together from a dense fog at high speed in echelon visibly impressed the Omani observers. In addition, thirty AAVs landed on two beaches. Subsequent waves consisted of fourteen additional AAVs, twenty-one LCAC loads, and thirty-two LCU loads. In total, four thousand Marines (the upper limit set by the Omanis) and 350 pieces of equipment were put ashore.[8]

IWO JIMA

The helicopter-carrier *Iwo Jima*, the first ship designed from the keel up to operate helicopters, was the Navy's oldest amphibious ship, nearly thirty years old at the time. All ships need repairs. Old ships like the *Iwo Jima* often require a lot of them, and the *Iwo Jima* class had a reputation for maintenance difficulties. She had developed a number of minor leaks in steam valves, which increased the heat stress for watchstanders in the engineering spaces. Then a forced-draft blower on the good boiler (the one without steam leaks) had a casualty. Rear Admiral LaPlante, Commander of the Amphibious Task Force, decided to send the *Iwo Jima* to Bahrain; repairing the ship while at anchor was impractical due to the monsoon-generated swells in the Gulf of Oman, and sufficient shore power was not available in Dubai. The *Iwo Jima* spent most of October tied up outboard of the *Blue Ridge* at the Mina Sulman pier in Bahrain, while the Arabian Ship Repair Yard worked on her. A week before the *Iwo Jima* left, the commanding officer, Captain Mike O'Hearn, USN, described to the author how the crew had been going through a continual cycle of fixing one thing only to have another thing break, fixing that, and having something else break.

Assessing the prognosis for the ship, LaPlante told Vice Admiral Mauz that the *Iwo Jima* had been the best of its class. Just six months previously, the *Iwo Jima* had undergone an Operational Propulsion Plant Examination (a major event in the life of a ship, of its commanding officer, and of its engineering officer). LaPlante described the result as having been the best ever for its class. He assessed the attitudes on the ship as good, and its personnel competent and committed. He predicted the *Iwo Jima* would continue to display symptoms typical of elderly single-plant ships in extended operations, but that the ship's crew could and would deal with them. Mauz visited the *Iwo Jima* and told LaPlante he found the ship to be positive in attitude and anxious to get on with the work.

On 30 October, after the repairs were completed, the *Iwo Jima* finally got under way. She barely got a mile into the channel before she suffered a major steam leak in her engine room. The superheated steam killed six crew members immediately. Four additional men in critical condition from burns and steam inhalation were taken to the hospital ship *Comfort*, anchored outside the harbor. Unfortunately, the four men died soon thereafter. The *Iwo Jima*, which had anchored in the channel, was towed back to the Mina Sulman pier.

Mauz appointed LaPlante (the *Iwo Jima* was part of his Amphibious Task Force) to conduct a preliminary inquiry regarding the circumstances surrounding the accident. LaPlante, then overseeing the start of the Sea Soldier II amphibious exercise from his flagship *Nassau* in the Gulf of Oman, immediately flew to the *Blue Ridge*. Ironically, less than one hour before the *Iwo Jima* had gotten under way LaPlante had sent a message to all his commanding officers urging them to pay great attention to safety: "Our most sacred responsibility is the lives and safety of the people entrusted to our care."[9] The next morning, LaPlante sat across from the author at breakfast in the Flag Mess on the *Blue Ridge*. He commented that when he was younger he had found it hard enough to deal with men dying who were about his age, but now, having young men die who were about his son's age was almost more than he could bear.

The subsequent court of inquiry concluded that a non-English-speaking repair person had used brass nuts (with a black coating to make them indistinguishable from the required steel nuts) to install a valve in the high-pressure steam system involved. When subjected to high temperatures, brass softens and loses its strength. Under the enormous heat and pressure of steam at 640 pounds per square inch, the valve had failed, releasing 865-degree steam into the compartment.

The *Iwo Jima* was repaired in Bahrain. She then rejoined the Amphibious Task Force for the rest of Desert Shield and all of Desert Storm.

OTHER DEVELOPMENTS

As we related earlier in this chapter, General Schwarzkopf agreed to Vice Admiral Mauz's plan to send the five ships of Amphibious Ready Group Alfa home to the West Coast on schedule. In early November, they left the North Arabian Sea accordingly. During the night of 7–8 November, as they approached the line near the tip of India where they were to shift operational control from the Central Command to the Pacific Command, General Schwarzkopf suddenly ordered them to hold their position. The next morning, Mauz said, the "smart money" in Washington was predicting they would be sent back to CentCom. Supposedly, Headquarters, Marine Corps, had proposed to the Joint Staff that the ships be brought back, because doing so would (1) retain the Special Operations Capable 13th MEU in the theater, (2) increase flexibility, (3) prevent sending the wrong message to Iraq. The next chapter reveals the reason for the mysterious order and what happened to these five ships.

NOTES

The primary sources for the Sea Soldier exercises were messages, CNA reconstruction reports, and interviews with Mauz, LaPlante, and Wickersham, For amphibious planning, sources included messages, the author's notes of briefings of the plans, and interviews with Mauz, LaPlante, and Gray. Primary sources for the *Iwo Jima* incident were the record of proceedings of the court of inquiry, messages, an article by Steigman, and the author's contemporary conversations with O'Hearn and LaPlante.

1. Consequently, Vice Admiral Mauz had his Fleet Marine Officer, Col. Frank Wickersham, try to make arrangements with the UAE for a site more suitable for future exercises. These arrangements took many months, but the UAE sites were used after the first of the year.

2. CTG 150.6 011652Z OCT 90, Personal for VAdm. Mauz from LaPlante, Amphib Ops Sitrep.

3. CTG 150.6 021345Z OCT 90, Personal for VAdm. Mauz info MGen. Jenkins from LaPlante, Amphib Ops Update.

4. ComUSNavCent 081704Z OCT 90, Amphibious Force Levels ISO [in support of] Desert Shield.

5. ComUSNavCent 130827Z OCT 90, Personal for General Schwarzkopf info Lt. Gen. Boomer from Mauz, End-Strength Ceiling.

6. CentCom DFH 161800Z OCT 90, Personal for Admiral Mauz and LtGen. Boomer from Maj. Gen. Moore, Amphibious Force Levels.

7. The terms "feint" and "demonstration" led to frequent confusion, especially by the USCinCCent staff. (The term "feint" is not defined in the Department of Defense's *Dictionary of Military and Associated Terms*. See Chapter 6 for the definition of the term "demonstration.") Col. Frank Wickersham perceived that the USCinCCent staff thought a "feint" was part of a psychological operation for amphibious forces, something that should be called a demonstration. Wickersham thought some used "feint" to mean a landing movement that turned away short of the beach and did not occur in conjunction with an actual assault. Some also used "demonstration" to mean "puffing about and making amphibious noises." All in all, everyone concerned could have benefited from using the terms defined by doctrine.

8. Though the Amphibious Task Force contained more than ten thousand Marines, the four thousand put ashore in Sea Soldier II represented almost a full-scale landing, because the ten thousand Marines in the landing force included many personnel who were in support, not "trigger-pullers."

9. CTG 150.6 300423Z OCT 90, Personal for Commanders and Commanding Officers info MGen. Jenkins from LaPlante, Sea Soldier II (Overview No. 16).

Part III

Preparations for Offensive War, 9 November–16 January

Saddam Hussein seemed to think the coalition was bluffing and would not risk war to eject Iraqi forces from Kuwait. Therefore, he could outwait the coalition. On 8 November, President George Bush raised the stakes. He announced a near-doubling of U.S. forces in the CentCom theater to allow for an offensive option to drive Iraq out of Kuwait. The increased forces would include the Army's armored VII Corps, another Marine division ashore, and many additional Air Force squadrons. NavCent forces would expand to six aircraft carriers, two battleships, and thirty-one amphibious ships with twenty thousand Marines embarked.

The following chapter explains how the escalation changed the situation and how the naval forces updated their command and control. Chapter 12 addresses the continuing maritime interception operations and Iraq's last attempts to circumvent the sanctions and embarrass the coalition. Chapters 13 and 14 describe the ever-quickening pace of planning for both offense and defense. The last chapter of this volume relates the final preparations for war and ends with the Execute Order for Operation Desert Storm.

Chapter 11

The Price of Poker Goes Up

Up to late October, all indications received by Vice Adm. Hank Mauz, ComUS-NavCent, suggested that the United States intended to allow plenty of time for sanctions to work. That month, Gen. Colin Powell, Chairman of the Joint Chiefs, visited Vice Admiral Mauz and spent the night on the *Blue Ridge*. In a private conversation in Mauz's cabin, Mauz asked Powell when they would go to war. Powell replied, "Why would we do that?" Mauz got the general impression that sanctions would be allowed at least a year to work.[1]

Soon after, Gen. Norman Schwarzkopf asked Mauz what assets he needed for an offensive option;[2] Schwarzkopf told him that General Powell had said he could have every carrier in the Navy if necessary.[3] Because Schwarzkopf had not given him much time to reply, Mauz did not have time for his staff to study the issue, though he did consult with his Chief of Staff, Capt. Bernie Smith. Mauz recommended to Schwarzkopf that a total of six carriers be assigned to NavCent.[4]

One of the arguments for asking for fewer than six carriers was that the amount of CentAF tanking likely to be available would support only four. Four carriers—two in the Red Sea and two on the Persian Gulf side—would allow twenty-four-hour-a-day operations from both locations, though only for a limited time.

On the other hand, three carriers in the Red Sea and three in the Persian Gulf would allow a rotation, with two carriers conducting strike operations and one carrier off line. With six carriers, NavCent forces could conduct strikes around the clock from both sides of the theater and sustain those operations indefinitely. If instead of the war starting at a time of the coalition's choosing (as it did) Iraq preemptively attacked in response to the coalition's buildup, sea-based air power would have a greater role to play. Mauz had observed Air Force aircraft lined up at Saudi Arabian bases wingtip to wingtip, extremely vulnerable to preemptive attack. If Iraq preempted and knocked out a significant number of Air Force aircraft, the ability of NavCent forces to sustain twenty-four-hour-a-day strikes from both sides of the theater would be even more important.

THE ESCALATION

The final decision on the number of carriers would be made in Washington, where the Navy Staff and Adm. David Jeremiah, Vice Chairman of the Joint Chiefs, discussed how many carriers would be appropriate. The Navy Staff provided estimates of the number of aircraft carriers that could be made available within various time frames. Jeremiah said he initially wanted to send six additional carriers to bring the total to nine, to get as many carriers into the operation as he could. According to Jeremiah, Powell suggested that with all the additional Air Force aircraft going to the theater, however, three additional carriers be sent rather than six. Thus, the final decision by Secretary of Defense Dick Cheney called for three additional carriers.

On 10 November, Mauz sent a message to his commanders titled "Price of Poker Goes Up," in which he explained what the expansion would mean to the naval forces. The present three carrier battle groups (including the one in the Mediterranean) would be joined by three more, centered on the aircraft carriers USS *Theodore Roosevelt* (CVN 71) and *America*, from the Atlantic Fleet, and the USS *Ranger* (CV 61) from the Pacific Fleet, for a total of six carrier battle groups. Mauz's plan was to form two three-carrier battle forces, one in the Red Sea and one in the North Arabian Sea or Persian Gulf. Already Mauz was thinking of moving some or all three carriers on the eastern side of the theater into the Persian Gulf rather than having them operate from the North Arabian Sea.

To carry out his plan, Mauz would have to move one of the Atlantic Fleet carriers—either the *Roosevelt* or *America*—to the Persian Gulf side of the theater. Previously, all the Atlantic Fleet battle groups operated in the Red Sea and all Pacific Fleet battle groups in the North Arabian Sea or Persian Gulf. This simplified logistics support, by retaining the battle groups' normal supply chain from their home fleets. Bringing one of the Atlantic Fleet carriers to the other side of the theater would complicate logistics support, but Mauz thought operational necessity required three carriers on the Persian Gulf side of the theater.

The thirty-one amphibious ships would have about twenty thousand Marines embarked. The thirteen amphibious ships of Amphibious Group Three, with 5th MEB embarked, would join the thirteen amphibious ships of Amphibious Group Two, with 4th MEB embarked. In addition, the five ships of Amphibious Ready Group Alfa (Amphibious Squadron Five, with 13th MEU[SOC] embarked), which had left the theater in early November, would eventually rejoin NavCent's Amphibious Task Force.

When President Bush made his announcement about the increase in forces, Amphibious Ready Group Alfa, which had been sailing in circles in the Indian Ocean, had been released. They resumed their journey to Subic Bay in the Philippines. When they passed the point at which they would normally switch control from the Central Command to the Pacific Command they remained instead under the control of USCinCCent, pending further word from the Joint Staff. Later it was decided to have this amphibious group stay in Subic Bay for a while (rather than continue to its home port in the United States) and then return to the CentCom theater in time for the 15 January deadline.

The battleship *Wisconsin* would be joined by a second battleship, the USS *Missouri* (BB 63). Mauz intended to use them in the Persian Gulf for Tomahawk launches and naval gunfire support.

Mauz urged his commanders to look at themselves through the eyes of Iraq. He warned that Saddam Hussein knew when the coalition would be ready for offensive operations and might well launch a preemptive attack, if for no other reason than to get maximum impact from his forces before the coalition destroyed Iraq's forces. Mauz listed the primary Iraqi threats that NavCent had to prepare to counter:

- Mines
- F-1s in a stream raid down the Persian Gulf firing Exocet antiship missiles
- Oil from the tankers off Kuwait
- Terrorism against shore facilities used by NavCent forces.

On 29 November, the United Nations Security Council passed Resolution 678. Under it, unless Iraq complied with previous resolutions and evacuated Kuwait on or before 15 January 1991, member states were authorized to use all necessary means to restore international peace and security in the area.

INTELLIGENCE

On 14 December, two CIA personnel came to the *Blue Ridge* to brief the ComUSNavCent staff on an evaluation of Saddam Hussein and the Iraqi leadership. The briefing began with the assertion that Saddam Hussein had two goals: to live, and to preserve what he had built in Iraq. From certain of Saddam's public speeches (not the ones with the flowery Arabic rhetoric), the CIA claimed, one could see what he intended to do. They now "saw" the invasion of Kuwait in Saddam's speeches earlier in 1990—but, they admitted, only with hindsight. They had not at the time. The CIA predicted that:

- Saddam Hussein would not start the war but would try to avoid war; he thought the United States would back down.
- He would involve Israel.
- He would try to destroy the Saudi oil fields, probably using Scud missiles with high-explosive or chemical warheads.

The CIA warned that Saddam Hussein's recent firings of generals should not be interpreted as a sign of weakness. Saddam had replaced "comfortable, non-dangerous" peacetime generals with the most capable ones. Furthermore, he had a firm hold on the Iraqi people. Although perceived weakness might snowball, as in Eastern Europe, at the moment Saddam remained fairly popular. People regarded his power as a point of Arab pride. Anybody replacing him as the leader of Iraq would have similar policies, including the development of nuclear weapons. Possession of nuclear weapons would be another source of Arab pride.

The Iraqi people could take a great deal of pain. They saw their current situation as being not as bad as what they had endured for the eight years of the Iran-Iraq War. The CIA believed that Saddam viewed the current situation as similar to Vietnam—he had to persuade the American people to give up. The United States might win a battle, but in the long run Iraq would win, in the geopolitical sense, because it would continue the struggle for many years. (The author understood this to mean that contrary to the then-current conventional wisdom, Saddam's rule would not collapse if his army were defeated. The coalition's troops would go away eventually, and then Iraq would win.) On the other hand, Iraq might conduct a partial pull-out from Kuwait. The briefers concluded that any peace talks would be major victory for Iraq.

In response to questions, the CIA warned that the Iraqis might launch a preemptive attack, but only if they became convinced an attack on them was just a few hours away. Alternatively, false reports might precipitate an Iraqi attack, or the Iraqis might fake an American or Israeli attack (even to the point of bombing their own people) to justify a preemption. Most ComUSNavCent staff members came out of the briefing rather sobered. One intelligence officer glumly declared that he had gotten the impression that the United States was getting into another war it had no chance of winning—like Vietnam.

In planning for war, Vice Admiral Mauz had to consider the wild card—Iran. For a decade, the U.S. Navy and Iran had opposed each other, often violently. The Joint Intelligence Liaison Element with the ComUSNavCent staff judged that Iran would follow a policy of calculated ambiguity in order to extract concessions from both Iraq and the coalition. Although Iran distrusted American intentions, it also feared regional dominance by Iraq. Iranian policy was to tolerate the presence of American forces as long as they were aimed at Iraq. JILE's evaluation portrayed Iran as less of a threat than in earlier evaluations, but the intelligence team hedged, adding that although it was unlikely, changes in the course of the Gulf crisis could cause Iran to support Iraq. Even in these instances, they judged, Iran was not likely to engage in hostilities on Iraq's side.

COMMAND AND CONTROL

With a major increase in forces and a shift in emphasis to the offense, Vice Admiral Mauz had to make a number of decisions. He had already decided where in the theater to deploy the major units—the six aircraft carriers—though he had not decided whether to send the three carriers on the eastern side of the theater into the Persian Gulf at the start of the war. Other issues concerned organizing the command and control of the forces and deciding whom to put in command of each force. The remainder of this chapter discusses these issues. (Chapters 13 and 14 examine the more tactical issues concerning plans for each warfare area.)

When the reinforcing naval units arrived, each battle group would bring an admiral. Mauz would have nine admirals, plus two generals, afloat in his command. When his staff started to work on the command-and-control structure for the expanded force, they asked Mauz whether he wanted to create a job for every admiral. Mauz said, "No." He wanted the most effective organization, not jobs to make everyone happy.

Choice of Commanders

On at least three occasions, ComUSNavCent chose a commander based on his perception of all relevant factors rather than solely on seniority, as done by some services. Rear Adm. Dan March, commander of the *Midway* battle group, was selected as Commander, Persian Gulf Battle Force (CTF 154), even though junior to Rear Adm. Bill Fogarty, commander of the Middle East Force. The primary reason for choosing March as the battle force commander was that he and his staff had trained to command Seventh Fleet's battle force and had experience in that role.

At the end of October, when the cruisers *Bunker Hill* and *Worden* relieved the two previous cruisers in the Persian Gulf, Vice Admiral Mauz had to decide which commanding officer to designate as antiair warfare commander in the Persian Gulf. On the one hand, the *Worden* was senior. The *Bunker Hill*, an Aegis cruiser, had the more capable air-defense system, however, and could generate a more comprehensive picture with which to exercise command and control of air defense. Second, the *Bunker Hill* and its commanding officer were known quantities; they had operated in Seventh Fleet as the antiair warfare commander in a number of exercises. Third, the ComUSNavCent staff thought the *Worden*'s crew might be "rusty," because reports indicated she had not operated in a battle group electronic data link environment for the past three years. Vice Admiral Mauz selected the commanding officer of the *Bunker Hill*, Capt. Tom Marfiak, choosing perceived capability over seniority. This pattern would be repeated.

Vice Admiral Mauz also had to decide whether to select as commander of the combined, thirty-one-ship Amphibious Task Force Rear Adm. Bat LaPlante, Commander, Amphibious Group Two, or Rear Admiral Stephen "Steve" Clarey, USN, Commander, Amphibious Group Three. Although both were one-star admirals, Clarey was senior to LaPlante. Clearly, Clarey expected to be named Commander, Amphibious Task Force.

Again Mauz considered factors other than seniority. Important factors in the selection included on-scene experience, collocation with the senior Marine in the amphibious force, and communications capability. Though Clarey had been in-theater as commander of the Maritime Prepositioning Force in August and early September, that experience had not involved planning for an amphibious landing. LaPlante, on the other hand, had had continuous on-scene experience as Commander, Amphibious Task Force since September, conducting the Sea Soldier I and II exercises and planning the options for employing the force. Plans needed to be made before mid-January, when Clarey was slated to arrive. The ComUSNav-Cent staff considered familiarity with the theater and operating environment a major factor. Also, LaPlante had better communications on his flagship, the *Nassau,* than Clarey would have on his own flagship, the USS *Tarawa* (LHA 1), though both were of the same class of general-purpose amphibious assault ships. In addition, Rear Admiral LaPlante was collocated with the senior general, Maj. Gen. Harry Jenkins, who would be commander of the Landing Force. Shifting LaPlante and Clarey and their staffs between the *Nassau* and *Tarawa* was considered briefly but rejected as much too disruptive.

LaPlante gave Mauz a fair rundown of the arguments for both himself and Clarey, adding that Clarey probably would remain in the theater longer. LaPlante then recommended that he (LaPlante) be designated commander of the Amphibious Task Force for the first exercise period to provide an orderly transition of the Pacific amphibious force into the theater. ComUSNavCent would then have the option of designating either LaPlante or Clarey as permanent commander of the Amphibious Task Force.

Capt. Gordon Holder, the ComUSNavCent amphibious expert, initially recommended a Solomonic solution that split the assignment, naming the senior person, Clarey, as commander of the Task Group and the person with the in-theater experience, LaPlante, as Commander, Amphibious Task Force. The operations officer, Capt. Bunky Johnson, disagreed and recommended that the senior person hold both positions. The Chief of Staff, Capt. Bernie Smith, concurred. Vice Admiral Mauz rejected his staff's recommendation and selected Rear Admiral LaPlante as permanent commander of the Amphibious Task Force.[5]

Flagship Rotation

Back in mid-October, the decision had been made for the *Coronado,* then the Third Fleet flagship, to relieve the *Blue Ridge* as the ComUSNavCent flagship, with the turnover scheduled for 13–14 January. This change would avoid violating the Chief of Naval Operations' personnel tempo guidelines for the *Blue Ridge*'s crew. Normally, although when such a decision is pending, everyone gets a chance to present his viewpoint, once it is made everyone is expected to support the decision and not bring it up for reconsideration. But the conflict between this decision and the mid-January arrival of so many additional naval forces, compounded by USCinCCent's rotation policy, was too much. Vice Admiral Mauz now asked that this decision be revisited. He argued that new factors applied: ComUSNavCent's span of control and associated command, control, and communication requirements would greatly increase, and the *Coronado*'s communications capability was not as good as that on the *Blue Ridge*. Also, the *Coronado* could not accommodate the staff plus all the augmentees. Most inconveniently, the *Coronado* was scheduled to arrive when ComUSNavCent would least like to be involved in a flagship switch—two days before the 15 January deadline. Mauz argued that because many ships were being extended beyond six-month deployments and turnaround ratios were being reduced, it did not seem consistent to send away the Navy's most capable flagship when she could be needed most.

Adm. Hunt Hardisty, commander in chief of the Pacific Command, agreed to extend the *Blue Ridge* as the ComUSNavCent flagship, with a late-January assessment of the tactical and strategic situation to determine how long to keep the *Blue Ridge* deployed.

Turnover of ComUSNavCent and NavCent-Riyadh

Commands such as USCinCCent, ComUSCentAF, and ComUSMarCent had no-rotation policies for their commanders. Notwithstanding, the Navy not only rotated people, it replaced two key admirals. In early November, Rear Admiral Conrad "Connie" Lautenbacher, Jr., USN, relieved Rear Adm. Tim Wright as NavCent-Riyadh, head of the ComUSNavCent liaison group in Riyadh. Wright, along with part of his staff, had gone to Riyadh in August with the understanding that he would be replaced after ninety days to return to his battle group command and prepare the USS *Abraham Lincoln* (CVN 72) battle group for deployment. Wright's staff had grown from the initial six to fifty-five people, about half of whom were reservists.

Despite a reputation as a quick study, Lautenbacher faced a formidable challenge. Even a two-week phased turnover could not substitute for three months of "working" the problems and becoming familiar with the issues, procedures, and personalities involved. In addition, most of NavCent's disputes with the USCinCCent staff concerned aviation matters. Whereas Wright wore the wings of an aviator, Lautenbacher was a surface warfare officer. He had several aviators on his staff to support him, but it was not the same thing. In any case, this switch of admirals paled in importance compared with the Navy's other change of command during this period.

On 1 December 1990, six and one-half weeks before the 15 January UN deadline, Vice Admiral Stanley R. "Stan" Arthur, USN, on previous orders from the Chief of Naval Operations, relieved Vice Adm. Hank Mauz as commander of both U.S. Naval Forces Central Command and Seventh Fleet. One might question why the Navy chose to change its commander just six weeks before the deadline.

The Navy had selected Arthur as Mauz's relief in early summer 1990, with the change of command to occur in late summer. In August, with the appointment of Mauz as ComUSNavCent, the Navy had decided to hold off. The Chief of Naval Operations, Adm. Frank Kelso, thought it would be good to wait a month or two to see what happened and allow Mauz to establish a rapport with Schwarzkopf.

In time, Kelso decided to proceed with the change of command, because he considered both Mauz and Arthur capable men, and it appeared that the Gulf standoff could persist for a long time. Also, Admiral William D. "Bill" Smith, USN, whom Mauz was scheduled to relieve, was going to Brussels for a NATO job that could not be left vacant. The job Mauz would go to, Deputy Chief of

Naval Operations for Navy Program Planning (OP-08), was regarded as the most important three-star billet on the Navy staff. Kelso believed that notwithstanding the Persian Gulf crisis, this was an important job for the Navy in view of coming force reductions. Arthur believed that one factor in this decision was that Kelso was comfortable with Mauz. In particular, Kelso had been commander of Sixth Fleet when Mauz's *America* battle group conducted the strikes against Libya. Kelso reinstated the change of command. In early September, long before the 15 January deadline was set, Mauz chose 1 December for the turnover.

In mid-November, Kelso visited the theater. Mauz thought that Kelso did not really believe there would be a war in the near term, that sanctions would be allowed at least a year to work. Indeed, Kelso felt that way because no clear time for offensive action had been set: Congress was holding hearings on whether to give sanctions more time, and a former CJCS was testifying that sanctions should be given time to work. Mauz, however, told Kelso the coalition might be going over to the offensive much sooner than expected. Because he had done all the planning and was familiar with General Schwarzkopf, Mauz told Kelso, he would like to stay. Kelso thought it over but said he would let the change occur as scheduled. If there was no war for some time, changing commanders would not be a problem. If there was fighting, Kelso thought it would be better to change commanders now, rather than just before the conflict started.

The next day, Mauz informed Schwarzkopf about the turnover. Schwarzkopf seemed concerned but not overly unhappy. He asked whether Mauz wanted him to help (presumably by demanding that he stay). Because he did not want to cause the Navy trouble, Mauz asked Schwarzkopf to "let it roll." Later, as Mauz watched Desert Storm from the Pentagon, he found it quite painful to be left out of the action.

If Schwarzkopf had made a big issue of changing commanders, Kelso later said, he would not have changed them. Why did Schwarzkopf let it happen, when he had a general policy of not changing key people? Rear Adm. Grant Sharp, General Schwarzkopf's Plans Officer, knew of no objection by Schwarzkopf or anyone on the USCinCCent staff. Sharp thought this was probably due in part to generally good reports of Arthur and the fact that he should have been familiar with the area, because he had served as the first ComUSNavCent in 1983. Admiral Hardisty noted that Vice Admiral Arthur, as ComUSNavCent, had spent more time in the CentCom theater than any of his successors and had become familiar with the theater's problems. But who was Stan Arthur?

Vice Admiral Stan Arthur

Vice Adm. Stan Arthur was born in San Diego and entered the U.S. Navy through the Naval Reserve Officer Training Corps Program at Miami University (Ohio). He was commissioned an officer in June 1957 and designated a naval aviator in 1958. Later he earned a bachelor of science degree in aeronautical engineering and a master of science degree in administration. Arthur was widely

Vice Admiral Stan Arthur. On 1 December 1990, he became Commander,
U.S. Naval Forces Central Command and Commander, Seventh Fleet.
Navy Photo by JOC Jim Richeson.

recognized as a distinguished combat veteran. During the Vietnam War he flew
more than five hundred combat missions in the A-4 Skyhawk and commanded an
attack squadron. Later, he commanded the USS *San Jose* (AFS 7), a combat logistics ship, and the aircraft carrier *Coral Sea*. As noted previously, he was the first
commander of U.S. Naval Forces Central Command. Curiously, he was senior to
Vice Admiral Mauz by a few months, having been promoted to vice admiral in
February 1988 when he became the Deputy Chief of Naval Operations for Logistics.

Arthur and Mauz had many similarities. Both believed in naval air power. Both
believed it was important to be close to the warfighters in the fleet. They were also,
however, very different. Mauz was a "blackshoe" from the surface Navy, Arthur
was a "brownshoe" aviator. (Now the admiral, the chief of staff [Capt. Bernie
Smith], and the operations officer [Capt. Bunky Johnson] were all aviators.) Mauz
was thought of as a strategic visionary, a political-military, big-picture man, while
Arthur was viewed as a "straight-stick operator." Arthur felt he was to be more a
component commander than a fleet commander; Mauz seemed to feel an affinity
for his fleet commander role. At a personal level, Mauz usually ate his meals alone
in his cabin; Arthur normally ate in the flag mess with his officers. Unlike Mauz,
who relaxed by playing golf and bridge, Arthur had no known hobbies. He seemed
totally consumed by the Navy and his job.

Arthur and Mauz had different leadership styles. Mauz wanted *complete* staff work and was willing to make a decision the first time the staff presented him with an issue. In contrast, Arthur wanted to be in on the development of issues rather than make decisions at the first presentation. When time allowed, he preferred to talk with the action officers and mull the ideas over in his mind before making a decision. Thus, not only did Arthur have to adjust to the command-and-control system in place, but the ComUSNavCent staff had to adjust to him.

Arthur immersed himself in detail. Most admirals have someone screen their message traffic and read only the most important items; Arthur insisted on seeing nearly every message that came into the command. Some early clashes ensued when the message handlers thought that Arthur really did not mean what he said about seeing every one of the more than three thousand messages a day received by the ComUSNavCent staff. When someone removed "unimportant" messages from his pile, Arthur noticed. When the message handlers borrowed a message to make a copy for someone else and forgot to return the original to the admiral's stack, Arthur noticed. Arthur did not read all the messages to make sure the staff would do their job; he read them to keep himself "calibrated," to stay in tune with what was happening. He seemed confident that he could separate the wheat from the chaff and, given the details, synthesize the big picture from the details.

Arthur possessed an incredible ability to recall the contents of messages. He didn't just read this mountain of message traffic, he absorbed and retained it. Once, in the midst of the war with everything happening at once, the frigate *Nicholas* reported an unexplained explosion near her. The next day, Arthur, reading the dozens of mission reports from attack aircraft, noticed one describing how two aircraft had fired antiradiation missiles. Arthur noted that the time and location were about the same as that of the *Nicholas* incident. (See chapter 8 of Volume II for that story.)

Arthur kept three-foot-high stacks of documents in his office. Whenever a draft message in routing could not be located, the staff suspected the admiral might have it. Captain Smith, the Chief of Staff, would ask Vice Admiral Arthur whether he had the message. If the answer was "no," the staff would suspect that Arthur had forgotten about the message but that it was somewhere in his stacks. Arthur refused to let anyone go through his stacks and mess them up—he knew where everything was. (He often demonstrated this by pulling a document he wanted out of the center of a stack.) The Chief of Staff would wait until Arthur left the ship and then lead a surreptitious expedition into the admiral's office to search for the missing document. He never found one there.

More than is typical of admirals, Arthur was willing to be criticized. He believed strongly in learning from the past by objectively analyzing operations. On at least two occasions he told the author that he found it extremely valuable to have someone on the staff that he did not "control" (that is, the author). Arthur commissioned a massive data-collection effort, and at the end of the war he asked the Center for Naval Analyses to conduct an extensive reconstruction and analysis of naval operations during Desert Shield and Storm. He ordered that in this review if his staff and the analysts could not agree on something, the analysts' version would stand. When some in the Navy objected to the findings of certain postwar analyses, Arthur backed the analysts fully.

Arthur was good at letting staff members do their jobs and at backing them up. When someone proposed an initiative to Arthur he would listen carefully, staring intently at the speaker with his penetrating blue eyes. Most often, he would approve it. One sometimes got the impression that even when he did not believe the proposal was the best course of action, he wanted to give people as much leeway as possible, to allow them every opportunity to make their idea succeed. Of course, if the idea did not succeed, he expected them to recognize the fact. If they did not, he would quietly put things back on track.

During the war, Captain Johnson, the ComUSNavCent Operations Officer, felt that when talking on the radio he could commit the command to a position without getting Arthur's prior approval. He knew Arthur was listening to the circuit and that if he did something Arthur really did not like, Arthur would correct it in a way that would not embarrass him. A few times, Johnson told a flag officer something he obviously did not want to hear. If the other flag officer objected, Arthur would jump into the radio conversation and back up Johnson.

Arthur Takes Command

One would think it was not easy for Arthur to take command six weeks before the UN deadline. It is not a criticism of either Arthur or Mauz to point out that they did not have identical views on how to organize the NavCent forces. In making plans for war, there is rarely a single correct answer. Plans made under two different admirals are unlikely to be the same. Thus, Arthur might have to change arrangements previously made or live with arrangements with which he was not completely comfortable. Nevertheless, Arthur later stated that although one always would prefer to start with a clean slate, he did not feel constrained by coming in so close to the 15 January deadline. He confirmed Mauz's choice of commanders, including the three cases where seniority had not been followed. Arthur spent most of his time during the first few weeks visiting his subordinates and refining the existing plans. He fussed with the details until he understood them. The ComUSNavCent Operations Officer, Capt. Bunky Johnson, later felt that the change of command resulted in a healthy reexamination of plans prior to the war.

Although the dominant theme during the change of commanders was continuity rather than change, Arthur altered or challenged arrangements in at least five significant areas: he questioned the location of ComUSNavCent headquarters on the *Blue Ridge* (see below); he adopted a new command-and-control organization (discussed later in this chapter); he questioned sending the carriers into the Persian Gulf (below, in this chapter); he tried to get the Air Force's Computer-Assisted

Force Management System (CAFMS) installed on the carriers (see chapter 14); and he changed some logistics plans (see chapter 14).

Location of ComUSNavCent Headquarters

After the war Arthur would say that he knew before he arrived in-theater that ComUSNavCent should have been located in Riyadh, but that by the time he got there it was too late to move. In the six weeks remaining until the 15 January deadline he did not have time to create the communications system he needed to operate from there. He would have had to create a new way to get information to the fleet. He thought that as the *Blue Ridge*'s forty-seven shore telephone lines were not keeping pace with peacetime operations, he could not hope to get by with the lesser communications capability he would have had in Riyadh. Arthur considered putting a mobile communications van in Riyadh, but even that could not have given him enough connectivity. The partial communications van already in Riyadh for the coordinating group had proven only marginally adequate for the liaison group's relatively modest needs. If he had arrived in August, Arthur thought, ComUSNavCent could have gotten enough communications gear to command the fleet effectively from Riyadh.

During his check-in meeting with General Schwarzkopf, Vice Admiral Arthur told him that he found the plans and command structure similar to those of his previous tour as ComUSNavCent. Arthur went on to say that as a component commander during his previous tour he had always travelled with the CinC whenever there were exercises in the theater. He had thought of himself as the CinC's naval advisor. Now he had an intermediary who stood in for him in Riyadh. If he could wipe the slate clean, Arthur assured Schwarzkopf, he would be in Riyadh. Schwarzkopf agreed.

Revised Command and Control Organization

With the doubling of forces announced in early November, ComUSNavCent had to decide how to organize his forces. Since August his subordinates had been organized primarily as a series of task groups, CTG 150.X (see chapter 2). Normally, the Navy called an aircraft carrier plus its escorts a battle *group;* conglomerations of more than one carrier were termed a battle *force*. Thus, it seemed inappropriate for the organization chart to call battle force commanders "task group commanders," carrier battle groups "task units," and for normal operating forces to have so many confusing decimals. Therefore, effective 1 January 1991, Vice Admiral Arthur reorganized his forces as depicted in Table 11–1. The most obvious change elevated most of the former CTGs to CTFs, with one fewer digit; for example, CTG 150.4 became CTF 154. By retaining his CTF 150 hat ComUS-NavCent indicated that he still had a warfighting role. Also, some of the names chosen had significance.

Table 11-1
Desert Storm Organization of ComUSNavCent

Command	Task Designator	Person	Location
Commander, U.S. Naval Forces Central Command	CTF 150	Vice Adm. Arthur	USS *Blue Ridge*
Command Liaison Group	CTG 150.0	Vice Adm. Arthur	USS *Blue Ridge*
U.S. Naval Forces Central Command Riyadh	CTU 150.0.1	Rear Adm. Lautenbacher	Riyadh
U.S. Naval Coordinating Group Riyadh	CTU 150.0.2		Riyadh
Commander, Flagship Unit	CTU 150.0.3	Capt. Henderson	USS *Blue Ridge*
Commander, U.S. Naval Logistics Support Force	CTG 150.3	Rear Adm. (Sel.) Sutton	Bahrain
Commander, Mediterranean Strike Group	CTG 150.9	Various	
Commander, Middle East Force	CTF 151	Rear Adm. Fogarty	USS *LaSalle*
Commander, U.S. Maritime Interception Force	CTF 152	Rear Adm. Fogarty	USS *LaSalle*
Commander, Battle Force Zulu	CTF 154	Rear Adm. March	USS *Midway*
Commander, Battle Force Yankee	CTF 155	Rear Adm. Mixson	USS *Kennedy*
Commander, U.S. Amphibious Task Force	CTF 156	Rear Adm. LaPlante	USS *Nassau*
Commander, U.S. Landing Force	CTF 158	Maj. Gen. Jenkins	USS *Nassau*

Source: ComUSNavCent 260731Z DEC 90, Task Designators Assigned to Component Commanders of ComUSNavCent.

CTG 150.4 had been the North Arabian Sea Carrier Battle Group, but this name was not used for CTF 154. CTF 154 was later known informally as the Arabian Gulf Battle Force;[6] nonetheless, ComUSNavCent did not adopt this designation at the time he developed the new organization—mid-December. He had not yet decided how often this battle force would operate inside the Persian Gulf, and did not want to change names every time it moved through the Strait of Hormuz. Hence, CTF 154 was given the name Battle Force Zulu. It would be commanded by Rear Admiral March (CTF 154), embarked on the *Midway*. (To aid the reader's geographic memory, we will refer to Battle Force Zulu as the Persian Gulf Battle Force, even though that was not one of its official names.) Rear Adm. Riley Mixson, CTF 155, on the *John F Kennedy* would command Battle Force Yankee (which we will refer to as the Red Sea Battle Force).

Some changes were substantive transfers of responsibility. For instance, CTG 150.3 was one of only two task groups not upgraded to a task force. Rear Adm. (Sel.) Bob Sutton continued as commander of the Naval Logistics Support Force. He would continue to coordinate shore-based logistics but would no longer have any operational responsibilities for such units as the logistics ships, hospital ships, and repair ships (tenders).

As Commander, Middle East Force (CTF 151), Rear Adm. Bill Fogarty would continue to control the roughly half a dozen ships normally assigned to the Middle East Force, plus the Aegis cruiser *Bunker Hill,* which Vice Admiral Mauz had removed from the *Midway* battle group and assigned to the Middle East Force. (The commanding officer of the *Bunker Hill* served as the Area Air Defense Commander of the eastern sector of the theater, under the control of the Air Force officer who was the Area Air Defense Commander for the entire theater.) In addition, Fogarty would now control some noncombatant ships, such as tenders and hospital ships, many of which came from the logistics support force. As commander of the U.S. Maritime Interception Force (CTF 152), Fogarty would continue to direct maritime interception operations, using assets he controlled in Task Force 151 and others provided by the battle forces.

The designator CTG 150.9 remained unchanged, but the name was now Commander, Mediterranean Strike Group, as opposed to the title Commander, Carrier Battle Group Mediterranean used early in Desert Shield. After 15 January there would no longer be any carriers in the Mediterranean Sea, only Tomahawk launchers—submarines, destroyers, and Aegis cruisers. Once the Alert Order for the air campaign was issued, the Mediterranean Tomahawk launchers would shift from the tactical control of Sixth Fleet to that of ComUSNavCent. The Sixth Fleet's submarine operating authority would coordinate movement of submarine Tomahawk launchers in the Mediterranean, subject to ComUSNavCent's requirements. Even though the ships and submarines of the Mediterranean Strike Group were not within the Central Command's area of responsibility, ComUSNavCent would directly control the details of who fired Tomahawk missiles, when they were fired, and the targets programmed into them. When JFACC ordered a strike by a specified number of Tomahawk missiles against a particular set of targets, ComUSNavCent would develop and send to the launch platforms both the launch-sequence plans and the messages (known as Indigos) ordering the Tomahawk launches.

Tactical Command and Control

In mid-December, because the ComUSNavCent staff expected at least some of the carriers on the eastern side of the theater to be in the North Arabian Sea during the war rather than in the Persian Gulf, they spent a lot of time delineating alternative command structures for various situations and the circumstances in which the alternatives would be employed. Most of these situations never came to pass.[7] In the actual event, when all carriers were inside the Persian Gulf they would use a fully integrated command structure that included Middle East Force ships and all the carrier battle groups. For example, the combined force would have a single antiair warfare commander. On the Red Sea side, things were simpler: the Red Sea Battle Force would operate under a single, integrated command structure at all times. Vice Admiral Arthur would let each battle force commander propose his own command structure and subordinate commanders—for example, who would serve as the strike warfare commander.

The Amphibious Task Force always would operate in associated, or mutual, support with the Persian Gulf Battle Force, no matter where the Amphibious Task Force and carriers were located. That is, the Amphibious Task Force and the carrier battle force would each retain its identity and its spectrum of warfare commanders. They would cooperate to achieve the same broad mission objectives, but each would have discretion on how best to support the other.

FORCE MOVEMENTS

In chapter 7 we described how "experienced naval officers" proclaimed that aircraft carriers could not conduct flight operations in the obstructed waters of the Persian Gulf, and how on 2 October Vice Admiral Mauz sent the *Independence* through the Strait of Hormuz. Figure 11–1 illustrates the timing of the movement of carriers in the theater. The *Independence*'s successful operations and several trips by the *Midway* battle group into the Persian Gulf convinced people that it was physically possible to steam aircraft carriers in the Persian Gulf and conduct flight operations there. However, would the threat of attack prohibit carrier operations in the Persian Gulf in wartime?

Carriers in the Persian Gulf

Mauz had been thinking of operating carriers in the Persian Gulf for some time. At the CinCCent map exercise in early October he briefed that he intended to oper-

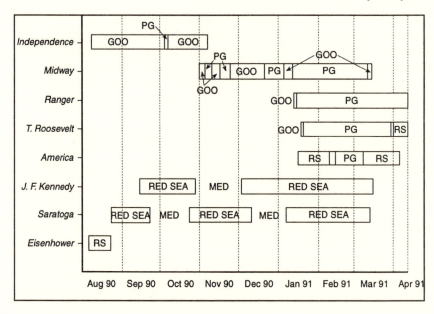

Figure 11–1. Movement of Carriers during Desert Shield and Storm

ate a carrier in the Persian Gulf as soon as the tactical situation permitted, perhaps two or three days after hostilities began. In his 10 November message "Price of Poker Goes Up," Mauz indicated he intended to operate some of the three Persian Gulf Battle Force carriers in the Persian Gulf in the event of war. Furthermore, he was "becoming persuaded we should have at least one inside before the war starts if possible. With the overwhelming naval power we will have, I think the deterrent effect on Iran will cause them to reconsider any mischief they might have in mind."[8] Mauz now says that well before he left he became convinced of the need to move carriers into the Persian Gulf when war came, including moving all three there from the North Arabian Sea at the start of the war.

Initially Vice Admiral Arthur, like most people arriving fresh in the theater, was not comfortable with this idea. Eventually, after carefully considering the pros and cons, he embraced the view. Arthur had thought about putting carriers in the Persian Gulf back in the late 1970s and early 1980s, but one would have needed to knock out a lot of Soviet attack aircraft first. When the Iranians changed their political structure, they had seemed to become erratic and vengeful. Thus for Desert Storm Arthur had to sort out whether Iran would try to make things hard for the United States. If so, he did not want to offer them the plum of all targets first. Arthur worried that if he brought the carriers into the Gulf he might have to tie up all his assets defending them (which could be the case if Iran threatened action). But the incentive to bring the carriers into the Persian Gulf was strong. Arthur felt that the lack of tankers for air-to-air refueling demanded such a move.

With carriers outside the Persian Gulf, air operations depended heavily on tanking from CentAF (which said there were not enough tankers). Arthur always felt he could not rely on CentAF tanker assets and that this restricted what NavCent could contribute. Inside the Persian Gulf, the carriers had much more flexibility. They needed less fuel themselves and some of the needed aviation fuel could be provided by small tanker aircraft operating from the carriers and controlled by Com-USNavCent.

As late as mid-December Arthur had not decided whether to move carriers into the Persian Gulf on D-day. By 1 January he formed the intention to establish a continuous carrier presence inside the Persian Gulf as soon as possible, with the remaining Persian Gulf Battle Force carriers staying in the North Arabian Sea. After hostilities began, he would direct them into the Persian Gulf. (He stated in a message that Iran did not pose a significant threat.) At one point during this process Arthur thought he might keep two carriers inside the Gulf and one outside, rotating them periodically. This would have been like the old Yankee Station operations during Vietnam, with two carriers on line and one back. This thought did not last long, however, because he realized that supporting two widely separated battle groups would mean complicated logistics. He decided it would be much easier if the off-line carrier stayed inside the Persian Gulf.

Arthur split the carriers three-three between the Red Sea and Persian Gulf, because he always thought NavCent forces had to be prepared for a sustainable long-term effort. It might be a long time before anything started, or the war might last a long time. A two-carrier battle force could sustain operations around the clock for several days but could not do so indefinitely, the way a three-carrier battle force could.

Timing of the Arrival of Additional Carriers

In mid-December General Schwarzkopf directed that all units must arrive *and be prepared to commence offensive operations* by 15 January, rather than simply be in the theater by then as the previous Navy plan had stated. General Schwarzkopf directed Vice Admiral Arthur to review the "closure" of forces and their employment schedules and to identify steps to ensure that all naval and amphibious forces were capable of conducting operations no later than 15 January. In previous years, having carriers in-theater had been a matter of naval presence, and staying within forty-eight hours of a notional launch position in the North Arabian Sea had been sufficient.

The *Ranger* had left the West Coast on 8 December. She was scheduled to arrive at the forty-eight-hour arc on 15 January, and the notional launch position in the North Arabian Sea on 17 January. The *Roosevelt* and *America* were scheduled to depart their home ports on 28 December. The *America* would arrive at her station in the northern Red Sea late on 15 January. The *Roosevelt,* with an additional eight-and-one-half-day transit from the Red Sea to the North Arabian Sea, was scheduled to arrive in the North Arabian Sea about 24 January.

Some thought that as a practical matter, being prepared to conduct strikes on 15 January required the carriers to arrive several days before that date, in order to conduct flight operations so as to accustom the aircrews to flying in that environment. Also, the carrier operations people needed to familiarize themselves with getting sorties into the ATO and arranging for tankers.

Arthur, however, did not believe the carriers needed to arrive before 15 January to train and acclimatize themselves to the environment and operating procedures. He thought they could begin combat operations as soon as they entered the area, without a warm-up period. In peacetime one had to learn how to work around the civilian air corridors in the Persian Gulf, but in wartime that was not a problem. Once the first carrier was plugged into the JFACC and ATO system, subsequent carriers would be easy to integrate.

Arthur believed that because the strike planning was based on two carriers in the Red Sea and one in the North Arabian Sea, additional carriers would not be needed immediately upon the start of the war. In particular, there was no need for a third carrier in the North Arabian Sea until about seven days into the war. Therefore, in response to Schwarzkopf's order to review the scheduled arrival of the additional carriers, Arthur recommended that the *Ranger*'s maintenance period in Subic Bay be cut short by one or two days, the *Roosevelt*'s transit be sped up by one day, and the *America*'s schedule not be changed.[9]

The Chief of Naval Operations and the Navy Staff exerted a great deal of pressure not to change the schedules, because they did not want the *America* and *Roosevelt* to leave home port before Christmas. Underlying much of this thinking was the perception that the coalition would not go to war until several weeks after 15 January; the Navy Staff in Washington seemed to believe that. Although we now know the war started only two days after the 15 January 1991 deadline, at the time most people, in and out of the theater, did not think it would. Reinforcing this perception, Schwarzkopf's Deputy, Lt. General Calvin "Cal" Waller, USA, told the press on 19 December that the Army would not be ready to go until February.

In the end, the *Midway* battle group entered the Persian Gulf for the third time on 21 December until 5 January, and for the fourth time on 11 January. The *Ranger* battle group entered the Persian Gulf on 15 January, as soon as it reached the theater. The *Theodore Roosevelt* shifted to the control of Central Command on 14 January and was en route to the Persian Gulf on the 17th.

COORDINATING WAR PLANS

One of the mechanisms the ComUSNavCent staff used to plan how to run the war was a series of conferences on the *Blue Ridge*. An Operations and Plans Conference took place on 13–14 December. The ComUSNavCent staff held an Amphibious Planning Conference 30–31 December, while the *Blue Ridge* visited Dubai in the UAE. (Chapter 13 describes the discussions at this conference.) On 8 January there was a second meeting of operations officers from ComUSNav-

Cent's subordinate commands. This was followed by a meeting of flag officers on 12 January, the *Blue Ridge* having got under way from Bahrain on 11 January.

The Operations and Plans Conference was a top-level session with mostly captains and colonels, and some commanders and lieutenant colonels. The purpose was to outline ComUSNavCent's warfighting strategy and the command, control, and communications structure and to assign the task force commanders (CTFs) to develop the force dispositions, tactics, and detailed command arrangements to implement that strategy. ComUSNavCent staff briefings included intelligence, the new overall command-and-control structure with the CTFs, air defense and data link architecture, strike plans, rules of engagement, combat search and rescue, amphibious plans, communications, and logistics. Attendees were told that Vice Admiral Arthur had not decided whether to move carriers into the Persian Gulf on D-day. The CTFs were tasked to prepare their battle force command structure and the detailed plans needed to implement Arthur's general plan. (These plans are described in chapters 13 and 14.) In several cases, such as combat search and rescue, sizable problems remained to be solved.

A second objective of this conference was to explain to people outside the theater how Arthur planned to run the war, so they would understand better what support ComUSNavCent would need. The ComUSNavCent Operations Officer, Captain Johnson, insisted, however, that the conference was not a request for input from others: it was a "transmit meeting." Attendees from outside the theater included representatives from CinCUSNavEur, ComSixthFlt, and CinCPacFlt.

ComUSNavCent held the 8 January Operations Officer Conference to allow the subordinate commands to present the detailed plans they had developed. No out-of-theater people were invited. Finally, Arthur hosted a 12 January Flag Conference to review the final arrangements with his senior subordinates before going to war.

THE FIRST REPORT IS *STILL* ALWAYS WRONG

As we have noted, military people have long known about the "fog of war" and its pernicious consequences, and people that hear a seemingly ominous report may initiate actions with potentially grave ramifications, only to learn later the report was wrong. One of Vice Admiral Arthur's contributions to the ComUSNavCent staff was instilling an attitude that "the first report is *always* wrong." The staff repeated this mantra so many times that it became second nature to question a report and diligently seek confirmation. On 30 November, the day before Arthur assumed command of ComUSNavCent, events conspired to demonstrate his point.

Oil Field on Fire

At 1145C on 30 November, the Middle East Force staff reported a "major" fire at Ras Tanura, a large refinery site about twenty miles southeast of al-Jubail, Saudi

Arabia. Sabotage was suspected. The Middle East Force staff directed one of its SH-3G logistics helicopters to investigate. The helicopter flew over the area about three hours later and found no evidence of fire. At that time, ComUSNavCent intelligence reported that its sources indicated the fire had been put out about 1215C.

Iraqi Troops on the Move

At the same time the fire was reported, the USCinCCent staff reported that twenty to thirty Iraqi vehicles were operating in the tri-border area (the former neutral zone where Saudi Arabia, Kuwait, and Iraq come together). Commander Dave Jennings, USN, the ComUSNavCent Battle Watch Captain at the time, wrote in the logbook that "[the USCinCCent staff] seems *very* concerned about this, although in absence of other indicators, does not seem to be that critical" (emphasis in original). A few hours later, the British Royal Navy cited this report as the reason for changing the status of its ships in port to "immediate sail." Nothing further came of this incident.

Bomb on the *Blue Ridge*

At 1420C, also on 30 November while at the pier in Bahrain, the *Blue Ridge*'s quarterdeck watch received a call warning that there was a bomb on board. The call probably came from inside the ship. Everyone except those on watch left the ship. Nothing was found.

Suicide Supertanker Headed South

Also on 30 November, at 1545C, the USCinCCent staff called the ComUS-NavCent Battle Watch to say that SOCCent (Special Operations Component, U.S. Central Command) had reported a supertanker "riding low in the water" one to two kilometers offshore at 28°30' north latitude, just below the border, moving south at four knots. The implication was that this was an Iraqi supertanker on some kind of suicide mission. The story did not make sense, because the Gulf was only five meters deep even five miles off shore in most places, and supertankers need water at least ten meters deep. Attempts were made to get Saudi patrol boats to investigate; for some reason, they would not. One Saudi organization denied anything was there; another said there was.

After several hours, the USCinCCent staff asked what the ComUSNavCent staff was doing about the supertanker. Capt. Gordon Holder, the ComUSNavCent Battle Watch Captain on duty, did not wish to react rashly. Holder said people had tried to start the war three times already that day, "getting spun up over nothing," and he did not want someone running across an Iranian tanker on legitimate business and shooting at it. The possibilities at this time appeared to be that the supertanker sighted was one of the following: (1) a figment of the imagination (unlikely in daylight), (2) a tanker legitimately loading at the oil terminal a few miles south of the border, (3) a tanker going into the channel there, (4) a tanker much farther out, or (5) a wrecked ship known to be in the area. The next morning, a helicopter from the frigate *Nicholas* searched the area and did not find the alleged super-tanker.

NOTES

Primary sources for the escalation were interviews with Mauz, Powell, Less, Bernie Smith, and Jeremiah. Powell's book and Mauz's message to his subordinates were also used. The description of the 14 December intelligence briefing comes entirely from the author's notes. Sources for the choice of commanders included messages and interviews with LaPlante, Connelly, Holder, Bernie Smith, and Johnson. For flagship rotation, sources were messages and interviews with Hardisty. For command turnover, sources included interviews with Mauz, Arthur, Kelso, Wright, Sharp, and Hardisty. The sketch of Arthur comes from interviews with his staff and the author's own observations. Interviews with Arthur were the primary source for the discussion of the location of ComUSNavCent's headquarters. Sources for force movements include messages and interviews with Mauz, Arthur, Zlatoper, and Edney and an article by Gellman. The ComUSNavCent Battle Watch Captain Events Log and the author's observations were the primary sources for the anecdotes at the end of the chapter.

1. Interview with Adm. Hank Mauz, 14 March 1996. Powell may not have been totally candid with Mauz. In his autobiography Powell states he and Schwarzkopf developed the left-hook plan on the evening of 22 October; on the morning of 23 October Powell suggested getting six aircraft carriers into theater. Powell, *My American Journey,* 486–7.

2. Admiral Mauz could not recall the timing of Schwarzkopf's request.

3. In January 1997 Powell vaguely recalled that Schwarzkopf had asked for four carriers initially but that Powell changed it to six when he found out more were available. Powell said his general policy had been to be sure that nobody ever said they needed more forces than they had been given.

4. Admiral Mauz could not recall the timing of his recommendation, except that it was in early November. Smith thought that Mauz got a phone call from the Navy Staff in the Pentagon that said "the answer is six carriers." Interview with Rear Adm. Bernie Smith, 23 April 1996. Mauz vigorously denied that he received any guidance from Washington.

5. LaPlante, noting that he had been the CinCPacFlt Logistics Officer while Mauz was there, thought that might have made him more a known quantity to Mauz.

6. The Arab nations call the body of water the "Arabian Gulf," but ComUSNavCent and his subordinates generally referred to it as the "Persian Gulf," though not with complete consistency, as in this case.

7. If any carriers were in the North Arabian Sea, they would always be "federated" with the Middle East Force ships and any carriers inside the Persian Gulf. That is, the forces inside and outside the Persian Gulf would each retain a complete set of warfare commanders, but the senior commander, March, would have overall tactical command.

8. ComUSNavCent 201437Z NOV 90, Personal for Admirals Carter, Howe, Larson and VAdm. Kelly from Mauz, Desert Shield Naval Update.

9. As an alternative, ComUSNavCent could have put three carriers into the Persian Gulf and three into the Red Sea on 15 January without any ship sailing early, by moving the *Kennedy* or *Saratoga* to the North Arabian Sea and keeping the *Roosevelt* in the Red Sea. This was not done because it would have wasted the four months of integrated strike training already carried out by the two Red Sea carriers. As an aside, Arthur's 21 December message indicated that the carriers on the eastern side of the theater would operate from the North Arabian Sea, perhaps in the Persian Gulf if the situation allowed.

Chapter 12

Maritime Interception Operations: The Paperwork War

The maritime interception operations were in their third month when the price of poker went up. As of 10 November ComUSNavCent forces had conducted 3,498 queries, 404 boardings, and 15 diversions. By mid-December more than 130 U.S. ships and sixty allied ships sailed in the region.

Because of the natural chokepoints, the maritime interception operations had two fronts—the Persian Gulf and the Red Sea. Forces on both fronts followed the same rules of engagement, had the same coordination requirements with coalition members (and their differing rules of engagement), and had to contend with suspect ships using territorial waters to avoid inspection. Even though Egypt, unlike Iran, was part of the coalition, there were territorial-water constraints. Chapters 3, 4, and 8 focused primarily on the Persian Gulf maritime interception operations and on stopping the flow of oil and other goods in and out of Iraqi ports. In this chapter we show how the Red Sea forces faced different challenges and obstacles.

RED SEA OPERATIONS

Although the Persian Gulf forces encountered many more ships than did the Red Sea forces, the latter conducted the majority of boardings. Large numbers of ships entered the Persian Gulf on legitimate business bound for countries other than Iraq or Kuwait. Coalition forces had to query each ship but needed to board relatively few, because traffic to Iraq nearly disappeared. Each ship needed to answer a series of questions regarding such topics as its port of registry, ports of embarkation and debarkation, cargo, and passengers.

On the other side of the theater, the Jordanian port of Aqaba was an active port and served as a transshipment point for goods to and from Iraq. Because the sanctions were not aimed at Jordan, the port could not be blocked off. Red Sea interception forces had not only to query but also board nearly every ship entering or leaving Aqaba, because they might contain cargo bound to or from Iraq. This is why although coalition forces on the Persian Gulf side conducted most of the queries and most of the high-interest boardings of Iraqi ships, forces on the Red Sea side conducted most of the boardings.

The intent of the operation was not to interfere with legitimate commerce but only to prevent smuggling and the circumvention of UN sanctions. Thus, as long as the paperwork was in order and correlated with the cargo and destination, a ship was allowed to proceed. It became a paperwork war. A bureaucrat's dream! Violators were stopped, but this often meant only that the ship would divert to a port long enough to make its documents correspond with the cargo, then set sail again. Because of the large number of ships travelling on legitimate business, the Red Sea operation frequently encountered particular ships multiple times. It would not take long for would-be smugglers to learn how to falsify ship documents to circumvent the sanctions. Ships could not be diverted on suspicion alone.

Vertical Insertions in the Red Sea

Omduran

The Sudanese merchant vessel *Omduran* was first encountered and queried by the Greek frigate HS *Elli* (F 450) on 9 November 1990 in the northern Red Sea. The *Omduran* offered that she was en route from Port Sudan to Aqaba carrying only ballast and had no intention of stopping. The local maritime interception operations commander, embarked on the cruiser USS *South Carolina* (CGN 37), directed the Aegis cruiser *Philippine Sea* to close in, and the Spanish frigate *Cazadora* voluntarily approached as well, to assist. While the *Philippine Sea* and *Cazadora* were en route, the *Elli* fired warning shots from her main battery. The master of the *Omduran* still refused to stop. At the request of the U.S. maritime interception operations commander, the *Elli* held off firing additional warning shots until the others arrived.

All parties agreed the *Philippine Sea* would be the on-scene commander, because of seniority. An SH-3H helicopter reported the *Omduran*'s cargo holds open and apparently empty. After the *Omduran* refused to heed more verbal warnings, the *Philippine Sea* fired .50-caliber warning shots across the vessel's bows and the *Elli* again fired her main battery. Three SH-3 helicopters launched from the aircraft carrier *Saratoga* with a U.S. Navy SEAL team embarked. The master steadfastly refused to stop, challenging the warships to "stop me any way you like."[1] The *Philippine Sea* then fired three five-inch rounds that the master acknowledged, but he again refused to stop.

When the *Philippine Sea* notified the master of the vertical insertion, he offered to help the team debark from the helicopter. The offer was declined. The *Omduran* altered her course slightly to delay entering Egyptian territorial waters, but she remained en route to Aqaba. SEALs from two of the helicopters boarded the *Omduran*, secured the bridge, and turned the ship south, away from territorial waters, from which the *Omduran* was now two miles away. Once the SEALs had secured the ship and mustered the crew, teams from the *Elli* and *Philippine Sea* boarded and began the search. A USCG LEDet led the *Philippine Sea* team. It found no cargo, declared the *Omduran* a cleared vessel, and allowed her to proceed to Aqaba.

This interception illustrates potential problems with an informal multinational command structure like this one. The U.S. policy at this time allowed ships to proceed to their destination (even to Iraq) if they were believed to be in ballast (or empty). In this case, the *Omduran* had been riding high in the water and her cargo holds had appeared empty. On a previous trip to Aqaba to pick up refugees, the *Omduran* had been cleared and allowed to proceed after a helicopter from a NavCent ship verified the holds were empty. But on 9 November, after she was asked to stop (a minor escalation) and *Elli* fired warning shots (a major escalation), letting the *Omduran* proceed without a boarding was no longer an option. The *Elli* was not required to obtain permission from higher authority for warning shots, but she did not have disabling authority.

Another interesting part of this multinational effort lies in the speed and efficiency of the stopping and boarding of this ship. The *Omduran* was getting close to Egyptian territorial waters. From the time of the initial call from the *Elli* to the *Philippine Sea* requesting assistance until the SEAL insertion teams were on board, only two hours and twenty-nine minutes elapsed. Several factors contributed to the success of this, the first vertical insertion in the Red Sea: first, by this time it was a well-practiced procedure; and second, the master, while not fully cooperative, was not altogether uncooperative.

Khawla Bint Al Zawra

The second Red Sea vertical insertion occurred on 27 November, and it resembled the *Omduran* interception in some ways. The *Khawla Bint Al Zawra*, an Iraqi roll-on/roll-off cargo ship (4,000 dwt), was first encountered by the cruiser *Philippine Sea* and the Spanish frigate *Diana* (F 32) on 26 November. The frigate USS *Thomas C Hart* and French destroyer FS *Dupleix* (D 641) also provided support. The *Philippine Sea* and *Thomas C Hart* were on "gateguard duty," that is, monitoring the entrance into the Gulf of Aqaba in the northern Red Sea. The *Khawla Bint Al Zawra* was en route from Aden, Yemen, to Aqaba, Jordan, via Port Sudan, Sudan. As with the *Omduran*, this interception required quick sequential action on the part of the Maritime Interception Force to prevent the ship from entering territorial waters.

Not only were territorial waters a problem, but Intelligence had indicated the *Khawla Bint Al Zawra* carried over a hundred Iraqi passengers composed of the crews of seven Iraqi merchant ships. For this reason, the Red Sea battle group commander wanted to divert the *Khawla Bint Al Zawra* without conducting a visit and search. Vice Adm. Hank Mauz rejected this idea, reasoning that personnel were not contraband cargo. He directed that the size of the boarding team be increased and that allies be included.

During the evening of 26 November, the *Philippine Sea* and *Thomas C Hart* proceeded south to intercept the *Khawla Bint Al Zawra*. The *Diana* and *Dupleix* accepted the invitation to participate, although the *Dupleix* did not wish to send a boarding party, because of a fear of jeopardizing their maneuverability while in their support role (for instance, it might not be able to fire its guns immediately while launching a small boat). The *Diana* advised NavCent forces that some actions on its part might require approval of higher Spanish authority. The four ships surrounded the *Khawla Bint Al Zawra* at a distance of five to ten thousand yards. The *Philippine Sea,* the on-scene commander, had tactical control of all ships involved.

Early in the morning of 27 November, the *Diana* and *Philippine Sea* attempted to contact the *Khawla Bint Al Zawra* using bridge-to-bridge radio, flashing lights, and top-side loudspeakers. The *Khawla Bint Al Zawra* refused to answer and continued on course. After getting permission, the *Philippine Sea* fired .50-caliber rounds across the bow. The *Khawla Bint Al Zawra* again did not respond. The *Philippine Sea* asked the *Diana* also to fire warning shots. The *Diana* fired two 76 mm rounds, neither of which provoked a response.

With no response from the *Khawla Bint Al Zawra*, the *Philippine Sea* increased the pressure by firing five-inch rounds and having the ships close inside 1,500 yards of the *Khawla Bint Al Zawra*. This show of force, intended to discourage further disregard of the challenges, indeed elicited a response. A little over two and one-half hours after the initial contact, the master of the *Khawla Bint Al Zawra* acknowledged the presence of the warships around him, said that he had no intention of stopping, and declared the Maritime Interception Force had no right to stop him. If she maintained her current course and speed, the *Khawla Bint Al Zawra* would enter territorial waters in half an hour. The *Philippine Sea* again instructed the *Khawla Bint Al Zawra* to stop and reemphasized to the master that he and the passengers would be allowed to proceed if no prohibited cargo was found. The *Khawla Bint Al Zawra*'s continued lack of cooperation prompted discussions on the use of disabling fire. To date, however, vertical insertions had solved the problem of stopping noncooperative ships.

The master now reported that though he could not stop, he was willing to slow to four knots. He also advised that he was under orders not to rig his boarding ladder. The *Khawla Bint Al Zawra* slowed, but she refused to turn south. By now a SEAL platoon from the carrier *Saratoga* was airborne in three SH-3H helicopters, and two F/A-18 aircraft had been launched. Shortly before sunrise, with the SEALs in a holding pattern awaiting daylight, the two *Saratoga* F/A-18s orbiting at twenty thousand feet, and the carrier's Marine security detachment on five-minute alert to reinforce the SEALs if necessary, the master began to cooperate. He agreed to muster the ninety-seven passengers and thirty-three crew members on board, but he required thirty minutes to do so.

Just minutes before the SEALs rappelled onto the deck, the *Philippine Sea* notified the master of their imminent arrival. It took only four minutes from that announcement for the SEALs to land and secure the bridge. Poor sea conditions prohibited small boats from transporting search teams from the *Philippine Sea* and *Diana;* therefore, the insertion team conducted the search. (The normal procedure was to have the SEALs secure the ship and then send a USCG LEDet to board and conduct the search and document inspection.) The search revealed no cargo, and all passengers and crew were accounted for. The *Khawla Bint Al Zawra* was cleared to proceed.

In this event, the firing of a graduated sequence of warning shots and the coordination of warning shots between warships from the United States and Spain occurred much quicker than in previous intercepts, perhaps because of the proximity to territorial waters, or because the procedures were so well established by then. This marked the first intercept in which an embarked Marine security detachment was a potential boarding party. Fortunately, its services were not required.

IMPROVING THE PROCESS

The Red Sea Maritime Interception Force faced two problems not shared to the same degree by the forces in the Persian Gulf and North Arabian Sea. First, as noted, Red Sea forces had to contend with an enormous number of boardings, whereas the Persian Gulf forces faced more often the tactical problem of stopping recalcitrant Iraqi ships without disabling them. The second problem, unique to the Red Sea side, was the potential for falsification of manifests.

Because of the criteria established in the Operations Order, all ships inbound to or outbound from Aqaba carrying cargo, or suspected of carrying cargo, had to be boarded. Considering the numbers boarded, remarkably few were diverted; as of 10 November, only fifteen of 404. The question naturally arose: Was there a more efficient way to cull out the ships that needed to be diverted?

To reduce the burden on the Red Sea forces, the people responsible for the interceptions (queries, boardings, diversions) suggested some changes. Instead of boarding all outbound suspect ships, a proposal called for boarding one randomly selected ship out of every four, as well as all suspect ships. The system would be more efficient but at the same time still provide a deterrent to would-be smugglers. ComMidEastFor recommended adoption of these changes and incorporated them into its policy, which now allowed inspections to be decided on a case-by-case basis. ComUSNavCent supported the changes and forwarded them with its recommendation to USCinCCent, where they were rejected—all outbound shipping from Aqaba was to be intercepted.

This same problem would be revisited when hostilities began. In fact, for the first two days of Desert Storm the maritime interception operations were suspended. Although the coalition continued to monitor merchant shipping activity closely, the start of the war brought changes to the maritime interception operations policy. Because NavCent ships now had warfighting responsibilities and there was increased concern about terrorist attacks, ComMidEastFor again altered the boarding policy so as to board only suspect ships and allow ships that frequently travelled the area and were known to comply with the UN sanctions to pass without a boarding after verification of their identity. Night boardings were also suspended; suspect ships that required boardings were directed to lie to in holding areas until daylight.

The second problem, falsification of ship's manifests, was summarized by Rear Adm. Nick Gee, commander of the *Saratoga* battle group in the Red Sea. Cargo manifests and container labels had become the prime tools of the boarding teams in deciding what to divert. By simply changing the written destination of the cargo or its container labels, ships could get prohibited cargo through. The stories in the following section illustrate how falsification of paperwork could be the Achilles' heel of the interception policy. The stories also show how NavCent forces met this challenge in the cases of the *Tilia* and *Dongola*.

TILIA AND *DONGOLA*

The *Tilia* and *Dongola* stand out from other interceptions not because of their refusal to stop and allow a boarding party to search them, but rather in the details of their trips into and out of Aqaba. The Cyprus-flagged *Tilia* was intercepted on 3 November, 5 November, 9 December, and 13 December 1990—each time either inbound to or outbound from Aqaba, Jordan. On 3 November, the French destroyer FS *Du Chayla* (D 630) intercepted the *Tilia* carrying automobiles to Aqaba. The French again intercepted the *Tilia* two days later outbound from Aqaba en route to Hodeida, Yemen. The visit and search team found twenty-two containers loaded with automobiles. The French cleared the vessel to proceed.

In the 9 December interception, the *Tilia* was bound for Aqaba from Hodeida carrying electrical supplies, acetylene gas, machinery, and automobile parts. The Greek frigate *Elli* conducted the interception and cleared her to continue to Aqaba. Four days later, the guided-missile cruiser USS *Mississippi* (CGN 40) intercepted the *Tilia*. This time she was outbound from Aqaba loaded with a variety of cargo including automobiles, construction material, cardboard, and plastic bags. By 13 December, the *Tilia* was familiar with the interception procedures. The master knew he would be asked questions about the cargo and his ports of embarkation and debarkation. He offered no resistance to the visit and search. The boarding team led by the USCG LEDet uncovered discrepancies in some of the manifests, discrepancies that indicated that the cars had been taken from Kuwait after the invasion. This evidence included Kuwaiti license plates and stickers on the windows. Some cars contained personal items, such as passports and newspapers, less than a month old. It was explained that the cars were privately owned by people who had fled Kuwait and Iraq; however, many of the cars, typically Mercedes and

BMWs, appeared to have been hot-wired and broken into. The *Tilia* was diverted back to Aqaba to discharge this suspicious cargo.

The *Tilia* reappeared on 15 December with the same cargo and was again intercepted by the *Mississippi* and diverted back to Aqaba. The following day the *Tilia* yet again attempted to sail to Hodeida with the same cargo. The *Mississippi*, with the concurrence of the chain of command as high as the Joint Chiefs of Staff, directed the *Tilia* to return to Aqaba; the *Tilia* turned around and headed back. On 18 December, the *Tilia* made a fourth attempt to reach Hodeida and for the fourth time failed, this time because of the frigate *Elmer Montgomery*. The cargo had changed a bit, and now a substantial number of containers were inaccessible and could not be searched. Therefore, the *Elmer Montgomery* escorted the *Tilia* to Yanbu, Saudi Arabia, for a more thorough search.

This pattern can be seen in other ships as well. For instance, the *Dongola*, a Cyprus-flagged cargo ship, made many passages through the Maritime Interception Force. In fact, she was one of the first ships intercepted and the first diverted back in August 1990. On 25 November, the *Elmer Montgomery* intercepted the *Dongola* while she was en route from Port Sudan to Aqaba. Carrying only ballast, she was cleared to proceed. The *Elmer Montgomery* again intercepted and cleared *Dongola* on 29 November as she steamed outbound from Aqaba en route to Port Sudan—her cargo, automobiles. On 9 December the *Dongola* set sail again, with the same pattern as before. She was intercepted by the Greek frigate *Elli* en route to Aqaba carrying only ballast. On 13 December—the same day on which the *Mississippi* diverted the *Tilia* with her load of stolen vehicles—the *Dongola* left Aqaba carrying vehicles and was intercepted again. This time, however, the *Dongola* was not cleared to proceed. She was diverted, like the *Tilia*. The *Dongola*'s next interaction with the maritime interception operations occurred on 28 December, when en route to Hamburg, Germany, carrying empty containers.

The master of the *Tilia* offered insight into regional smuggling operations. Ships would carry stolen Kuwaiti vehicles to Yemen, where they would be sold at a fraction of their value. The master admitted that he himself was waiting for a Land Cruiser—"It's good business." Only the persistence of the multinational force and the detailed search led by the USCG LEDet produced the evidence of the continuing plundering of Kuwait.

The stolen cars from Kuwait provide an example of smuggling schemes by which Iraq attempted to circumvent the UN sanctions. Intelligence estimated that Iraq had only $1.5 billion in hard currency left. In addition, Iraqi imports were down to only 5 percent of their pre-invasion levels. Smuggling had evidently picked up across the land borders with Jordan and Iran. A report claimed that whereas in October 1990 the highway between Baghdad and the Jordanian border had been virtually free of traffic, in late December the same highway saw dozens of covered freight-carrying trucks with Jordanian license plates streaming toward the Iraqi capital. Also, considerable truck traffic was reported to be entering Iraq from Iran at a number of points along the seven-hundred-mile frontier.

The relentless pursuit of potential violators on the part of NavCent and coalition forces at sea made the smuggling by sea a much riskier proposition than by land.

IRAQI SHIPS STILL CAUSE PROBLEMS

Although the *Tilia* and *Dongola* offered no resistance to being repeatedly intercepted, Iraqi ships continued to resist. As the reader will recall with the interceptions of the *Omduran* and *Khawla Bint Al Zawra*, not all ships intercepted in the Red Sea were cooperative. The Iraqi cargo ship *Altaawin Alarabi* (13,634 dwt) is another example. The cruiser USS *San Jacinto* (CG 56) and French destroyer *Du Chayla* intercepted the *Altaawin Alarabi* in transit from Port Sudan to Aqaba on 23 December. Both the U.S. and French ships repeatedly attempted to communicate with the *Altaawin Alarabi* via radio calls, ship's whistle, and flashing lights, to no avail. Only after these attempts failed and the *San Jacinto* had fired .50-caliber warning shots across the bow did the master finally agree to stop and allow the vessel to be searched. The French conducted the visit and search and found passengers, but no cargo. They cleared the *Altaawin Alarabi* to proceed to Aqaba.

The Iraqi cargo ship *Ibn Khaldoon* (12,650 dwt), a self-proclaimed "peace ship," proved a challenging boarding and illustrates a different kind of Iraqi resistance. The *Ibn Khaldoon* received international media attention throughout her journey, which began in Algeria and ended in Iraq. On board the *Ibn Khaldoon* were 241 passengers and forty-one crew members. Included in the passengers were sixty women, a U.S. Congress staff member, and an American lawyer. Evidently, the Iraqis wanted to embarrass the coalition by forcing them to harm a civilian ship carrying baby food and women. If the American citizens on board were harmed, it might induce protests in the United States. If on the other hand, the coalition let the peace ship pass unmolested, Iraq would gain propaganda points because it would have broken the sanctions.

The multinational force knew the *Ibn Khaldoon* would be transiting through the Red Sea down to the Gulf of Oman and up into the Persian Gulf (see Figure 12–1). This knowledge allowed extensive planning and rehearsal of a vertical insertion. The planners anticipated the type of resistance most likely to be employed by the activists. For this reason, the insertion team was briefed in and armed for crowd-control measures. The USS *Trenton* (LPD 14), part of the Amphibious Task Force, provided the helicopter-insertion team.

Warning shots were not fired at the *Ibn Khaldoon*. After an inquiry by the Australian guided-missile frigate HMAS *Sydney* (FFG 03) and the master's refusal to stop, the master was advised that a vertical insertion team was en route to rappel onto the ship. Passengers used both active and passive resistance in an attempt to prevent the boarding. A flare gun was fired in the direction of the starboard-side helicopter providing cover. Later, nonmilitary 9 mm shell casings were found on the deck of the *Ibn Khaldoon*. Passengers and crew gathered on the flight deck to

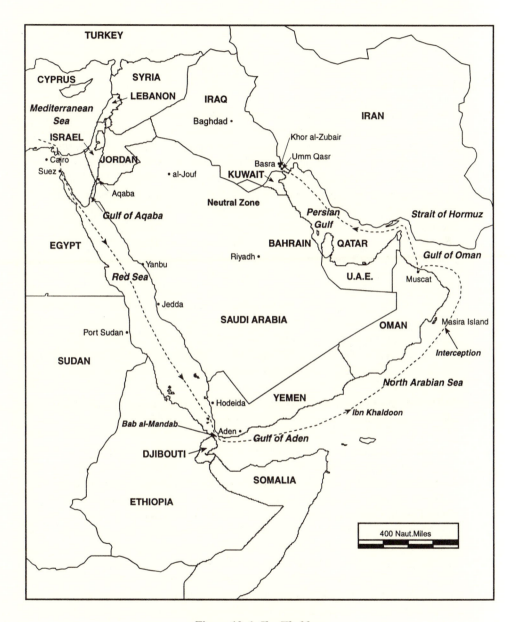

Figure 12–1. *Ibn Khaldoon*

prevent the insertion team from rappelling onto the after cargo deck, forcing the insertion forward past the deckhouse. The passengers seemed to know they would be intercepted; they held up banners obviously not made in the short time between the announcement of the vertical insertion and the execution. To complicate the interception further, after the insertion team rappelled onto the ship, passengers formed a human chain to deny access to the bridge. Some women grabbed at weapons when the boarding party tried to push through. They even knocked one man in the boarding party down.

The insertion team restored order by firing warning shots and throwing a smoke grenade and a flash grenade. Using crowd-control tactics, the team threw the grenades against a bulkhead, not in the direction of the passengers. Once the ship was secured, boarding parties arrived and began to search the *Ibn Khaldoon*. The boarding parties consisted of U.S. Navy personnel and USCG LEDet members from the destroyers USS *Oldendorf* (DD 972) and USS *Fife* (DD 991), as well as personnel from the *Sydney* and the British frigate *Brazen*. They found prohibited cargo and offered the master the choice of returning to his port of origin or to divert to an allowable port. The prohibited cargo included cooking oil, noodles, rice, sweetener, tea, sugar, milk, rock salt, flour, and grain. The cargo also included medical supplies, which were not prohibited.

The master accepted the fact that the cargo was prohibited and that once it was offloaded the ship would be allowed to proceed. The master opted not to return to his port of origin; rather, he chose to let the multinational force find a port for the cargo to be offloaded. Thus, diplomatic efforts began to find a port that would accept the *Ibn Khaldoon*. Because of its present location off Masira Island, the options were either the UAE or Oman. The government of Oman, in the *Tadmur* and *Zanoobia* diversions, had demonstrated its reluctance to accept diverted Iraqi ships.

The process dragged on, and time became a concern, because fresh water on the ship was limited. The problem of provisions, mostly fresh water, was not the only concern on the *Ibn Khaldoon*. After the scuffle on 26 December to secure the ship, the master had reported several passenger injuries, including two heart attacks and two miscarriages. A medical officer from the *Trenton* went aboard to examine the alleged injured. He found no evidence of heart attacks or miscarriages or any of the abuse claimed, but there were some passengers running low on prescribed medications. Arrangements were made for replenishments where possible. The medical officer concluded that none of the ill required medical evacuation. The master was briefed on the situation and concurred.

The *Ibn Khaldoon* steamed north and approached the Omani port of Mina Qaboos, just outside Muscat. This placed the Omani foreign minister under pressure to accept the ship. The Omanis recognized the lack of ports in the area to use as diversion points but did not want to set a precedent by which future diverted ships would be sent to Mina Qaboos. Nonetheless, on 4 January Mina Qaboos accepted the *Ibn Khaldoon*. While she was in port, observers saw small vehicles going to and from the ship. But when the U.S. ambassador inquired about what was being done to offload the cargo, he received a vague answer from the foreign minister, who said the ship would still be in port the next day and he would address that question then. During the night of 4 January, the *Ibn Khaldoon* left the port and anchored six miles off the coast, with the *Oldendorf* standing by. The ship's master stated he intended to remain anchored until he received word from the Iraqi government regarding the cargo.

On 9 January, cleared by the Omani government and with the agreement of the Iraqi government, the *Ibn Khaldoon* again entered Mina Qaboos to offload her cargo. The United States requested that an officer from the *Oldendorf* be present while the cargo was being unloaded, as this would obviate the need to reintercept the *Ibn Khaldoon* on its way to Iraq, but the *Oldendorf* was not given clearance to enter the port of Mina Qaboos. By 11 January, however, an agreement was reached that allowed a team of two Americans and three Omanis to inspect the *Ibn Khaldoon* before it sailed. The U.S. Coast Guard officer had to be transferred by helicopter from the *Oldendorf* to the *Trenton,* which was then coincidently in Mina Qaboos.

Later that same day, the inspectors found that some of the prohibited cargo had been removed but that a substantial amount still remained on board. The master stated that the cargo would be removed. Several hours later, the inspection team went through the ship a second time and found that three of the four holds still contained a large amount of prohibited cargo. The master promised that all prohibited cargo would be removed by 12 January; the officer in charge of the USCG LEDet boarded and inspected the *Ibn Khaldoon* on that date and found no prohibited cargo. When the *Ibn Khaldoon* set sail for Iraq she carried provisions for the passengers and crew, as well as the medical supplies. Before she sailed, the Americans warned the master about Iraqi mines in the Persian Gulf.

NOTES

Primary sources for the interceptions were the after-action and situation report messages. For the remainder of the chapter, sources included CNA's reconstruction report, messages, and an article by Tyler.

1. ComDesRon 24 092300Z NOV 90, After Action Report on Boarding of M.V. *Omduran.*

Chapter 13

Preparations for Amphibious Warfare

In this chapter, we describe the amphibious exercises and the evolution of planning that took place during the buildup to Desert Storm from early November 1990 through mid-January 1991. These preparations began with Vice Adm. Hank Mauz as ComUSNavCent and continued under the leadership of Vice Adm. Stan Arthur after he took over on 1 December. Because this and the next chapter discuss various topics of the buildup from early November through mid-January, the decision maker is sometimes Mauz, sometimes Arthur. Although this might cause some confusion, we deem it important to treat each issue in a coherent way over the whole period.

IMMINENT THUNDER

Late in October, Gen. Norman Schwarzkopf, USCinCCent, directed that Vice Admiral Mauz, ComUSNavCent, conduct an amphibious exercise, to be called "Imminent Thunder," from 15 to 21 November along the north Saudi coast. Giving so little notice for a major exercise was unusual. Furthermore, Schwarzkopf ordered that the landing take place near al-Mishab, Saudi Arabia, only about twenty miles south of the Kuwaiti border (see Figure 13–1).[1] This order caused great consternation on Mauz's staff. As Iraqi aircraft sometimes flew as far south as the border, the amphibious ships standing off the beach at al-Mishab filled with Marines would be within Exocet range. Iraqi aircraft could fly the same routes they had been flying, turn on their radars at the last minute, pick a target out of the crowd of ships, and fire a missile before U.S. forces could react. The Iraqi aircraft could then hope to duck into Kuwait to escape under the Iraqi air-defense umbrella. This potential tactic presented an impossible air-defense problem. In addition, ships would have difficulties approaching the beach, because of restricted areas, uncharted waters, and offshore oil wells. These constraints might

require ships to sail past al-Mishab and come in from the north, a track that would
bring them even closer to the Iraqi Exocet threat. Closely packed, thin-skinned
amphibious ships crammed with Marines would make a tempting target for a foe
that believed the American people would give up as soon as U.S. forces suffered
a few hundred casualties.

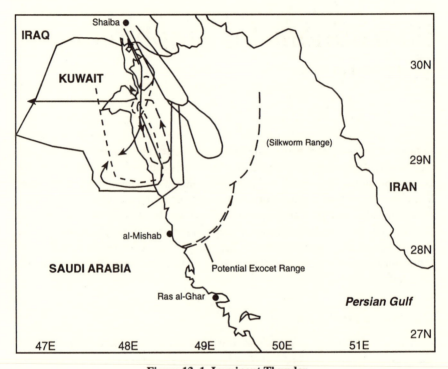

Figure 13–1. Imminent Thunder

Iraqi air tracks in and near Kuwait are shown

The initial USCinCCent plan did not include air support (strikes and close air
support). Mauz's staff added exercise air support at a hurried conference in Riyadh. Capt. Gordon Holder, ComUSNavCent's exercise officer and amphibious
expert, described the conference as getting done in one day things that normally
took nine months of planning.

The official objectives for Imminent Thunder were the usual generalities that
could apply to any exercise—training and interoperability. Another avowed purpose of the exercise was to "send a message" to Iraq by demonstrating that the

United States possessed both the capability and the will to bring amphibious ships into the Persian Gulf and land troops far up in the Gulf. This was fine, but why conduct an exercise under the guns of the enemy and allow an easy shot at ships loaded with Marines? The ComUSNavCent staff suspected hidden objectives. The author's notes for 7 November read: "Imminent Thunder: something is rotten."

The ComUSNavCent staff started speculating. For example, some thought Imminent Thunder might provide cover for a real attack. That is, when the Amphibious Task Force sailed north, it might be told to go farther north and land in Kuwait. Though farfetched, this might be the only way to achieve surprise when the newspapers seemed to print most of what was on yesterday's secret message board. But the idea of conducting a complex amphibious assault with only a few days' planning (from the time they were told it would be a real attack) was simply ludicrous. Some on the ComUSNavCent staff suspected that the USCinCCent staff simply had not carefully thought through the consequences of conducting the exercise landing near al-Mishab and did not realize the problem with stationing ships within missile-launch range of Iraqi aircraft. Others wondered whether perhaps someone wanted to provoke a "Gulf of Tonkin" incident. This notion seemed inconsistent, however, with measures being taken to be nonprovocative—like the restrictions on surveillance. Holder speculated that Imminent Thunder might be a cover for "something" occurring on the western part of the border at the same time. With the benefit of hindsight, we see that Holder was correct, though a bit off in the timing. Most likely, Schwarzkopf, having decided on the left hook in the desert as the centerpiece of his plan, wanted the Iraqis to concentrate on the amphibious threat to their eastern flank, so they would not improve their western defenses. Generals Colin Powell and Norman Schwarzkopf agreed on the left-hook strategy about 22 October; USCinCCent issued the warning order for Imminent Thunder on 28 October.

In a briefing to Schwarzkopf's staff, Mauz's staff said that Imminent Thunder was a good idea, but in view of air-defense problems (such as extremely short warning times) they recommended the exercise be moved forty miles farther south, to Ras al-Ghar (about 27°30' north latitude and sixty miles from the Kuwaiti border), as shown in Figure 13–1. Schwarzkopf's staff said it had another agenda. It would not say what, but in any case, that agenda evidently did not include starting the war in November. USCinCCent ordered Imminent Thunder moved to Ras al-Ghar.[2]

Imminent Thunder seemed designed to impress the news media. The exercise was not part of the Sea Soldier series and did not rehearse any particular landing plan. It was not even a full-scale exercise, one that landed everything the Amphibious Task Force would land in a real assault. The initiating directive for Imminent Thunder emphasized media aspects: "Extensive public affairs coverage . . . is planned. USCinCCent will control media coverage. Amphibious operations will receive priority coverage over other aspects of Exercise Imminent Thunder. . . . Media coverage . . . [is] essential to achieving USCinCCent's objectives."[3]

Thus, the exercise was widely publicized. Before it started, one newspaper reported that U.S. Marines would storm Saudi Arabian beaches less than thirty miles south of the Kuwaiti border in a mock amphibious landing and that the exercise would simulate a tactic likely to be used in any actual U.S. military offensive.[4] An article datelined Baghdad reported the Iraqi government had accused the United States of trying to provoke an attack by scheduling a Marine assault exercise near the border.[5]

Helicopters and LCACs were scheduled to land troops on 18 November in simultaneous assaults at Ras al-Ghar. The Amphibious Task Force would launch both assaults from over the horizon; that is, to enhance surprise, the ships would stay so far from shore that they could not be seen. Even if the enemy realized a landing was about to take place, he would not know where—it could be anywhere along perhaps fifty miles of coastline.

Near the shore the seas were relatively calm, but out at sea where the amphibious ships sailed, they were not. The Amphibious Task Force experienced twenty-five-knot winds and eight-foot waves. To test conditions, one LCAC was launched, under the most experienced craftmaster. Usually the air-cushioned landing craft can take higher seas than the older, displacement-hull LCU landing craft. But today, the LCAC had a lot of trouble, and the craftmaster judged conditions too bad to proceed. He strongly recommended against further LCAC operations. Because the seas were short and choppy, the LCAC would plow its bow into them and throw spray through its propellers, which risked damaging them. As he would not be able to replace the propellers easily or quickly, Rear Adm. Bat LaPlante wanted to preserve the equipment for the real thing. The LCAC landing was postponed and eventually canceled due to the high seas. Later LaPlante stated that if it had been wartime, he would have sent the LCACs in to the beach. Also, if he had known that the primary objective of the amphibious forces was deception, he would have insisted on sending the LCACs in during Imminent Thunder.

Other problems arose. The Amphibious Task Force requested additional, unscheduled CentAF sorties with which to practice procedures, but the flight crews did not have the handbook or the CentAF special instructions needed to carry out the mission effectively. Communications problems were minor in exercise conditions, but, LaPlante warned, they might have become major problems in a real-world assault. Using the same radio frequency for two purposes would not work in a war when the amount of communication traffic increased. Also, because hospital ships would have to stop using cryptographic systems when hostilities started (to comply with the Geneva Convention), it would be vital to have InMarSat (the commercial International Maritime Satellite telephone system, for talking with ships at sea) installed in his flagship.

On the positive side, LaPlante was pleased with the 190 close-air-support sorties flown and with the familiarity of most pilots with the proper procedures. He considered it the high point of the exercise to have seen eighteen aircraft from all components, plus the British and French, in the pre-assault beach preparations.

Landing Craft, Air Cushion (LCAC). The speed and range of the LCAC could allow an amphibious task force to achieve surprise by launching an assault from beyond the horizon, but during Imminent Thunder unusual seas prevented the LCACs from being used. Navy Photo.

LaPlante judged the air assault of six scheduled waves, twenty-two helicopters in the first wave, to have been textbook perfect. A total of 494 Marines and nineteen vehicles had been landed, all from more than twenty-five miles offshore. LaPlante recommended the next exercise include mine countermeasures, operational deception, and silent, predawn landings. Finally, he thought the greatest value of Imminent Thunder had been the exposure of the Amphibious Task Force to the joint and combined environment.

Iraqi aircraft did not threaten the amphibious ships during Imminent Thunder. They made only one overwater flight on 17 November and none on the 18th.

DESERT SABER

As described in chapter 10, in mid-October Vice Admiral Mauz directed the Amphibious Task Force to formulate plans for a landing at Ras al-Qulaya, Kuwait, which is about twenty miles north of the Saudi border. Although Mauz was skeptical that an assault on Ras al-Qulaya was a good idea, in late October he issued a letter of instruction that directed the Amphibious Task Force to prepare a feasibility statement, with a detailed time line, for such an assault. The objectives would be to interdict enemy lines of communication south of Kuwait City, fix enemy forces along the coast, and establish a beachhead or port area to sustain American forces in Kuwait. The operation was given the code name "Desert Saber."

Plans for Ras al-Qulaya Assault

In response to Mauz's letter of instruction, Rear Admiral LaPlante, commander of the Amphibious Task Force, and Maj. Gen. Harry Jenkins, commander of the Landing Force, reported that they believed a single MEB could conduct raids but was an insufficient force to conduct an assault. A single MEB could not capture and defend a beachhead for the thirty-six to seventy-two hours estimated to be required before they could link up with MarCent forces. After 8 November, however, LaPlante and Jenkins knew that 5th MEB would be joining them in mid-January. Therefore, they elected to plan the mission using both 4th and 5th MEBs.

The plan called for naval gunfire and air strikes to precede the landing. Six direct-support gunnery ships (one for each maneuvering element ashore) and two general-support gun ships (one for each ground combat element), including at least one battleship, would support the landing. Planners identified ninety-seven primary targets for air strikes. The landing would be on two beaches. An armor-heavy force would land north of Ras al-Qulaya and establish blocking positions to the north and west; heliborne troops would reinforce it. Simultaneously, a mechanized force would land farther south and attack to isolate and seize the naval facility and port of Ras al-Qulaya. Heliborne troops would reinforce this attack as well.

Concerns surrounding the assault at Ras al-Qulaya included: naval mining, shallow-water mining, chemical attack during the assault, beach obstacles, oil discharged from tankers and shore facilities to foul landing areas and create walls of fire, and the use of electric cables in the surf zone to electrocute troops coming ashore.

Sea Soldier III

Sea Soldier II, completed 8 November, had exercised some aspects of an early version of the Ras al-Qulaya plan. Sea Soldier III, conducted from 8 to 18 December off the coast of Oman, rehearsed a later version of the plan. It was not a full rehearsal, because not all the amphibious forces expected were in the theater (5th MEB would not arrive until mid-January), and because the Omanis once again imposed a four-thousand-man ceiling on the number of Marines ashore. The hydrography and coastal topography from the Ras al-Qulaya area were again superimposed on the exercise area, west of Ras Madraka. Despite minor navigation and timing difficulties, the first wave landed within two minutes of schedule. Rear Admiral LaPlante bragged that to his knowledge, this was the first time anyone had ever attempted a night, electronically silent MEB-size assault.

Desert Saber Moves to Ash Shuaybah

In early December, at MarCent's request, the actual intended landing site was shifted from Ras al-Qulaya to Ash Shuaybah, an industrial area about thirty miles north of the Saudi-Kuwaiti border and ten miles farther into Kuwait than Ras al-Qulaya (see Figure 13–2). The Marines wanted to land at Ash Shuaybah because that would allow better support logistics for MarCent forces; Vice Admiral Arthur agreed the landing would be there. The code name for the assault would remain Desert Saber. Planning would include options to induce the Iraqis to believe the assault might be directed against Bubiyan Island or the al-Faw area of Iraq. Ash Shuaybah was a better landing site than Ras al-Qulaya in that it lay farther behind Iraqi lines and had more favorable hydrography. But Ash Shuaybah was a built-up area, which is usually considered to be a poor place for an amphibious assault.

General Schwarzkopf had briefed his left-hook strategy to his component commanders on 14 November and again on 12 December. Thus, Arthur knew that at the theater-strategic level, the primary role of the amphibious force would be to deceive the Iraqis about the location of the main attack.[6] Schwarzkopf's theater-level strategy did not contain a preplanned amphibious assault, but about this time, a clandestine operation began with the aim of convincing Iraq that the coalition did plan to conduct an amphibious assault, into the area north of Kuwait Bay. Arthur was informed of the aim of this operation. Meanwhile, Gen. Al Gray had a team of Marines in Quantico, Virginia, wargaming various options. Gray's choice for a decisive role for the amphibious forces—the decisive strategic reserve, in his mind—was an assault on the Iraqi peninsula of al-Faw. In October, Gray had travelled to Saudi Arabia and told Lt. Gen. Walt Boomer, ComUSMarCent, about the al-Faw option.

However, an amphibious assault might be needed at a tactical level, to support MarCent forces. On 14 November, Schwarzkopf said he would allow Boomer to decide whether to use a landing as part of his attack into Kuwait.

About 20 December, Schwarzkopf and his component commanders briefed Secretary of Defense Dick Cheney and General Powell on their overall war plans in Riyadh. Arthur's briefing included the amphibious assault plans. Although he received no specific direction, Arthur concluded from the body language of and dialog among Schwarzkopf, Powell, and Cheney that there would be no amphibious landing as a "piece of the action," meaning as a preplanned assault. Arthur perceived that a landing would take place only if there was an emergency, that is, if Boomer got into trouble. Arthur believed, however, that there was a good chance Boomer would in fact encounter difficulties that might necessitate an amphibious landing.[7] Even if an assault was unlikely, military prudence required development of plans. These plans might also be useful for a deception; thus, planning continued.

After the change of landing site in early December, various commands rapidly developed plans for their portion of the operation. On 30–31 December, ComUS-NavCent held an Amphibious Planning Conference on the *Blue Ridge* in the port

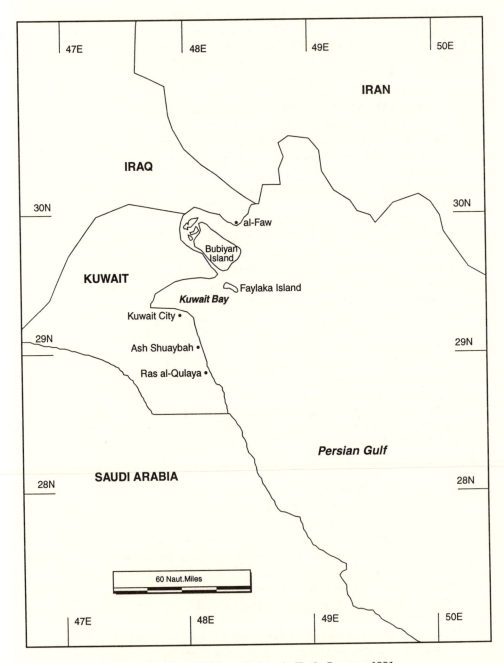

Figure 13–2. Amphibious Options in Early January 1991

of Dubai, UAE. Representatives, typically operations officers, from the Amphibious Task Force, the Landing Force, ComUSMarCent, and the Mine Countermeasures (MCM) Group attended. In the following, we summarize the state of the planning as of that time.

First, conference attendees were told they needed to understand how an amphibious operation would fit into Schwarzkopf's grand scheme. The main thrust of the ground attack would be the left hook by ArCent forces; MarCent's effort into Kuwait would be a supporting attack. An amphibious assault would be, at least in part, a diversion in support of MarCent's effort; amphibious raids or demonstrations might in turn provide diversions for the assault. The various layers of diversion would have to be coordinated so that, for example, the diversion for the amphibious landing did not fake the Iraqis into the ArCent or MarCent sectors. ComUSNavCent's objective for an assault was to tie down Iraqi forces in eastern Kuwait, support MarCent, establish a beach or port for supplying ground forces, and link up with MarCent forces.

In his opening remarks to the conference, Capt. Bunky Johnson, ComUSNavCent Operations Officer, knowing that many people thought the assault was a bad idea, said that the attendees should assume the landing would take place and that some risk from mines was acceptable. One of the objectives of the conference was to determine when the landing should occur relative to the air and ground attacks. Captain Holder added that it was now too late to keep looking at options.

The ComUSNavCent Intelligence Officer, Cdr. Wayne Perras, described the main threat as hundreds of little boats, patrol boats capable of firing antiship missiles, five tankers loaded with oil, and millions of barrels of oil in shore terminals. In addition, the ComUSNavCent staff had evidence of mining activity off Kuwait in November and December, but intelligence personnel thought they knew the approximate location of the mines.

A representative from ComUSMarCent explained Boomer's scheme of maneuver. His objective was to isolate, not take, Kuwait City. The MarCent assault would be a predawn attack and would take twenty-four hours to get at the second line of Iraqi defenses. The Marines would need naval gunfire support on their right flank, primarily to suppress Iraqi artillery. They expected to link up with the amphibious beachhead in about forty-eight to sixty hours.

The representative from 4th MEB, the Landing Force, described its mission as being to seize the port of Ash Shuaybah to allow follow-on forces and logistic sustainment, join in the attack to isolate Kuwait City, and be prepared to seize Kuwait International Airport. He said Iraq was vulnerable to deception, because it lacked the means to collect information and had no experience against a mobile foe.

Commander Joe Greene, USN, Rear Admiral LaPlante's Operations Officer, laid out three options for the amphibious force:

- Strategic: two brigades could tie down six Iraqi divisions by making feints.
- Tactical: two brigades could engage one or more divisions (the assault).
- Administrative: two brigades could reinforce MarCent through Saudi Arabia.

Greene stated that either the strategic or the administrative option was preferable to the assault. One of the problems with the assault was that mine-clearance operations would take a long time and could not even begin until the threat to the mine countermeasures forces had been reduced. This presented a timing problem: mine clearance would take twelve days for 60 to 70 percent clearance, but on the other hand, the timing of the assault was tied to the MarCent and ArCent attacks. He went through the times needed for clearing several types of mines in different areas. For naval gunfire support, he wanted seven direct-support ships, one for each maneuver element, plus two gunnery ships for general support of the landing. Greene concluded that the circumstances were very risky, not the way to do an amphibious operation.

Johnson now felt the meeting was turning into a whining session. Too many people were still in a peacetime mode. He felt he had to jolt the audience and make them realize that people were going to get killed. Therefore, he got up and interjected that the ComUSNavCent staff had gone through all the problems just mentioned; it had made that argument with USCinCCent—and lost. The assault was going to happen.

The MCM representative said the counter-mine force ships were not designed to search in mixed influence and magnetic minefields without a precursor sweep by AMCM (airborne mine countermeasures) MH-53 helicopters. He wanted an LPH (Landing Platform Helicopter, a large amphibious ship) dedicated for use by the MH-53s. He estimated the force needed eleven days to sweep the transit lane, the gunfire support areas, and the sea echelon area (where the amphibious ships would unload) to 60 percent clearance. This assumed ten hours per day (daylight only), a benign environment, a low sea state, and winds less than thirty knots. It also assumed the Iraqi mines were set to detonate the first time a ship passed over them.[8] If the Amphibious Task Force reduced the area to be cleared and British MCM forces also participated, the MCM forces would require six days for 60 percent clearance, thirteen days for 80 percent. He emphasized the vital importance of British participation in MCM, in part because British ships, due to their lower magnetic signature, did not require precursor sweeps as the American ships did.

Although there were problems (some of which we discuss below) and many people had reservations about the wisdom of an amphibious assault, planning would continue. Chapter 6 of Volume II describes the evolution of plans for an assault at Ash Shuaybah after 15 January 1991.

Faylaka Raid

Major General John J. "Jack" Sheehan, USMC, was MarCent Forward. He arrived on board the *Blue Ridge* with about a dozen other Marine officers a few days before the war started to provide liaison between ComUSMarCent and ComUSNavCent. On 14 January he briefed Vice Admiral Arthur on a proposed initiating directive for a raid on Faylaka Island (see Figure 13–2). This raid could be an alternative to an assault at Ash Shuaybah. The objectives of the proposed Faylaka raid were to return the island to Kuwaiti control, fix the enemy in northern Kuwait, and apply "psychological methods."[9] If executed, the raid would be launched after the start of the ground campaign. Faylaka is surrounded by one-meter-deep water extending one or two miles offshore. A five-meter channel exists, but it is too narrow to be useful. Intelligence indicated that a 2,500-man Iraqi brigade occupied the island. (In chapters 6 and 7 of Volume II, we will see how the plans for a raid on Faylaka Island developed over time.)

PROBLEM AREAS

Any amphibious landing faces many challenges. Three problem areas here merit elaboration.

Rivers of Fire

Saddam Hussein had publicly threatened "rivers of fire" and to set the Persian Gulf on fire. Intelligence described several ways in which Iraq might use petroleum to thwart an amphibious landing. Dangers included fire, toxic fumes, and clogged machinery, especially cooling systems. Marines thought this threat was not much of a problem at all; Navy operations people thought it was probably not a bad problem but were not certain. Intelligence personnel considered it potentially serious.

The ComUSNavCent operations analyst (the author of this book) did a simple calculation to determine how large an area the Iraqis could set on fire. Intelligence estimated that crude oil could not be set on fire unless it was relatively fresh (within less than three hours of being dumped) and at least three millimeters thick. The most severe threat would be if the five Iraqi tankers, aggregate 653,000 dwt, simultaneously dumped their entire load by blowing holes in their own sides. In the worst case, this could cover an area of about seventy square nautical miles—a circle of radius slightly less than five nautical miles—to a depth of three millimeters. Vice Admiral Mauz's reaction was that this was a much smaller area than he had been led to believe, one that could be easily avoided and was not a serious problem.

Harrier Carriers

During the evening discussions at the amphibious conference at the end of December, the Marines said they wanted the twenty AV-8 Harrier jump-jets on the *Nassau* and the six more on the *Tarawa* kept there, so those two ships could serve as "Harrier carriers" to provide dedicated close air support. Vice Admiral Arthur did not like this. He believed the Persian Gulf aircraft carriers could and would provide sufficient close air support when the ground campaign began and that

Harriers would be better employed from ashore bases, in accordance with doctrine. The Marines said shore air bases had no room for the Harriers; ComUSNavCent staff officers countered that the Harriers were designed to operate from rough, "expeditionary" airfields. Marines also complained that ComUSNavCent was not supplying ordnance for Harriers. The ComUSNavCent Logistics Officer, Capt. Ross Hendricks, explained that because the ships were not designed for twenty Harriers, they did not have large enough magazines for more than two or three days' worth of bombs.

In early January, Arthur proposed that the six Harriers on the *Tarawa* be offloaded at Sheikh Isa air base in Bahrain as soon as the ship arrived in the theater, in mid-January. Off-loading the Harriers from the *Tarawa* at that time would alleviate the problem of identifying a dedicated helicopter carrier for the MCM helicopters. The Harriers on the *Nassau* could remain there until the completion of any amphibious assault; then they would be phased ashore. Arthur promised to provide ten days' supply of ammunition for the Harriers to support the assault.

Lt. General Boomer, ComUSMarCent, concurred with offloading the Harriers from the *Tarawa* but wanted them to go to the King Abdul Aziz naval base (just south of al-Jubail in Saudi Arabia), not Sheikh Isa air base in Bahrain. Also, he was adamant that no forward basing site could accommodate the twenty Harriers on the *Nassau*, not even after the landing, unless the coalition liberated a suitable one. He gave several specific arguments for the advantages of keeping the Harriers on a ship: excellent maintenance support for the aircraft, and air support for a second operation if the Marines had to "backload" after an assault. Boomer's general argument was that the flexibility provided by a forward base that could easily move and be virtually always on the enemy's flank would be a force multiplier.

Mines

Two mine problems were high on NavCent's worry list at this time: minefields in the Persian Gulf off Kuwait, and drifting mines in the area of the Persian Gulf in which NavCent ships were steaming. On 21 November ComUSNavCent Intelligence reported evidence of mining activity off Ras al-Qulaya in southern Kuwait, perhaps since 7 November. A potential Iraqi minelayer had made at least four or five short trips. On 13 December, Intelligence personnel concluded there was a 90 percent likelihood that Iraq had laid mines during the previous four weeks. As of 17 December, they believed Iraq had laid 80 to 180 moored and bottom mines in the water; by the end of the year, they estimated there were 180 to 250 moored and bottom mines in the Persian Gulf. They thought, however, they knew the general location of the mines. By the time Desert Storm began, ComUSNavCent Intelligence believed that Iraq planned to lay two semicircles of mines off the coast of Kuwait. Iraq had completed the inner circle in December; the outer circle was nearing completion.

USS *Nassau*. This amphibious assault ship served as command ship of the Amphibious
Task Force and as a "Harrier carrier" for the AV-8 Harrier jump jets. Navy Photo.

USCinCCent rules of engagement required catching Iraqi minelayers in the act,
even though USCinCCent did not allow surveillance in the areas where Iraqis
were laying the mines. General Schwarzkopf rejected every request by ComUS-
NavCent to allow surveillance assets farther north—even remotely piloted vehicles (RPVs) were not allowed north.[10] It was the ComUSNavCent staff's
perception in mid-November that Iraq was not anxious to start a war and would
not have done so if NavCent forces attacked one of its minelayers. In retrospect,
because the coalition allowed Iraq to mine the Persian Gulf without opposition,
Iraq's perception of the United States as a "paper tiger" may have been reinforced.
Of course, the minefields greatly increased the risk in any amphibious operations
in the northern Persian Gulf.

On 21 December, the first drifting mine was found. One possibility was that it
had broken loose from an old minefield dating from the Iran-Iraq War; such a mine
should have had a lot of biological growth on it from the warm waters, and the
shackle holding it to the chain should have shown signs of wear. Reports indicated
this mine had no growth. The ComUSNavCent mine expert, Commander Pete
Burdett, USN, judged that the mine had been in the water less than a week.

Reports also indicated that it was a mine of a type manufactured indigenously by the Iraqis and previously unknown to the NavCent forces.

On 26 December, a second floating mine was found. Initial reports were that this one had some growth on it, indicating it had been in the water for some time and thus might have been left over from the Iran-Iraq War. Later, however, when pictures arrived, the ComUSNavCent staff judged the mine to be quite clean and fairly recent.

The third and fourth floating mines were found on 30 December. The pace picked up in the new year; by the end of 1 January, a total of six floating mines had been reported. The Saudis found number seven in the eastern half of the Persian Gulf, lending credibility to reports that the Iranians also might have found several mines. When a floating mine was found, the typical procedure was to put an explosive ordnance disposal or SEAL swimmer in the water to attach a time-delay explosive. After the swimmer got out of the water, the charge exploded the mine. Usually, the mine was exploded immediately rather than captured, towed ashore, and studied, because it was too dangerous to let it drift overnight. Of the first seven reported mines, three were exploded, two could not be located (perhaps these were duplicate or spurious reports), and two were towed ashore and studied.

By 13 January, the drifting-mine count reached twenty. The staff did not believe all twenty reports were valid. Only after there had been a dozen reports had the staff realized that it needed to systematize collecting the data (where, when, type, amount of growth), carefully eliminate duplicate reports, and assign a number to each. The ComUSNavCent staff believed some drifting mines were moored mines that had broken loose due to poor Iraqi adaptation of a Soviet design. Some drifting mines had no evidence of wear on the shackle, however, and ComUSNavCent Intelligence concluded that they had never been moored. Evidently Iraq had deliberately set them adrift where they would enter international waters—an act of war. Much later, Iraqi prisoners of war confirmed this conclusion.

The ComUSNavCent staff made numerous efforts to determine the location of the minefields. For example, in early January intelligence indicated that an Iraqi minelayer was loaded with about three dozen naval mines, suggesting minelaying was imminent. Therefore, Vice Admiral Arthur directed that a P-3 maritime patrol aircraft conduct radar searches as soon as the potential minelaying ship was reported absent from port. "Expeditious determination of location of [minelayer] and associated minelaying [operations] is considered essential to counter mine effort [in support of] fleet defense and *is currently top NavCent [intelligence] collection priority*" (emphasis added).[11] In addition, the battleship *Missouri* was directed to move to 27°40' north latitude. If the P-3s or other sources detected movement of a minelayer they would notify the *Missouri*, which would reposition as necessary to conduct RPV operations to observe areas farther north. Her mission would be to survey the suspected areas for Iraqi minelaying activity and to gather intelligence as feasible to determine the nature of the activity. (Chapter 15 describes the results of this effort.)

By not allowing aggressive surveillance in the international waters of the northern Persian Gulf, USCinCCent made it virtually impossible to catch Iraq in the act of minelaying or to determine where Iraq laid the mines. By this decision USCinCCent may have effectively precluded an amphibious landing, without realizing it. Of course, there is a counterargument: if NavCent forces caught an Iraqi minelayer in the act and sank it, that might precipitate a war (though, as the ComUSNavCent staff argued, a similar incident—when the United States sank the *Iran Ajr* just a few years previously—had not started one). Even if patrolling ships and aircraft did not detect an Iraqi minelayer, the act of patrolling the international waters of the northern Persian Gulf risked an incident with Iraqi ships and aircraft patrolling the same areas. (Again, since numerous shooting incidents in the past had not precipitated wars—for example, shooting down Libyan aircraft—the ComUSNavCent staff thought this was an acceptable risk. Furthermore, allowing Iraq to lay mines unmolested ran the risk of Iraq thinking the coalition was not serious about military action—thus *increasing* the risk of war.) Assuming General Schwarzkopf knew of the implications of allowing Iraq to lay mines without opposition, he might still have felt the advantage of not starting a fight until all coalition forces were ready was too great an advantage to risk.

If Schwarzkopf would not allow NavCent to prevent or observe the minelaying, perhaps the Iraqis would "tell" ComUSNavCent the location of their minefields. In mid-January, after the "peace ship" *Ibn Khaldoon* unloaded prohibited materials, the coalition allowed her to leave Oman and proceed to Basra. As she approached Iraq, ComUSNavCent watched her track as closely as possible, expecting that the Iraqis would direct the *Ibn Khaldoon* to go around any minefields. The plan was to use all possible means, including super-secret methods, to track the *Ibn Khaldoon*. ComUSNavCent Intelligence thought it gained valuable information from this effort.

MEDICAL

By deploying two hospital ships and a fleet hospital, the Navy had provided much of the initial medical capability in the theater. By mid-November its 1,500 beds were more than half of the beds available in-theater. The Navy is responsible for supplying not only its own medical needs but also those of the Marine Corps ashore. The additional forces ordered in early November included increasing the capacity of the hospital ships and deploying two more fleet hospitals. Fleet Hospital 6 deployed to Bahrain from storage in Japan. Fleet Hospital 15, previously stored in Norway, deployed to al-Jubail, Saudi Arabia. Each provided an additional five hundred beds when it achieved full capability in mid-February, prior to the ground war. Also, the two hospital ships *Comfort* and *Mercy* were fully staffed, to increase their capacity from five hundred beds to a thousand beds each. These

Navy assets provided a total of 3,500 beds. In addition, the Amphibious Task Force had 1,332 beds for receiving and treating casualties.

Evidently, during the turnover of ComUSNavCent commanders no one told Vice Admiral Arthur that Captain Cook, USN, physically located at the Naval Logistics Support Force post ashore in Bahrain, was the ComUSNavCent Surgeon. Naturally, the admiral assumed that Captain Ken Andrus, USN, the Seventh Fleet Surgeon, who was present on the flagship and attended the daily briefings, was also the ComUSNavCent surgeon, and he dealt with him accordingly. He regarded Cook as being in charge of only shore medical facilities. Everyone else (including the ComUSNavCent Chief of Staff, Andrus, and Cook) understood that Cook was the NavCent Surgeon. As far as is known, this error caused no problems.

OPERATION EASTERN EXIT

Though there had been a period of growing unrest in Somalia, the first warning message to military forces was received by the ComUSNavCent staff on 1 January. Although there was no tasking yet, Vice Admiral Arthur wrote a note to his Operations Officer on the message: "Better have the Amphib crowd take a look at a helo NEO [Noncombatant Evacuation Operation] of Mogadishu!"[12] Arthur's direction never made it to Rear Admiral LaPlante, however. Thus, despite Arthur's foresight, when General Schwarzkopf's orders arrived on 2 January, it caught the Amphibious Task Force by surprise.[13]

Arthur sent two amphibious ships, the *Guam* and *Trenton*, carrying Marines, SEALs, and helicopters, to the area. When the situation deteriorated rapidly, they launched two CH-53E helicopters with a combined SEAL and Marine team in the middle of the night for a flight of more than 450 miles to Mogadishu. After two night aerial refuelings (with fuel spilled over the occupants of one helo) the CH-53Es arrived at the city, spent twenty minutes searching for the embassy due to outdated and inaccurate information on its location, and landed in the embassy compound, even as looters were at the walls. Despite intermittent harassing fire, the team secured the compound and held their own fire. After many other adventures, described in detail by Adam Siegel in a forthcoming book, the team conducted the final evacuation in the middle of the same night via ten CH-46s from the *Guam*, which had steamed closer to the coast.[14] The team evacuated 281 people from over thirty nations, including twelve heads of diplomatic missions, from amidst a bloody civil war.

One of Arthur's concerns was that any amphibious ships sent to Somalia might be lost to the Amphibious Task Force for an extended period, with no guarantee of when they could return. After considerable negotiation, the two amphibious ships were directed to take the evacuees to Oman, which allowed the ships to return to the Amphibious Task Force before the 15 January UN deadline.

NOTES

Primary sources for information in this chapter were messages and interviews with Arthur, Holder, LaPlante, Johnson, Manthorpe, Barnett, Gray, Boomer, and Powell. Books by Powell, Schwarzkopf, and Woodward were sources of additional information. We also used CNA reconstruction reports and articles by Healy and Sisler. The description of the Amphibious Planning Conference came from the author's notes, an interview with Johnson, and briefing slides. Information on "rivers of fire" came from the author's notes and an internal memorandum he wrote in December 1990. Siegel's report was the primary source for Eastern Exit.

1. The Kuwaiti border is at 28°32' north latitude; the geographic cape Ras al-Mishab is at 28°10' north latitude; the town of al-Mishab is at 28°05' north latitude.

2. Capt. Gordon Holder and Capt. Joe Greene, the Amphibious Task Force operations officer, went to Brigadier General Richard "Butch" Neal, USMC, the deputy operations officer at USCinCCent, and said they could not make the landing at al-Mishab. Neal asked where they could; Greene and Holder looked at a chart and picked a site in five minutes— Ras al-Ghar. Neal agreed to the site. Interview with Rear Adm. Gordon Holder, 22 April 1996. Afterwards, Rear Adm. Bat LaPlante was told that Imminent Thunder was initially designed to provide cover for an operation involving special operations forces going in and relieving the American embassy in Kuwait. After the Kuwaiti resistance provided supplies, this operation became unnecessary. In 1990, LaPlante did not know about the plan to relieve the American embassy. Some people at ComUSNavCent did know about the special operations plan at the time.

3. CTF 150 111154Z NOV 90, Initiating Directive for Exercise Imminent Thunder.

4. Melissa Healy, "Marines to Hold Mock Raid on Saudi Beaches," *Los Angeles Times,* 14 November 1990.

5. Peter F. Sisler, "Iraq Says U.S. Is Trying to Provoke Attack," *Washington Times,* 15 November 1990.

6. Vice Admiral Mauz, not Vice Admiral Arthur, attended the 14 November briefing, of course, but almost certainly both Mauz and Schwarzkopf told Arthur about it when he arrived in-theater at the end of November.

7. Arthur was not certain of the date of this meeting but recalled it as after his initial trip to Riyadh. The 19–20 December briefings are the only ones that seem to fit. Woodward, *The Commanders,* 333–37, states Schwarzkopf's briefing said the amphibious forces would be only a feint. We believe Arthur's account is more reliable.

8. Some mines can be set with "ship counters," which cause them not to explode the first time a ship passes over them but on a subsequent pass. For example, if the ship counter is set at five, the first four ships pass over that mine safely and the fifth ship detonates it. When ship counts are used, to pass a device that simulates a ship's acoustic or magnetic signature over the minefield will not detonate all the mines. This ploy greatly complicates mine countermeasures operations.

9. The author did not then and does not now understand how raiding Faylaka would send a useful message to the Iraqi leadership, or what that message would be.

10. Evidently, these requests were verbal. We have not located any hard-copy messages containing ComUSNavCent requests to change the policy.

11. ComUSNavCent 072028Z JAN 91.

12. Siegel, *Eastern Exit,* 8.

13. Gen. Colin Powell said the Marines were chosen rather than the Army's 82nd Airborne Division (on alert in case the Marines could not get there in time) because the Marines could come out the same way they went in, whereas the 82nd would have to have aircraft sent to take them out.

14. Adam B. Siegel, *An American Entebbe: The Non-Combatant Evacuation Operation from Mogadishu, Somalia, January 1991,* forthcoming.

Chapter 14

Preparations for Air Warfare

As the prospects for war increased, several issues in air warfare needed to be resolved. Dealing with these issues frequently caused friction between Navy and Air Force personnel. They disagreed about what constituted realistic strike rehearsals and how to organize combat search and rescue (of the many air crews expected to be shot down). Relations with JFACC reached a low in a dispute over the issue of the rules of engagement—especially those pertaining to missile shots "beyond visual range." In air defense, the challenge came from the complexity of combining the different data links, procedures, and philosophies of the Navy and Air Force.

STRIKE REHEARSALS

During the period leading up to the 15 January deadline, NavCent forces participated in a series of strike rehearsals. A common denominator had been NavCent complaints about coordinating with CentAF tankers. Thus, ComUSNavCent, both Vice Adm. Hank Mauz and then Vice Adm. Stan Arthur after 1 December, continued to push for more comprehensive rehearsals to test all aspects of the strike plans. Although the rehearsals were not as comprehensive as ComUSNavCent wanted, their pace increased. As both CentAF and NavCent learned each other's problems, terminology, and procedures, many of the minor glitches went away, and complaints about tanker problems declined.

Imminent Thunder

In conjunction with Imminent Thunder, three "mirror-image" strike rehearsals by the *Midway* air wing were planned for the night of 15–16 November. For each strike the ship and air wing practiced putting all the bombs and missiles together and loading them on the aircraft. They encountered no significant problems. To duplicate the drag on the aircraft, they carried all the bombs and fuel tanks that would be carried on the actual mission. The flights validated all fuel-consumption estimates, with no surprises. Because they could not get clearance to use the altitude they planned to use to fly to the target, however, the route did not totally replicate the mission.

One strike went well; two did not, because of tanker problems. In the first strike, the *Midway*'s air wing understood the Air Tasking Order (ATO) as directing the CentAF tanker to accompany the strike part of the way to the target, but the tanker pilot refused to do so, insisting he was to provide fuel at only one location and not again on the way to a target. This made it impossible for the *Midway*'s aircraft to complete their mission. Rear Adm. Connie Lautenbacher, NavCent-Riyadh, thought this was a simple case of a tanker element leader failing to read his portion of the special instructions. He was convinced that it represented an isolated case, with little chance of recurrence.

JFACC scheduled the third strike to refuel twice, once before the new day (Zulu time) and once after. JFACC's procedures dictated that this strike be scheduled on the ATO for 16 November, even though it started on 15 November, because it had a "time over target" after the start of the new day. The tanker crew missed the mission, because they thought the event was for the next night. About seven hours before the first tanking time NavCent-Riyadh discovered that the tankers did not intend to cover the event and called CentAF, but it was told that no CentAF crews were available for the tanker. Worse, NavCent-Riyadh had anticipated the possibility of a date mistake and discussed it with the JFACC staff when the events had been scheduled; the JFACC staff had given them vigorous assurance that the date would be accounted for correctly. Lautenbacher reported many red faces in the JFACC ATO cell and no shortage of command attention. He was confident that Lt. Gen. Chuck Horner, the JFACC, had made this so big an issue with his people that if Vice Admiral Mauz weighed in, it might be counterproductive. Mauz wrote a note to his staff on Lautenbacher's message to allow him to "work the problem" without further intervention.

These events tended to confirm the ComUSNavCent staff's concern that an unwieldy, centralized ATO, combined with human frailties, might be a disaster waiting to happen.

Free Lunch

The *Midway* air wing participated in another series of mirror-image strike rehearsals, "Free Lunch," on 28 to 30 November. Once again, most complaints concerned tanking. On two of the four strikes fewer CentAF tankers showed up than the *Midway* air wing expected. In one case, this slowed the tanking; as a result, four aircraft that were to have fired antiradiation missiles and decoys missed their ordnance-launch times. As these defense-suppression weapons must be closely coordinated with other strike aircraft, delays can result in aircraft being shot down in a real strike. For three strikes the tankers were not on station at the time and location expected by the *Midway* air wing, potentially causing delays in the time over the target; in a real strike, setting back the time over target would not have been possible, and the entire strike would have had to be cancelled. The *Midway* air wing concluded, however, that they had demonstrated they could load, launch, tank, and execute the ATO strikes with no major air wing–level difficulties.

In view of the problems during Free Lunch, the ComUSNavCent staff was incensed by a ComUSCentAF message saying that everyone needed to practice together. The ComUSNavCent staff claimed that ComUSCentAF had been the one refusing to participate in practice strikes and that ComUSNavCent had been the leader in trying to hold them. For example, back on 24 November, Vice Admiral Mauz had asked why everyone who had to be over the target could not get together to practice; the CentAF liaison officer on the *Blue Ridge* had said he thought that ComUSCentAF believed that type of practice was not needed, since everything was all planned out.

Three-Carrier Mirror-Image Strike Rehearsals

In view of the upcoming force deployments, Vice Admiral Mauz accelerated the *Saratoga-Kennedy* turnover in the Red Sea by two weeks. He wanted to allow an earlier start in preparing the air wings for strike operations, and he scheduled a dual-carrier strike rehearsal for 5 to 7 December. In addition, the *Midway* air wing would conduct similar exercises at the same time; thus it was in effect a three-carrier strike rehearsal, though the *Midway* did not have the same targets as the two Red Sea carriers.

The *Midway*'s air wing reported more tanker problems, though they seemed less severe than on the previous evolution. For two of four strikes the CentAF tankers were not at the position expected by the *Midway* air wing. Also, the air wing complained that it had not received the ATO before launch in two cases, and that there had been abrupt heading and altitude changes by the tankers. Overall, however, the air wing evaluated the exercise as the smoothest to date.

The Red Sea carriers had a similar experience. In one case the tankers were more than twenty miles from the position expected by the NavCent aircraft. Despite minor glitches, however, the overall evaluation of Rear Adm. Riley Mixson, commander of the Red Sea Battle Force, was that strike practice execution had been the best to date.

About a month later, when the carrier *Saratoga* rejoined the carrier *Kennedy* in the Red Sea, they again conducted dual-carrier strike rehearsals, with three large strikes over a twenty-nine-hour period on 8–9 January 1991. In some respects, a series of tanker problems made this rehearsal seem like a step backwards. Nevertheless, Mixson thought the exercise had provided excellent training.

COMBAT SEARCH AND RESCUE

Gen. Norman Schwarzkopf designated Lt. Gen. Chuck Horner, ComUSCentAF, as the combat search and rescue coordinator, directing him to establish a Joint Rescue Coordination Center to coordinate all combat search and rescue operations. In addition, each component would conduct combat search and rescue in support of its own operations—just as joint doctrine specified. Therefore, ComUSNavCent established the NavCent Rescue Coordination Center aboard the *Blue Ridge* and designated two regional coordinators: ComMidEastFor in the Persian Gulf, and the commander of the battle force in the Red Sea. ComUSNavCent had three concerns: the time needed to coordinate a rescue, a policy of not dispatching rescuers until the downed aircrew had been located and authenticated, and the status of combat search and rescue as only a secondary mission for SOCCent.

Based on the plan, it might take a long time to get rescue assets to a downed airman. For example, if a NavCent aircraft went down over land, the wingman would radio the airborne controller, who in turn would radio the carrier. The carrier would call the regional coordinator, who then had to call the NavCent Rescue Coordination Center on the *Blue Ridge*. The NavCent Rescue Coordination Center would call the Joint Rescue Coordination Center in Riyadh. Then the Joint Rescue Coordination Center would attempt to coordinate a rescue. The primary source of rescue assets would be SOCCent; it was the best prepared and equipped command for the mission. Because the Joint Rescue Coordination Center passed most cases to SOCCent, eventually the NavCent Rescue Coordination Center encouraged its two regional coordinators to contact SOCCent directly at the first report of a downed aircraft and report up through the formal chain later. SOCCent had limited communications, however, which caused a problem: sometimes its few communications lines were saturated when more commands than just the Joint Rescue Coordination Center began calling.

Use of SOCCent assets involved other constraints. SOCCent had several primary missions, and combat search and rescue for other services was only a secondary one. Also, SOCCent generally refused to dispatch assets for a rescue until the survivor had been located and authenticated—they would not do the search part of combat search and rescue. The ComUSNavCent Chief of Staff, Capt. Bernie Smith, believed that a lesson wrongly learned from Vietnam was that one needed to be sure a downed aviator was alive and know his position before sending in a combat search and rescue helicopter. Smith thought the decision to move in a combat search and rescue helicopter should be based on the assessment of the on-scene commander. He felt strongly that time was critical, because the chances for a successful rescue were greatest in the first few hours after an aircraft went down.

Vice Admiral Mauz was unhappy with the combat search and rescue arrangement. He did not know, for example, how many rescue helicopters SOCCent possessed. Mauz went to see the colonel in charge of combat search and rescue at

SOCCent and asked questions. He considered the answers "soft." When he asked what assets SOCCent had for rescues, he was told that it would use whatever assets were available at the time, but that it did not have any dedicated for that purpose. Mauz asked to see the command center from which rescues would be coordinated. The "command center" was the colonel's desk. Mauz was concerned that SOCCent hedged "promises" of assets and other support as being subject to other missions; he regarded that as unsatisfactory. As a result he hit hard about getting Navy HH-60 rescue helicopters, because they would have only one mission—combat search and rescue. Mauz later recalled that Horner objected to bringing the HH-60s in-theater because of the lack of ramp space; eventually, Mauz did manage to do it.

In late November, Mauz proposed to ComSOCCent that he assume responsibility for all overwater combat search and rescue—not just for NavCent's aircrews but for those of all services—thereby allowing SOCCent forces to focus on the near-land and overland missions for which its assets were better suited. Eventually, this proposal was adopted.

When hostilities were imminent, naval rescue assets in the Persian Gulf would be consolidated in Surface Action Group Alfa, which would include two frigates with SH-60 helicopters and Army OH-58D helicopters embarked, one destroyer with two SH-3 helicopters, a Kuwaiti self-propelled barge, and SEALs. (Chapters 4 and 5 of Volume II describe the adventures of SAG Alfa during Desert Storm.)

JFACC AND STRIKE PLANNING

A variety of problems plagued relations between NavCent forces and JFACC. Three core problems were: compartmented planning, lack of trust in and understanding of the ATO process, and the absence of interactive access to the ATO system. We also discuss two problems we consider to be symptoms of the difficulties between NavCent forces and the JFACC staff.

Restricted access to sensitive war plans and limited communications led to a lack of understanding. Late in Desert Shield, people worked on two types of ATOs. Everyone saw the ATO that covered the daily training and defensive sorties; very few people saw the highly classified offensive strike ATO that a dedicated staff in the "Black Hole" had worked and reworked for months. It covered the first three days of Desert Storm. The highly restricted access to this plan, combined with limited direct communications between ashore and afloat planners, meant that most members of the afloat staffs did not understand what the Black Hole planners were trying to do. Lack of communications and understanding was not restricted to Black Hole planning, however.

As the 15 January deadline approached, the ComUSNavCent staff was concerned that not all the air power scheduled to come into the theater would be applied effectively, in a joint manner. They felt that the ATO was too detailed—a funnel going into a very narrow pipe at JFACC—and would have to be decentralized, perhaps by a geographic division. Attendees at ComUSNavCent's 8 January Operations Officer Conference were told that the ATO process would probably fall apart on the third day, and if that happened they should be prepared to go back to the tried-and-true method of dividing up the area. Someone suggested the ATO could be simplified by not scheduling every single tanking evolution, instead just telling NavCent forces where tanker orbits would be and how much fuel would be there and letting its air wings schedule accordingly. The ComUSNavCent staff conceded, however, that the ATO was good enough for the first few days, which could be planned in detail, and perhaps was also needed for deep-strike targets.

Because of the size of the ATO, the ComUSNavCent staff continued to try to find a better way to get it distributed to all players in a timely manner. Vice Admiral Mauz had wanted to explore getting the Air Force's Computer-Assisted Force Management System (CAFMS) on board the carriers. Doing so required a particular type of satellite link; the staff told Mauz it could not be done. When Vice Adm. Stan Arthur arrived he did not accept that answer, and he pushed the issue hard for several weeks. He made the point that getting CAFMS would allow NavCent forces access to the interactive system that built the ATO. It turned out that putting an SHF link (super-high-frequency satellite circuit) on the carriers would require placing a van on them. This involved giving up flight-deck or hangar space, which was a problem, but Arthur believed that it could be solved and was not a limiting factor. In the end, the real problem was satellite access. On land, CentAF could use satellites for one part of the link and land lines for the other part, but NavCent forces at sea would have to do it all by satellite. They needed more satellite channels than were allocated to NavCent. In the end, Arthur too had to give up.

One measure that often prevents misunderstandings is an exchange of liaison officers. At this time, ComUSNavCent had more than fifty people at NavCent-Riyadh performing liaison, mostly with the JFACC staff. Early in Desert Shield, Colonel Stu Mosby, USAF, was ComUSCentAF's liaison officer with ComUS-NavCent. Later, Colonel Brian Wages, USAF, relieved Mosby. They were given access to essentially all ComUSNavCent meetings and had done much to reduce misunderstandings in both directions. Perhaps CentAF liaison officers at the battle force level would also help.

In December, Rear Admiral Mixson, the prospective commander of the three-carrier battle force in the Red Sea, asked Lt. General Horner in person and then by message to send him two Air Force liaison officers—one for AWACS, one for tanking—to join his strike planning cell on the *Kennedy*. This seemed like a good effort to cooperate and be joint. The ComUSCentAF reply lauded Mixson's idea but stated that the planning and coordination could best be done if instead he sent liaison officers to Riyadh. From the NavCent point of view, an attempt to improve communications and understanding with JFACC had been rebuffed; from the JFACC point of view, NavCent had failed to understand how planning would be done. This incident illustrates a contrast between the Air Force and Navy planning methods; the Navy emphasized detailed planning on the ship, close to the opera-tors; the Air Force emphasized centralized planning. The Desert Storm air cam-paign would be done the Air Force way.

NavCent forces periodically complained that the JFACC staff failed to take their requirements into account. For example, JFACC had devised quick-reaction strike plans for retaliation if Iraq launched a preemptive attack against coalition forces. Vice Admiral Mauz noticed that the targets did not include Iraqi ships or aircraft that threatened naval forces. Mauz's most direct concern was a raid of Mirage F-1 aircraft equipped for strikes against naval targets. If Iraq launched such an attack, Mauz wanted to be able to go after its source. Therefore, in November Mauz directed his carrier strike planners to prepare plans, for adoption by JFACC, for striking the F-1 airfields and naval bases involved within a few hours. The battle groups proposed suitable packages.

RULES OF ENGAGEMENT

Few things upset Vice Admiral Arthur as much as the ComUSCentAF rules of engagement (ROE). He had two objections: he believed that USCinCCent rather than ComUSCentAF should promulgate the ROE, and he did not like the rules about firing air-to-air missiles beyond visual range (BVR). Although these two disputes occurred simultaneously, we will discuss them separately for clarity. We examine both at length, because they illustrate how the ComUSNavCent staff felt that General Schwarzkopf had elevated Lt. General Horner above the other com-ponent commanders and that the ComUSCentAF staff was abusing its privileged position and preventing NavCent forces from contributing fully to what should have been a joint effort.

ComUSCentAF ROE

ComUSCentAF first provided a draft of the ComUSCentAF Wartime ROE to Vice Admiral Mauz on 17 October and requested comments. Mauz's response noted that the draft ROE applied only to U.S. aircraft not operating in support of seaborne forces. He recommended that to enhance interoperability joint ROE be proposed for all air and surface-to-air capable forces, but that USCinCCent should promulgate them. ComUSCentAF's "final coordination" version was labeled "ComUSCentAF Wartime Rules of Engagement." The reply by Vice Admiral Arthur (now ComUSNavCent) repeated the recommendation that USCinCCent rather than ComUSCentAF promulgate the ROE. Arthur argued that the range of issues addressed, the scope and magnitude of their application, and the pivotal importance of these ROE warranted USCinCCent promulgation. In particular, the ROE contained rules governing sea-based surface-to-air platforms and sea-based command-and-control platforms. ComUSCentAF ushered in the new year with a revision titled "Joint Force Air Component Commander (ComUSCentAF) Wartime Rules of Engagement: Desert Shield." Most references in the text to ComUSCentAF had been changed to JFACC—with at least one notable exception that concerned minelaying.

The ROE governing attacks against Iraqi minelayers represented a symptom of the problem of having ComUSCentAF promulgate the rules. Unless the tactical situation precluded doing so, a NavCent aircraft that encountered minelaying in international waters had to ask *ComUSCentAF* for permission before attacking the ship. Arthur and his staff understandably regarded this as absurd. Several unsuccessful attempts to get Lt. General Horner to make changes in the definition emphasized the fact that Horner's staff knew little about minelaying and the international law applicable to it. Arthur recommended deleting the requirement to consult either ComUSCentAF or ComUSNavCent before engaging platforms conducting minelaying in international waters. He regarded the substitution of JFACC for ComUSCentAF in some sections as a cosmetic change that failed to address the fundamental issue: that USCinCCent, not ComUSCentAF, should promulgate the ROE.

At this point, Horner tried to calm the waters with a personal message to Arthur. Horner felt the promulgation issue was purely administrative and that releasing the ROE was part of his charter as JFACC. He pointed out that General Schwarzkopf had the final review and approval. Arthur responded that promulgation of ROE was *not* simply an administrative matter, because it affected all aircraft and surface-to-air weapons assigned to USCinCCent, as well as to multinational forces. Arthur did not want to have to go to more than one staff for ROE changes. (Requests for ROE changes had to be submitted to ComUSCentAF, who would coordinate the issues with all the components *before* presenting them to USCinCCent.) Arthur was already having to deal with both staffs on the minelaying ROE. Arthur wrote that he thought Horner would do a better job than USCinCCent but that it was time for the USCinCCent staff to mature and do its job.

Schwarzkopf approved the ROE, except for a few changes. One of the changes (as requested by Arthur) was to alter the conditions under which minelaying could be considered a hostile act; Schwarzkopf also deleted the requirement to consult ComUSCentAF if such conditions were encountered. On the major issue, Schwarzkopf made it clear that ComUSCentAF (as JFACC) would remain executive agent for ROE governing air and air defense operations.

Arthur appealed the decision to Lt. General Cal Waller, General Schwarzkopf's deputy. Because of the importance of the issue, we quote the entire message:

Cal, need to reclama decision made by your [Operations Officer] in ref A. I am sure you are aware that there has been considerable debate over issuance of ROE. I can address issues relative to JFACC when we all have more time, but for purposes of these rules neither USCentAF nor JFACC should be issuing ROE that extend well beyond [their] level of interest or expertise. Mining is a prime example.

I am disturbed that an issue of this importance appears to have been handled strictly at the staff level. I feel strongly that CinC should not abrogate his responsibility to make personal decisions on hostilities ROE of this magnitude. Moreover, his personal involvement is even more important when, as is the case here, components differ on rules which should apply. Chuck Horner and his folks have done a great job in trying to bring this together but in my mind it is not his job.

If you cannot revisit this situation I will do my best to make it work. However, this is an important issue that needs correction. It is too awkward to work. I don't think you can find anywhere where a component commander has to go to another component commander before he goes to the unified commander for a ROE change.

Very Respectfully, Stan.[1]

Waller's reply was negative.[2] ComUSCentAF published the wartime ROE on 14 January. Two days later, Schwarzkopf put out a message stating that these ROE had been approved by him but had been inaccurately titled "ComUSCentAF Rules of Engagement"—they should have been "The CentCom Hostility ROE for Air/ Air Defense Forces: Desert Shield."

This dispute involved more than just who set ROE for minelaying. The real battle concerned the ROE for firing missiles beyond visual range.

ROE for BVR Shots

Everyone—including both Lt. General Horner and Vice Admiral Arthur—feared a large number of fratricidal air engagements when the war started. It seemed impossible to have so many aircraft from different services and nations operating in the same area without numerous fratricide incidents. Arthur wanted geographic separation of the services. Horner's solution prohibited firing on an aircraft beyond visual range unless there were two independent electronic forms of identification. Targets could also be procedurally identified as hostile by designating an activated "BVR" zone.

Air Force aircraft, designed largely to operate in a melee with the Warsaw Pact in Central Europe, had multiple means of identifying aircraft as hostile or friendly. The Navy, whose aircraft had been built for mid-ocean, where every aircraft approaching from a particular direction would be hostile, had spent its money on other capabilities. One of those capabilities was the F-14 fighter's powerful radar and Phoenix missile system. The F-14 could track and engage multiple targets simultaneously at extremely long ranges—well beyond visual range. Air Force aircraft had no capability comparable to the Phoenix missile. However, although the F-14 could interrogate friendly Identification, Friend or Foe (IFF) systems, it did not have a second, independent way to identify aircraft electronically. Therefore, it could never meet the ComUSCentAF requirement for a BVR missile firing. The Navy's F/A-18 also had only one of the identification systems needed. Thus, NavCent aviators felt that the ComUSCentAF ROE would prevent the F-14 from using its best weapon and thus effectively preclude JFACC from assigning Navy F-14s and F/A-18s to the forward CAP stations, which had the greatest likelihood of encountering Iraqi aircraft.[3] From the CentAF point of view, relaxing the

criteria for BVR shots to accommodate the capabilities of Navy aircraft would run
unacceptable risks of fratricide.

An exception to the criteria described above was that an AWACS could declare
an aircraft hostile. Many on the ComUSNavCent staff believed, however, that the
(Air Force) AWACS would never do so for a Navy aircraft.[4]

ComUSNavCent argued that the ROE must consider the capability of the
Navy's fighter aircraft. He argued also that BVR authority would protect American forces and minimize losses, by allowing fighter aircraft to engage multiple
threats outside the weapon "envelopes" of hostile aircraft. Otherwise, in some circumstances NavCent aircraft would have to allow enemy fighters to fire first.
ComUSNavCent did not request blanket BVR authority, only authority for some
NavCent stand-alone strikes. He also wanted special BVR zones—geographic
areas with set time limits. He noted that this would be similar to the authorization
already granted for BVR shots at any low-flyer in the path of certain Air Force aircraft.

Late in December, Brig. Gen. Buster Glosson visited the *Blue Ridge* to discuss
BVR ROE with the ComUSNavCent staff. Arthur believed that on this occasion
he reached an agreement with Glosson, that Glosson would change the BVR ROE
to what ComUSNavCent wanted—that they had his word on it. When that change
was not made, the staff felt betrayed by Glosson.

In the 1 January revision of the ROE, Horner let stand the basic BVR ROE but
included special BVR zones that could be activated in the ATO. In a personal message, Horner explained to Arthur that although he was philosophically sympa-
thetic to Arthur's position he believed it prudent to go the extra mile to guard
against fratricide, because he expected friendly aircraft greatly to outnumber hostile aircraft. Arthur was not satisfied. He felt that if one had a positive hostile ID,
one should not need to check for the absence of friendly IFF:

My position on BVR is uncomplicated. Positive hostile ID is positive hostile ID. If a Navy
airplane cannot positively ID a particular contact as hostile then that contact does not have
a positive hostile ID. . . . I will bow to your wisdom but I sure hope neither of us lose an
aircrew because we didn't take the good shot.[5]

The Navy complained that its aircraft had no BVR zones in the ATOs for the
first few days of Desert Storm. Horner replied that there would be days when no
BVR zones could be established, but he promised that wherever possible, special
BVR zones would be established to allow coalition aircraft to take advantage of
their technically superior systems. Navy personnel later claimed that during
Desert Storm no special BVR zones were *ever* established.

AIR DEFENSE

When the *Midway* first went into the Persian Gulf early in November, her
battle group did not join the Persian Gulf electronic data link; it maintained its own

link. The battle group commander, Rear Adm. Dan March, admitted that his ships needed more work prior to hostilities to solve the problems of coordinating air defense. Although there were a number of options for command and control, March suggested that it was important to select the best solution quickly so that forces could train the way they intended to fight. He argued that the battle group commander should have the responsibility for air defense. He proposed a solution based on the belief that the situation in the Persian Gulf was similar to that experienced by his battle group in Team Spirit (an exercise with the unified Korean command and the Koreans).

Vice Admiral Mauz did not think Desert Shield was the same as Team Spirit. Desert Shield was a near-land situation with many more players over a much greater area. The task in the Persian Gulf required air and surface defense for a great variety of participants, including shore facilities, hospital ships, and commercial ships. The extensive structure for command, control, and communications already in place had been built on a series of international and interservice agreements that had taken three months of hard bargaining, eventually requiring Mauz's personal intervention with Lt. General Horner.

Capt. Tom Marfiak, commanding officer of the cruiser *Bunker Hill* and the air-defense commander in the Persian Gulf, reported to Rear Adm. Bill Fogarty, commander of the Middle East Force. He observed that carrier operations in the Persian Gulf differed radically from those commonly encountered in the open ocean. Because of constrained air space, land-based forces might replace long-range pickets and even combat air patrol aircraft. The environment seriously affected communications and the reliability of the electronic data link. Marfiak suggested using distinct links for each sector and forming separate defense zones around each carrier if two or three operated in the Persian Gulf simultaneously. On a broader scale, he also suggested that the eastern sector of the entire theater have an electronic link separate from the rest of the theater, despite ComUSCentAF's desire for a single electronic data link for the entire area. Marfiak felt that his suggestion would not significantly impede ComUSCentAF's objective, while it would materially aid naval operations. If sectors were not adopted, limitations on track numbers and participating units might drastically affect the ability to integrate forces and provide a stout defense.

ComUSNavCent and Marfiak were unhappy with the proposed scheme for connecting the various pieces of the electronic data link. To transmit electronically the AWACS picture to the forces at sea required several ground relay stations. Two alternative arrangements, "Coconut" and "Hollywood," for the relays were devised. NavCent forces used the five months of Desert Shield to work with the ground stations to get as good an air picture as possible. Marfiak experimented with various options to determine the best way to overcome the extremely poor radio propagation conditions and to develop an effective way to interchange information electronically with the joint system. By the end of Desert Shield, he thought he had a workable solution.

Moving the *Midway* battle group into the Persian Gulf during Imminent Thunder in mid-November afforded an opportunity to exercise command-and-control plans. The organization established by Marfiak would be left intact, so that when the battle group left the Persian Gulf a functioning air-defense organization would remain. When the battle group was inside the Persian Gulf, had joined the data link, and was fully familiar with Persian Gulf air-defense methods and procedures, March would assume control over Marfiak and the Persian Gulf air-defense organization for as long as his battle group remained there.

After the *Midway* had operated in the Persian Gulf for a while, March expressed concern to Marfiak about the data link. March thought the scheme for relaying the link to the battle force via ground stations was a very fragile, easily disrupted connection. His primary concern was the AWACS-cruiser link option, which he felt gave him a tenuous link picture. Also, March did not feel the E-2Cs were being used effectively.

Marfiak sought to reassure March. He was working to make the link more robust, experimenting with various frequencies to overcome the peculiar transmission characteristics of the area. He needed airborne surveillance for coverage of the air over inland Iraq as well as over the northern Persian Gulf. The direct AWACS-cruiser link would be vital if the ground relay stations were lost. To get this air picture he was operating in a receive-only link from AWACS while simultaneously linking with NavCent air-defense units. That is, Marfiak did not transmit his own picture to the AWACS but simply received its data.

In December, Iraqi air activity took on a new character, with few flights below thirty degrees north latitude. Most flights now were around Tallil airfield in Iraq and near Baghdad, and one-third flew at night. Iraqi aircraft did not appear to emit much electronically; there were no communications or radar emissions. Intelligence concluded that Iraqi air training was getting more complex.

On the first day of the new year, Vice Admiral Arthur gave his subordinates comprehensive guidance in his concept of operations for use in the event of hostilities. The Persian Gulf antiair warfare commander (Captain Marfiak) reported to Fogarty. Arthur directed March and his Persian Gulf Battle Force to establish air-defense surveillance, coordinating with Marfiak.

March did not seem happy with part of these orders. He felt the level of detail involved and the command relationships tied his hands just where he needed flexibility. He objected to the perpetuation of the Persian Gulf air-defense commander as a distinct entity rather than as a subordinate in March's own command-and-control structure. He argued that as the battle force commander he was responsible for forming a battle force, taking tactical control of it, and defending the Gulf; he wished Arthur's message had said that specifically.

LOGISTICS

While amateurs talk about strategy and tactics, successful generals and admirals worry about logistics. NavCent's unheralded role was to provide the sea control necessary for safe delivery of the immense stream of ships carrying the equipment and supplies for the massive buildup. In a narrower sense, much of the success of the naval forces in Desert Storm resulted from very high readiness rates for ships, aircraft, and equipment, which resulted in part from having the right supplies on hand. This did not happen by accident. The decision to deploy six carrier battle groups, two battleships, and thirty-one amphibious ships dramatically increased the logistics requirements. By mid-January more than a hundred ships and a hundred thousand personnel would operate under ComUSNavCent. They all would need "beans, bullets, black oil," and spare parts.

In late November, Vice Admiral Mauz outlined his logistics support plan for the expanded naval forces in support of Desert Shield. Capt. Ross Hendricks, ComUSNavCent Logistics Officer, estimated that they required nine ammunition ships, fifteen oilers, eight combat stores (especially food) ships, and up to five tenders. An AOE (fast combat support ship, combination oiler and ammunition ship) was assumed to be equivalent to an AO (oiler), half an AE (ammunition ship), and one-quarter of an AFS (combat stores ship). An AOR (replenishment oiler) was considered equivalent to an AO plus one-quarter of an AE and a quarter of an AFS. ComUSNavCent would locate one or two tenders in the Red Sea and three in the North Arabian Sea or Persian Gulf for maintenance and battle-damage repair. Hendricks generally wanted one tender for every two carrier battle groups—plus an extra for the amphibious ships and mine countermeasure ships, because they seemed to need more upkeep. (As of 27 November, twenty-five of thirty-two serious [C-3 and C-4] casualty reports in NavCent came from amphibious ships and minesweepers.) Also, ships being extended in their stay in the theater and ships that had come without time to prepare for deployment needed extra work.

ComUSNavCent's original plan assigned overall operational control of the combat logistics ships in the North Arabian Sea and Persian Gulf to Rear Adm. (Sel.) Bob Sutton, the Commander of the U.S. Naval Logistics Support Force (CTG 150.3). Operational control of the combat logistics ships in the Red Sea went to the Red Sea Battle Force commander (CTG 150.5), Rear Admiral Mixson.

After Vice Admiral Arthur relieved Vice Admiral Mauz on 1 December, there was a general review of logistical plans. In particular, Arthur brought his experience as head of Navy logistics and a keen interest in the subject. As a result of his review, Arthur cancelled the 21 November logistics plan and issued a revised one. He did not change estimated requirements but significantly altered the organizational structure.

Arthur's overall concept was to maintain what he felt were the well-established and time-proven relationships between logistics assets, principal logistics agents, and the afloat commanders. The Sixth and Seventh fleets' logistics commands, as principal logistics agents for ships in the Red Sea and North Arabian Sea or Persian Gulf, respectively, would manage the flow of material into the CentCom theater. The NavCent task group commanders (CTGs 150.1, 150.4, 150.5, 150.6), rather than the Naval Logistics Support Force commander, would now have operational control of combat logistics assets associated with their battle groups.

The Naval Logistics Support Force would manage all logistics support *ashore*, including airhead and Forward Logistics Support sites. The latter would include both an airhead (a place where logistics aircraft delivered supplies for further transportation and distribution) and a collocated surface resupply port, as shown in Figure 14–1. These primary logistics sites would include existing sites at Jedda (Saudi Arabia) in the Red Sea, and Bahrain in the Persian Gulf, plus a new one at Fujaira, UAE, on the coast of the Gulf of Oman. Airheads, considered secondary logistics sites, would include an existing site at Masira, Oman, for the North Arabian Sea, as well as new ones at Hurghada, Egypt, for the Red Sea and Doha, Qatar, for the Persian Gulf. Another resupply port would also be established at Jebel Ali, UAE, in the Persian Gulf. One reason for establishing an airhead at Hurghada was that Jedda was too far from the carrier operating areas in the northern Red Sea for daily helicopter flights; Hurghada was more convenient.

The west-to-east air channel ran from Norfolk to Jedda, Hurghada, and Bahrain. The east-to-west air channel went from Clark Air Force Base in the Philippines to Masira and Fujaira. Intratheater air channels would link Masira, Fujaira, and Doha to Bahrain, and Bahrain to Jedda and Hurghada. Logistics during Desert Storm followed this plan, except that the airhead in Doha was never established.

The possibility of a closure of the Suez Canal concerned logistics planners. Intelligence frequently warned of possible attempts to close the canal. For example, on 21 December, intelligence reports indicated that five tankers might be scuttled in the Suez Canal. Although no one on the ComUSNavCent staff thought that closing it was easy—or likely, they could not dismiss the possibility. As a hedge against loss of the Suez Canal Hendricks stored enough food, parts, and consumable items in Jedda to fill a supply ship (and thus several warships). He placed a similar cache in Jebel Ali in the UAE in case the long supply line from Subic Bay was disrupted. One of the reasons for establishing an airhead at Hurghada was that if the Suez Canal were closed, supplies could be unloaded at Alexandria on the Mediterranean Sea and trucked to the Hurghada airhead on the Red Sea.

Aircraft and ship readiness in general exceeded expectations, especially when one considers the long supply lines and limited opportunities for maintenance. For example, as of 9 January all six carrier air wings reported overall mission-capable rates of at least 84 percent; 94 percent of all ships reported they were in the two highest readiness categories.

INFORMATION CONTROL AND DISPLAY

One important tool the Navy uses to exercise command and control is a system for integrating all available information on the locations of friendly, neutral, unknown, and enemy ships and aircraft. This system is called the Officer in Tactical Command Information Exchange System (OTCIXS). The Joint Operational

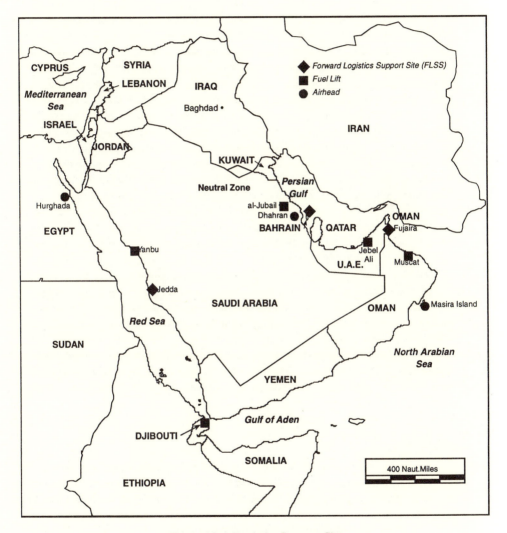

Figure 14–1. Logistics Support Sites

Tactical System (JOTS)—a network of computers—allowed the information gathered to be displayed and manipulated. In the case of the flagship *Blue Ridge,* the JOTS displays were two large screens and several monitors in the command center.

ComUSNavCent was warned that when the naval forces in the theater approximately doubled in January, the load on OTCIXS would exceed design specifications. At best, this overloading would cause long delays in passing information; at worst, the system might crash. Procedural changes to reduce the burden on it were suggested. In addition, many software engineers back in the United States worked hard to accelerate development of a follow-on system, JOTS2; they developed an adaptation for use in the unique NavCent situation, with multiple track coordinators—a decentralized way to keep the database current and accurate. The system involved several levels of JOTS and JOTS2 local area computer networks on the *Blue Ridge.* At least one of the software engineers, however, felt it was too risky to deploy the system without more testing; the ComUSNavCent operations analyst also argued against introducing a new system just before the command went to war—a programming bug could blind the command. Capt. Bunky Johnson, the Operations Officer, recognized that installing new software less than one month before the 15 January deadline was a risk, but he believed it was a calculated one, necessary because otherwise the system would be greatly overloaded when the forces in-theater approximately doubled in January. Johnson thought he had no choice, but he was holding his breath.

Therefore, in late December JOTS2 software and hardware were installed in ComUSNavCent's command center on the *Blue Ridge.* Initially, JOTS2 sometimes automatically rebooted (shut itself off and restarted without human intervention) at inconvenient times, precluding use of the system for several minutes. Over time, this problem was largely fixed. Then, early on 1 January, the times for every entry in the system went bad; it seems the new year had confused the JOTS2 program, which did not recognize January as coming after December. This somewhat unsettled the battle watch. Nevertheless, in the end, the system performed well throughout Desert Storm.

ALLIES

For any nation to give another nation tactical control over its military forces is a major step. In January, after lengthy negotiations of the conditions, several of the coalition partners agreed to give ComUSNavCent tactical control of their ships.

- The Netherlands agreed to pass tactical control of its Task Group 429.9 units in the event of a preemptive Iraqi attack or upon commencement of military operations in accordance with UN Resolution 678.
- Australia assigned tactical control of the destroyer HMAS *Brisbane* (DDG 41), the frigate *Sydney,* and the replenishment ship *Success* (A 304)—the first two for escort of battle groups, the *Success* for logistic support of the battle groups.

- Canada assigned tactical control of Task Group 302.3 and the destroyer HMCS *Athabaskan* (DDH 282) and the frigate HMCS *Terra Nova* (DD 259).
- France assigned operational and tactical control of the destroyer FS *Jean de Vienne* (D 643) to the Persian Gulf Battle Force for general escort of logistic and combat units south of 26°20' north latitude.
- Britain delegated tactical control of the destroyers HMS *Gloucester* and HMS *Cardiff* to the Persian Gulf Battle Force for forward air defense. The British also offered Royal Navy mine countermeasure assets for federated operations with the NavCent forces, subject to some conditions that will be detailed in Volume II.

NOTES

Primary sources for this chapter were messages, including both the planning messages and the exchange of "Personal For" messages. We also used CNA's reconstruction report and interviews with Mauz, Arthur, Bernie Smith, Marfiak, and Johnson.

1. ComUSNavCent 131705Z JAN 91, Personal for LTGen. Waller fm. Arthur, ROE.

2. Arthur did not remember getting either a message or a specific reply from Waller. He recalled that word more or less filtered down through Maj. Gen. Bob Johnston, Schwarzkopf's chief of staff.

3. Many NavCent officers became convinced that parochial Air Force officers sacrificed fighting effectiveness in order to give all the kills to the Air Force and make the Navy look bad. For example, one Navy aviator serving in Riyadh made the following claim: "No F-14s were offered the forward CAP stations until 18 days into the war (fifteen days after the last F-15C bogey contact). The original reason the Tomcat [F-14] was denied CAP stations was its electronic suite, then the reason became gas. To save tanker sorties, the CAP forward stations were going to go 'untanked' (however 'emergency fuel' was available from the AWACS KC-10). Untanked CAP lasted for the first twenty-four hours of the war, then the KC-10 dedicated to AWACS additionally was tasked to support the F-15C HVAA CAP and the rules/guidance were established—the Navy was not allowed to man forward CAP stations." Operation Desert Storm [USN Strike Planning], written by a Navy strike planner, undated, 5. We can neither verify nor refute the claim.

4. After the war, it was claimed AWACS had never done so for a Navy aircraft, that even when a Navy aircraft was closer than an Air Force aircraft, AWACS had never vectored a Navy fighter onto an Iraqi aircraft. For example, one Navy aviator serving in Riyadh made the following claim: "In the period of time that there was active Iraq air, no USN fighter CAP was even vectored towards a 'bogey' by a USAF AWACS, even in those few cases that the F-14 was closer." Operation Desert Storm [USN Strike Planning], written by a Navy strike planner, undated, 5. We can neither verify nor refute the claim, except to note that in at least one case, described in chapter 3 of Volume II, AWACS vectored a NavCent F-14 for a kill of an Iraqi helicopter.

5. ComUSNavCent 112120Z JAN 91, Personal for LTGen. Horner from Arthur, Rules of Engagement (ROE).

Chapter 15

Countdown to War

At the start of the new year, the battle group led by the aircraft carrier *John F Kennedy* sailed in the Red Sea, the *Midway* battle group in the North Arabian Sea. The *Saratoga* battle group was in the Mediterranean Sea but would soon rejoin the *Kennedy* in the Red Sea. The *Ranger, America,* and *Theodore Roosevelt* battle groups were approaching the CentCom theater. Thirteen amphibious ships steamed in the North Arabian Sea, and eighteen more were on the way. Two hospital ships, currently with only enough personnel to activate five hundred beds each, were in the Persian Gulf. Mine countermeasure ships and helicopters were operating from their base in the UAE and training in the southern Persian Gulf. The air defenses had been tested and were in place. Offensive strike plans were nearly set.

As the UN's 15 January deadline approached, many people thought that Saddam Hussein would make some kind of face-saving deal at the last minute to avoid war. Even if he did not, it seemed unlikely that hostilities would begin soon after 15 January.

5 JANUARY

SEALs began nightly patrols along the coast from Ras al-Mishab, Saudi Arabia, up to Mina Saud, Kuwait, to prevent infiltration by Iraqi small boats and collect intelligence.

7 JANUARY

Eight days before the UN deadline, the aircraft carrier *Saratoga* and her escorts left the Mediterranean Sea, passed through the Suez Canal, and joined the *Kennedy* battle group in the Red Sea.

8 JANUARY

A drifting mine was reported about thirty nautical miles northeast of Bahrain. Because of this and other indications of minelaying activity, Vice Adm. Stan Arthur, ComUSNavCent, ordered the battleship *Missouri* to get under way and fly her RPV to look for the minelayer. SOCCent forces reported minelaying activity just south of the Saudi-Kuwaiti border, but because of many previous SOCCent reports that the ComUSNavCent staff perceived as totally invalid (for example, the previously mentioned "supertanker" reported on 30 November), they did not take this report seriously. They believed that one of these reports was a commercial ship from the Arabian-American Oil Company.

The ComUSNavCent staff held the second Operations and Plans Conference on board the *Blue Ridge* to review its war plans. Operations officers from all of ComUSNavCent's direct subordinate organizations attended. Arthur got the attention of everyone when he told the attendees there was a 95 percent chance there would be a shooting war. Furthermore, rather than being delayed until long after the 15 January deadline, the war would start between the 15th and the 20th—unless Iraq launched a preemptive attack first. In that case, they should expect helicopters and small boats hiding under the oil platforms to jump out at the NavCent ships. Arthur warned his subordinates that they should also guard against possible attacks by Iran, because although Iran had not been a problem during Desert Shield, he could not be sure how it would react to hostilities. Arthur expected the ATO process to fall apart on the third day, forcing USCinCCent to go back to the tried-and-true method of dividing up the area.

9 JANUARY

Gen. Norman Schwarzkopf held a conference in Dhahran with his senior commanders to review their plans. He gave them preliminary attack orders, with a 17 January 0300C start time for war if no progress occurred on the diplomatic front.

A Marine Corps planning team, Maj. Gen. Jack Sheehan plus fourteen officers, arrived on the *Blue Ridge*. The Commandant of the Marine Corps, Gen. Al Gray, had sent them to provide additional amphibious warfare expertise. They came from the Marine Corps Combat Development Command at Quantico, Virginia, where they had been studying and wargaming various options for amphibious landings. This program was somewhat analogous to what the Air Force's Checkmate program in Washington had done in planning a strike campaign—with differences (Schwarzkopf had not requested the Quantico effort) and similarities (people in the theater resented plans made back in the United States and derided them as unrealistic).

As Vice Admiral Arthur and General Gray had known each other and worked together previously, Gray asked Arthur to take Sheehan on the *Blue Ridge* as an advisor and liaison. Because one of Arthur's objectives was to have the Navy and Marine Corps work together as closely as possible, and as Lt. Gen. Walt Boomer,

ComUSMarCent, did not object, Arthur agreed to this arrangement. Boomer designated Sheehan MarCent Forward.

On the diplomatic front, in a final attempt to achieve a peaceful settlement, Secretary of State James Baker met with the Iraqi foreign minister, Tariq Aziz, in Geneva. Iraq still refused to withdraw from Kuwait.

10 JANUARY

The battleship *Missouri* reported that she had flown her RPV seven times, for a total of twenty-six hours. She had searched for minelaying activity, keeping the RPV south of 29°00' north latitude and east of 048°50' east longitude (see Figure 15–1). She had observed no minelaying activity. Nor had she found any evidence of activity in the Durra and Hout oil fields off the coast of Kuwait, or on Qaruh Island, also off Kuwait. The *Missouri* warned that the RPV would have had to get quite close to a ship to determine whether it was laying mines. Also, if minelaying were occurring west of 048°50' east longitude, the RPV could not get close enough to observe it. This message tended to confirm the estimate that Iraqi minelaying was confined to areas west of 048°50' east longitude.

A mine was found drifting in the northern Persian Gulf with no evidence of wear on its shackle. The ComUSNavCent staff concluded that this was not a moored mine that had broken free but a mine that Iraq had deliberately set adrift. SOCCent forces stood by their story of a small ship dropping mines south of the border. Frustrated by USCinCCent's repeated refusal to allow NavCent to prevent minelaying activity, Vice Admiral Arthur vowed that if he caught the Iraqis doing it, he would blow them out of the water without asking anyone.[1]

The ComUSNavCent Intelligence Officer, Cdr. Wayne Perras, predicted that if Iraq launched a preemptive attack it would include Scud missiles against Israel, Riyadh, and Manama (Bahrain), followed by perhaps eighty kamikaze aircraft. Terrorist attacks would follow twenty-four hours later.

Iraq's so-called peace ship, the *Ibn Khaldoon,* was unloading its prohibited cargo in Oman and would be ready to sail again in a few days. Arthur directed that the master be told that the United States had found drifting mines in the Persian Gulf and that he would be sailing at his own risk.

At a meeting the previous day on security for the Suez Canal, participants discussed the Iraqi ship *Balqees*, scheduled to go through the canal on 11 January. It was feared that she might try to lay mines covertly during her passage. Therefore, the Egyptians would either hold up the *Balqees* until the aircraft carrier *Theodore Roosevelt* went through or let the *Balqees* go through quickly so that several other ships would pass through the canal between the *Balqees* and *Roosevelt.*

A question was raised concerning how long ships could stay at sea, with respect to the trash problem. Ordinarily, ships were not allowed to dump trash close to a coast, which would include all of the Persian Gulf; later, trash was dumped at sea. Ships were supposed to be sure to puncture all black plastic garbage bags to ensure

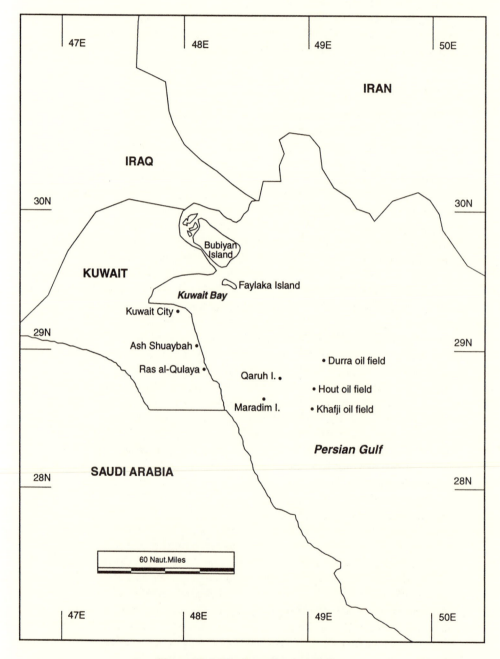

Figure 15–1. Northern Persian Gulf

they sank. Many bags did not sink, however, and ships steaming in the Persian Gulf found that these black garbage bags complicated their search for other round, black, floating objects—mines.

The commander of the Mine Countermeasures Group estimated that even with British participation, he would need seventeen and a half days to clear mines from the areas that would be used by amphibious ships and naval gunfire support ships in an amphibious assault. This seemed to be an increase over the six or thirteen days estimated (for 60 and 80 percent clearance levels) at the 30 December amphibious conference.

11 JANUARY

Intelligence repeatedly predicted that terrorists would be a serious threat, and tying the flagship to the pier would have made her an easy target for them. Vice Admiral Arthur wanted to leave no such cheap targets; he had decided well in advance he wanted all ships at sea. He told General Schwarzkopf he would do it in stages, but four or five days before the expected start of the war they would all be at sea. The *Blue Ridge* would be one of the last to go. At 0600C she got under way. When asked why the ship got under way, Arthur cited the terrorist threat, his desire to be near the fleet operating in the Persian Gulf, and—he then added facetiously—to cut the telephone lines to get fewer stupid questions from the USCinCCent staff. Notwithstanding the admiral's frustration with the USCinCCent staff, substituting one InMarSat circuit for the forty-seven phone lines the *Blue Ridge* had when tied to the pier was a handicap in dealing with it.

The *Midway* battle group entered the Persian Gulf for the fourth time—and stayed.

The amphibious ships *Guam* and *Trenton* returned to the Gulf of Oman after completing Operation Eastern Exit off Somalia.

Intelligence reported that Iraq had constructed a sixteen-inch oil pipeline that led into the sea, presumably to dump oil into the sea and perhaps set it afire.

12 JANUARY

The Iraqi "peace ship" *Ibn Khaldoon* sailed from Muscat, Oman. As she approached Iraq, ComUSNavCent Intelligence reported that all possible methods, including highly classified means, would be used to determine her track so they could estimate where Iraqi mines were located and where they were not.

Vice Admiral Arthur hosted a meeting on the *Blue Ridge* of all his flag officers to review the plans for war. When Rear Adm. Connie Lautenbacher, NavCent-Riyadh, gave his briefing, he had the impression that most battle group commanders did not understand how the centralized air war would be run. Lautenbacher's briefing ran far past his allotted time as they peppered him with questions about how the JFACC process would work and how targets would be selected.

Amphibious Group Three, with 5th MEB(SOC) embarked, and Amphibious Squadron Five, with 13th MEU(SOC) embarked, arrived in the CentCom theater. Arthur now had a thirty-one-ship Amphibious Task Force.

Starting on 12 January, the AWACS orbit over the western part of the Saudi border would be covered twenty-four hours a day. The significance for NavCent forces was that this would allow the AWACS aircraft covering the eastern part of the Saudi border to move farther east, where it could better cover the Persian Gulf.

The U.S. Congress endorsed the use of force (in the House 250–183, in the Senate 52–47). At least some on the ComUSNavCent staff found the closeness of the vote in the Senate disconcerting and incredible. All previous indications had suggested that the country solidly supported the operation; perhaps that perception had been wrong. This vote seemed to indicate that if things started to go even slightly awry, the thin margin of support might evaporate overnight. They found the vote incredible because it seemed then so obvious that the United States could not allow Saddam Hussein to get away with blatant aggression, that sanctions would not work any time soon, and that the coalition forces could not be maintained in the theater indefinitely.

A personnel augmentation for the hospital ship *Comfort* gave her a thousand-bed capability. Four days previously, an augmentation had brought the hospital ship *Mercy* to thousand-bed capability.

13 JANUARY

The total of drifting-mine reports had now reached twenty. To minimize the danger of running over a drifting mine, the *Blue Ridge* steamed at only three knots. She set Condition Zebra below the third deck, which meant that most watertight doors were kept "dogged" but could be opened by anyone needing to move about the ship. The third deck was slightly above the waterline.

The *Ranger* battle group shifted control to ComUSNavCent; it would reach the Strait of Hormuz in two days.

Vice Admiral Arthur later recalled that either Lt. Gen. Cal Waller (Schwarzkopf's Deputy) or Maj. Gen. Robert Johnston (Schwarzkopf's Chief of Staff) called Arthur about this time to tell him that General Schwarzkopf thought Arthur was not doing enough to "advertise" the amphibious forces. Schwarzkopf wanted the Iraqis to see these forces everywhere. Arthur thought Schwarzkopf and his staff did not realize all he had done with them. He agreed that one of his primary taskings was to convince Iraq he would conduct an amphibious landing.

Arthur sent Schwarzkopf a message describing what he had done to make the amphibious forces conspicuous. Arthur claimed there had been an almost continuous presence of amphibious ships in the Persian Gulf.

Granted we haven't been rushing ashore everywhere but I think that would be a little too obvious that it's all show—no go. . . . The Gulf newspapers have been full of stories. The MEB enroute left the States with big PR coverage, again in Hawaii and then in the Philippines. The Sea Soldier III exercise in Oman should have filtered back to him . . . as a rehearsal. . . . We see intel of his increasing presence on Faylaka Island and that could only be because he's expecting a raid or landing.[2]

Part of the theater deception was to make Iraq think the amphibious forces would head for Bubiyan or north of Kuwait City. A raid on Faylaka Island would fit in, because in order to assault Bubiyan or al-Faw one first needed to take Faylaka.

Later, Arthur gave television reporter Sam Donaldson an interview as part of his effort to "advertise" the amphibious forces. Arthur realized that if the attempt to convince Iraq of this was successful, it was hard to see (with limited coastline to choose from) how a real landing would make sense. Nonetheless, Arthur thought, MarCent was flanked by coalition troops that might leave MarCent's flanks exposed. The Army was farther away and might not be ready. Thus, the only source of help for MarCent might be the amphibious forces.

In a message to the Chief of Naval Operations, Adm. Frank Kelso, Arthur indicated his thoughts shortly before the start of the war:

NavCent is tasked to . . . conduct naval and amphibious feints and demonstrations along the east coast of Kuwait in support of theater deception operations.

[NavCent is also tasked to] be prepared to conduct amphibious operations to seize specific objectives with Marine forces in Kuwait. Planning priorities for other amphibious operations are a landing at the port of Ras al Qulaya [in southern Kuwait] and raid or assault at al-Faw [in Iraq]. . . .

[The movement of carriers into the Persian Gulf] reflects inability of Air Force to provide sufficient tankers to support full participation of naval air. . . .

I will be moving MCM capability up north as soon as we can assure the air threat and shore batteries are knocked down. . . .

The configuration and readiness of the Army and coalition forces will almost certainly require a landing to support MarCent. . . .

Mines are a problem and CinCCent finds it too hard to let me go after the smoking gun. I keep the pressure on. They'd find it easier if they found Saddam putting land mines in their parking lot at Riyadh.[3]

14 JANUARY

Lt. Gen. Chuck Horner, ComUSCentAF, published the wartime rules of engagement, ending Vice Admiral Arthur's battle to have USCinCCent issue the ROE and effectively denying NavCent aircraft the right to fire missiles beyond visual range using their own sensors.

Major General Sheehan presented a briefing to Vice Admiral Arthur in which he proposed that Arthur issue an initiating directive for an amphibious raid on Faylaka Island.

The *Theodore Roosevelt* passed through the Suez Canal and entered the USCinCCent area of responsibility, but still more than a week away from her launch position in the Persian Gulf. She headed in that direction at high speed.

15 JANUARY

The UN deadline came and went without Iraq withdrawing from Kuwait.

More than half a decade after the war, it is difficult to remember that the coalition expected—and greatly feared—that Iraq would use chemical weapons. At the time, all indications were that Iraq would use chemical, and perhaps biological, weapons. Information was mixed as to whether Iraq had developed chemical or biological warheads for its Scud ballistic missiles. Of course, the threat to naval forces at sea from Scud missiles or any other delivery method was far less than that to ground forces.

Nerve gas paraphernalia was issued to all hands on the *Blue Ridge* and other ships in the Persian Gulf. In addition to the gas masks, gas-mask filter cartridges, and chemical warfare suits, which had been issued in August, all hands were now given prophylactic pills to ameliorate the effects of exposure to nerve gas, and a set of self-injection antidote syringes. Ship policy required all to carry their gas masks with them at all times. Some noted, however, that Iraq had no way to target the *Blue Ridge* while she was at sea and possessed no weapon system that could effectively deliver nerve gas in the middle of the Persian Gulf.

The ComUSNavCent intelligence briefing on this day made the following points:

- Iraqi aircraft had done almost no flying the previous day. This raised suspicions, because air forces often "stand down" prior to important operations.
- When the war started, Intelligence expected Iraq to keep its aircraft in hardened shelters and to use surface-to-air missiles rather than aircraft to defend against air attack.
- Israel had gone to its highest state of alert.
- The Iraqi merchant ship *Balqees* (suspected of intending to lay mines in the Suez Canal) had been held up one day, had got under way on 14 January, and was expected to pass through the Suez Canal on 17 January.
- Intelligence repeated its belief that Iraq was laying two semicircles of mines off the coast of Kuwait. The inner semicircle had been completed in December; the outer semicircle was nearing completion. Capt. Bernie Smith, the ComUSNavCent Chief of Staff, interrupted to say that the drifting mines that had been found had been more in the center of the Persian Gulf and did not correlate with the suspected locations of the minefields.

The aircraft carrier *Ranger* entered the Persian Gulf. The *America* passed through the Suez Canal from the Mediterranean Sea and joined the *Saratoga* and *Kennedy* in the Red Sea.

16 JANUARY

The *Theodore Roosevelt* steamed at high speed in the southern Red Sea en route to the Persian Gulf. The *Ranger* and *Midway* battle groups had already sailed into the Persian Gulf. Amphibious Squadron Five and 13th MEU(SOC) entered the Gulf. The Amphibious Task Force now contained approximately 17,000

Marines afloat, 25 fixed-wing and 141 rotary-wing aircraft, 39 tanks, 115 AAVs, and 51 landing craft, including 17 LCACs. MarCent strength ashore was 72,000 personnel (including 4,000 from the Army's Tiger Brigade, attached to MarCent), with 190 fixed-wing and 172 rotary-wing aircraft ashore.

A Military Sealift Command (civilian-manned) cargo ship refused to enter the Persian Gulf without an escort. With all the coalition combat ships in the Persian Gulf, a ship in the southern Persian Gulf faced essentially no danger at this time. Vice Admiral Arthur, demonstrating remarkable forbearance under the circumstances, held his temper and directed that the ship be given a "voice escort" rather than an "alongside escort"—that is, a combatant ship would talk to them on the radio every once in a while.

Tomahawk-equipped ships in the Mediterranean Sea were placed on a twelve-hour alert for Tomahawk launch and were proceeding to their launch areas. The previous night, the ComUSNavCent staff had sent out messages that specified the sequence of Tomahawk missile launches and the targets assigned to each missile. Cdr. Geno Nielsen, ComUSNavCent's Strike Officer, worked furiously to complete the "Indigo" messages with the final launch instructions.

Three hundred messages with priority "Operational Immediate" (very high priority) addressed to ComUSNavCent were backed up at the communication center.

ComUSNavCent received the top secret Execute Order for Operation Desert Storm about 1100C. The order set H-hour at 0300C on 17 January—less than twenty-four hours away.

Arthur directed the two hospital ships, *Mercy* and *Comfort*, to shift to unclassified communications upon commencement of hostilities as required by the Geneva Convention.

On the evening of 16 January, everyone on the *Blue Ridge* (including the ComUSNavCent staff) was ordered to take one "nerve gas pill" then and one every eight hours thereafter, in addition to carrying their gas masks at all times. (The prophylactic pills were pyridostigmine bromide.) According to Capt. Ken Andrus, the Seventh Fleet Surgeon, taking these pills gave one "a mild case of reversible nerve gas poisoning." Loosely speaking, the pills work by coating the nerve synapses temporarily so as to prevent nerve gas from doing so permanently. Side effects of the pills can include diarrhea, nausea, slight fever, tingling in the extremities, headaches, lethargy, and muscle cramps. Some people experienced none of these symptoms, most had some side effects, a few reported all of them. As a result, for the first few crucial days of the war, some on the ComUSNavCent staff had headaches and felt lethargic. Most stopped taking the pills after two or three days.

FINAL INSTRUCTIONS FOR COMBAT

In a prewar message to the Persian Gulf Battle Force, Rear Adm. Dan March emphasized damage control. In a superb example of being a naval officer first and an aviator second, March told his battle force:

We are committed to not taking the first hit, but also must be able to withstand battle damage once the conflict starts. The damage control lessons of World War Two, Korea, Vietnam and the Falklands should not be lost on us. Missile hazards [loose objects that could fly about] in shipboard spaces must be ruthlessly eliminated. Battle dress including flash gear must be complete. Fire hazards must be purged to the maximum extent possible consistent with readiness for combat operations. Damage control equipment must be in peak condition and our teams fully ready and able to use it correctly.[4]

In the Red Sea, Rear Adm. Riley Mixson also emphasized damage control in his message to the Red Sea Battle Force. He deemed either taking the first hit or firing on friendly forces to be equally unacceptable. Mixson finished on an inspirational note:

I expect each and every one of us will be tested to new limits and in the end will be better for it. Those of us who will be doing the fighting did not ask for this war, but deep down we realize it is the right thing to do, for as Alexander Solzhenitsyn wrote in his book about the gulag: ". . . then gradually it was disclosed to me that the line separating good and evil passes not through states, nor between classes, nor between political parties, but right through every human heart—through all human hearts." . . . And, when all the rhetoric is boiled away and we're left with the cold, hard facts, my conclusion is that's what this crisis is really all about—good versus evil.[5]

NOTES

Messages and the author's notes were the sources for most of this chapter. We supplemented this with information from interviews with Arthur and Lautenbacher, Schwarzkopf's book, an article by Dwyer, and CNA reconstruction reports.

1. We report this statement to show how frustrated Vice Admiral Arthur was. We do not believe he would have violated the rules of engagement. The staff would not have taken such a statement as an order.

2. ComUSNavCent 130836Z JAN 91, SpeCat Exclusive for Gen. Schwarzkopf fm. Arthur, Amphib Movements.

3. ComUSNavCent 131335Z JAN 91, SpeCat Exclusive for Adm. Kelso fm. Arthur, Status Report. Despite his mention of al-Faw as a possible amphibious objective, Arthur later said that in his view al-Faw was never a viable objective.

4. CTF 154 021620Z JAN 91, Personal for commanders and commanding officers from RAdm. March, Preparations for Combat Operations.

5. CTF 155 141220Z JAN 91, Personal for Commanders, Commanding Officers and Masters info VAdm. Arthur from RAdm. Mixson, Preparations for War.

Bibliography

Primary sources included the messages and logs in CNA's Desert Shield and Desert Storm archives. A manuscript copy of this book with complete sources will be maintained at CNA, as well as a file of the sources themselves.

BOOKS

Arnett, Peter. *Live from the Battlefield: From Vietnam to Baghdad: 35 Years in the World's War Zones*. New York: Simon & Schuster, 1994.

Atkinson, Rick. *Crusade: The Untold Story of the Persian Gulf War*. Boston: Houghton Mifflin, 1993.

Baker, James A., with Thomas M. DeFrank. *The Politics of Diplomacy: Revolution, War, and Peace 1989–1992*. New York: G. P. Putnam's Sons, 1995.

Bichowsky, F. Russell, Ph.D. *Is the Navy Ready?* New York: Vanguard Press, 1935.

Cohen, Eliot A. *Gulf War Air Power Survey,* Volumes I–V plus an unnumbered summary by Thomas A. Keaney and Eliot A. Cohen. Department of the Air Force. Washington, D.C.: Government Printing Office, 1993.

de la Billiere, General Sir Peter. *Storm Command: A Personal Account of the Gulf War*. London: HarperCollins, 1992.

Fair, Charles. *From the Jaws of Victory*. New York: Simon & Schuster, 1971.

Gordon, Michael R., and General Bernard E. Trainor. *The Generals' War*. Boston: Little Brown, 1995.

Grossman, Mark. *Encyclopedia of the Persian Gulf War.* Santa Barbara, Calif.: ABC-CLIO, 1995.

Hallion, Richard P. *Storm over Iraq: Air Power and the Gulf War.* Washington & London: Smithsonian Institution Press, 1992.

Hufbauer, Gary Clyde, Jeffery J. Schott, and Kimberly Ann Elliott. *Economic Sanctions Reconsidered: History and Current Policy*. 2d ed. Washington, D.C.: Institution for International Economics, 1990.

Human Rights Watch. *Needless Deaths in the Gulf War: Civilian Casualties during the Air Campaign and Violations of the Laws of War, A Middle East Watch Report*. New York: 1991.

Keaney, Thomas A., and Eliot A. Cohen. *Revolution in Warfare? Air Power in the Persian Gulf*. Annapolis, Md.: Naval Institute Press, 1995.

Khaled, HRH General bin Sultan, written with Patrick Seale. *Desert Warrior: A Personal View of the Gulf War by the Joint Force Commander*. New York: HarperCollins, 1995.

Mandeles, Mark D., Thomas C. Hone, and Sanford S. Terry. *Managing "Command and Control" in the Persian Gulf War*. Westport, Conn.: Praeger, 1996.

Mann, Colonel Edward C., III, USAF. *Thunder and Lightning: Desert Storm and the Air-power Debates*. Maxwell Air Force Base, Ala.: Air University Press, April 1995.

Matthews, James K., and Cora J. Holt. *So Many, So Much, So Far, So Fast: United States Transportation Command and Strategic Deployment for Operation Desert Shield/ Desert Storm*. Washington, D.C.:Office of the Chairman of the Joint Chiefs of Staff and the United States Transportation Command, 1995.

Miller, Commodore Duncan (Dusty) E., and Sharon Hobson. *The Persian Excursion: The Canadian Navy in the Gulf War*. Clementsport, Nova Scotia: Canadian Peacekeeping Press; and Toronto: Canadian Institute of Strategic Studies, 1995.

Momyer, William W. *Air Power in Three Wars: World War Two, Korea and Vietnam*. Washington, D.C.: Government Printing Office, 1978.

Moore, Molly. *A Woman at War: Storming Kuwait with the U.S. Marines*. New York: Charles Scribner's Sons, 1993.

Morin, Major Jean, and Lt. Commander Richard H. Gimblett. *The Canadian Forces in the Persian Gulf: Operation Friction, 1990–1991*. Toronto, Ontario: Dundurn Press, 1997.

Palmer, Michael A. *Guardians of the Gulf: A History on America's Expanding Role in the Persian Gulf, 1833–1992*. New York: Free Press, 1992.

———. *On Course to Desert Storm: The United States Navy and the Persian Gulf*. Washington, D.C.: Naval Historical Center, 1992.

Pape, Robert A. *Bombing to Win: Air Power and Coercion in War*. Ithaca, N.Y., and London: Cornell University Press, 1996.

Powell, Colin, with Joseph E. Persico. *My American Journey*. New York: Random House, 1995.

Pyle, Richard. *Schwarzkopf in His Own Words: The Man, the Mission, the Triumph*. New York: Penguin Group, 1991.

Reynolds, Colonel Richard T., USAF. *Heart of the Storm: The Genesis of the Air Campaign against Iraq*. Maxwell Air Force Base, Ala.: Air University Press, 1995.

Salinger, Pierre, and Eric Laurent. *Secret Dossier: The Hidden Agenda behind the Gulf War*. Translated by Howard Curtis. New York: Penguin Books, 1991.

Schwarzkopf, General H. Norman, USA (Ret.), written with Peter Petre. *The Autobiography: It Doesn't Take a Hero*. New York: Linda Grey Bantam Books, 1992; Bantam paperback edition, October 1993.

Siegel, Adam B. *An American Entebbe: The Non-Combatant Evacuation Operation from Mogadishu, Somalia, January 1991*. Forthcoming.

Summers, Colonel Harry G., Jr., USA (Ret.). *On Strategy II: A Critical Analysis of the Gulf War*. New York: Dell Publishing, 1992.

Warden, Colonel John A., III, USAF. *The Air Campaign: Planning for Combat*. New York: Pergamon-Brassey, 1989.

Wiener, Robert. *Live from Baghdad: Gathering News at Ground Zero*. New York: Double-day, 1992.

Winnefeld, James A., and Dana J. Johnson. *Joint Air Operations: Pursuit of Unity in Command and Control, 1942–1991*. Rand Research Study. Annapolis, Md.: Naval Institute Press, 1993.

Woodward, Bob. *The Commanders*. New York: Pocket Books, 1991.

OTHER PUBLICATIONS

Agnew, Lt. Cdr. D. K. [Canadian Forces], Lt. Cdr. A. M. Wallington Smith, RN, and Flt. Lt. K Haysom, RAF. *Operation Granby: Iraqi Merchant Ship Incident Summaries 24 August–22 October 1990*. Fleet Operational Analysis Staff Northwood Report 33/90.

Department of Defense. *Conduct of the Persian Gulf War: Final Report to Congress*. 3 vols. Washington, D.C.: Government Printing Office, April 1992.

———. *Department of Defense Dictionary of Military and Associated Terms*. Joint Pub 1-02. Washington, D.C.: Government Printing Office, 23 March 1994.

———. *Joint Warfare of the US Armed Forces: Joint Warfare is Team Warfare*. Joint Pub 1. Washington, D.C.: Government Printing Office, 11 November 1991.

———. *Unified Action Armed Forces (UNAAF)*. Joint Pub 0-2. Washington, D.C.: Government Printing Office, 24 February 1995.

Fleet Operational Analysis Staff Northwood. *HMS Gloucester Sea Dart Engagements*. FOAS Report 36/91, 17 May 1991.

Harper, Lt. Cdr. W. B., RN, and D. Rees. *Operation Granby: LYNX/Sea SKUA Engagements*, Fleet Operational Analysis Staff Northwood Report 17/91.

Leland, Joe, and Daniel Gonzales. *Command, Control, Communications and Intelligence Support of Air Operations in Desert Storm*. Project AIR FORCE Analysis of the Air War in the Gulf. RAND Note N-3610/4-AF, February 1994.

Lloyd's Maritime Directory 1993. London: Lloyd's of London Press, 1993.

Lloyd's Ports of the World 1995. London: Lloyd's of London Press, 1995.

Lockwood, Major William C., USA. "Command and Control of Land Forces During Joint Operations." Thesis, U.S. Army Command and General Staff College, Fort Leavenworth, Kans., 1989.

National Defense University, Armed Forces Staff College (AFSC). *The Joint Staff Officer's Guide 1993*. AFSC Pub 1. Washington, D.C.: Government Printing Office, 1993.

Naval Special Warfare Command. *Naval Special Warfare Lessons Learned Case Study Operation Desert Shield/Storm*, August 1996.

Navy Operational Intelligence Center. *Iraq: Merchant Marine Identification Guide*. Washington, D.C.: August 1990.

Office of the Chief of Naval Operations. *The United States Navy in Desert Shield/Desert Storm*. Washington, D.C.: Department of the Navy, 15 May 1991.

Record of Proceedings of a Court of Inquiry to Inquire into a Major Steam Leak Which Occurred on Board USS IWO JIMA (LPH 2) on 30 October 1990.

ARTICLES

Arnett, Eric H. "Surgery with a Tomahawk." *Bulletin of the Atomic Scientists,* November 1990, 7.

Arthur, Vice Admiral Stanley R., and Marvin Pokrant. "Desert Storm at Sea." U.S. Naval Institute *Proceedings* 117, no. 5 (May 1991): 82–87.

Canby, Thomas Y. "After the Storm." *National Geographic* 180, no. 2 (August 1991): 2–33.

Delery, Cdr. Tom, USN. "Away, the Boarding Party." U.S. Naval Institute *Proceedings* 117, no. 5 (May 1991): 65–71.

Department of State. Bureau of Public Affairs. "UN Security Council Resolutions on Iraq's Invasion of Kuwait." *Dispatch* 1, no. 2 (10 September 1990): 76.

Dwyer, John B. "SEALs in Desert Storm." U.S. Naval Institute *Proceedings* 118, no. 7 (July 1992): 95–98.

Earle, Sylvia A. "Persian Gulf Pollution." *National Geographic* 181, no. 2 (February 1992): 122–34.

Fortin, Lt. Ernest, USNR. "Those Damn Mines." U.S. Naval Institute *Proceedings* 118, no. 7 (July 1992): 30–34.

Froggett, Commander Steve, USN (Ret.). "Tomahawk in the Desert." U.S. Naval Institute *Proceedings* 118, no. 1 (January 1992): 71–75.

Gellman, Barton. "General: Troops Not Ready by Jan. 15." *Washington Post,* 20 December 1990.

Getler, Michael. "Are U.S. Forces Really Ready for War?" *Washington Post,* 14 October 1990.

Goshko, John M. "U.N. Approves Use of Force for Iraqi Embargo." *Washington Post,* 26 August 1990.

———. "US Pushes for New Vote in U.N." *Washington Post,* 23 August 1990.

Healy, Melissa. "Gamble Seen in U.S. Carrier's Entry into Narrow Gulf." *Los Angeles Times,* 28 September 1990.

———. "Marines to Hold Mock Raid on Saudi Beaches." *Los Angeles Times,* 14 November 1990.

Leonard, Terry. "Iraqi Tanker, Shadowed by U.S. Warship, Reaches Aden." Associated Press, 22 August 1990.

Locke, Rear Admiral Walter M., USN (Ret.), and Kenneth P. Werrell. "Speak Softly and . . ." U.S. Naval Institute *Proceedings* 120, no. 10 (October 1994): 30–35.

Moore, Molly. "U.S. Delays Action against Iraqi Tankers." *Washington Post,* 20 August 1990.

Nagle, Commander R. J., USN. "Having a Blast in the Persian Gulf." U.S. Naval Institute *Proceedings* 118, no. 10 (October 1992): 104–107.

Owens, William A. "Living Jointness." *Joint Forces Quarterly,* no. 3 (Winter 1993–94): 7–14.

"Plan for Carrier in Persian Gulf." *New York Times,* 26 September 1990.

Powell, General Colin L., USA. "Dealing with the Changes." U.S. Naval Institute *Proceedings* 118, no. 7 (July 1992): 11–15.

Reed, Fred. "Worth Watching If the Shooting Starts." *Air Force Times,* 5 November 1990, 70.

"Resolution Sets Jan. 15 Deadline for Withdrawal." *Washington Post,* 30 November 1990.

Scarborough, Rowen. "Carrier to Sail within Attack Distance of Iraq." *Washington Times,* 27 September 1990.

Sisler, Peter F. "Iraq Says U.S. Is Trying to Provoke Attack." *Washington Times,* 15 November 1990.

Steigman, David S. "10 Killed in Boiler Accident." *Navy Times*, 12 November 1990.

Tanik, Lt. Commander Joseph T., USN (Ret.). "Welcome to El Dorado Canyon." U.S. Naval Institute *Proceedings* 122, no. 4 (April 1996): 57–62.

Trainor, Lt. General Bernard E., USMC (Ret.). "Still Go-ing . . . Amphibious Warfare." U.S. Naval Institute *Proceedings* 118, no. 11 (November 1992): 30–33.

Truver, Scott C. "Exploding the Mine Warfare Myth." U.S. Naval Institute *Proceedings* 120, no. 10 (October 1994): 36–43.

Tyler, Patrick E. "Iraqis' Food Rations Are Reduced As Trade Embargo Cuts Supplies." *New York Times*, 2 January 1991.

CNA DESERT STORM RECONSTRUCTION REPORTS

Pokrant, Marvin. *A View of Desert Shield and Desert Storm as Seen from ComUSNavCent*, October 1991. Center for Naval Analyses Research Memorandum 91-271.

Perla, Peter P. *Desert Storm Reconstruction Report, Volume I: Summary*, December 1991. Center for Naval Analyses Research Memorandum 91-219.

Schwamb, Frank, et al. *Desert Storm Reconstruction Report, Volume II: Strike Warfare*, October 1991. Center for Naval Analyses Research Memorandum 91-178.

Chambers, Charles E., et al. *Desert Storm Reconstruction Report, Volume III: Antiair Warfare*, October 1991. Center for Naval Analyses Research Memorandum 91-179.

Passarelli, Ralph, et al. *Desert Storm Reconstruction Report, Volume IV: Mine Countermeasures*, October 1991. Center for Naval Analyses Research Memorandum 91-180.

Griffis, Henry S., et al. *Desert Storm Reconstruction Report, Volume V: Amphibious Operations*, October 1991. Center for Naval Analyses Research Memorandum 91-181.

Lutz, Jeffrey, et al. *Desert Storm Reconstruction Report, Volume VI: Antisurface Warfare*, October 1991. Center for Naval Analyses Research Memorandum 91-182.

Carroll, Timothy J. *Desert Storm Reconstruction Report, Volume VII: Maritime Interception Force Operations*, October 1991. Center for Naval Analyses Research Memorandum 91-183.

Ward, Robert W., et al. *Desert Storm Reconstruction Report, Volume VIII: C^3/Space and Electronic Warfare*, October 1991. Center for Naval Analyses Research Memorandum 91-184.

Nickel, Ronald, et al. *Desert Storm Reconstruction Report, Volume IX: Logistics*, October 1991. Center for Naval Analyses Research Memorandum 91-185.

Rodney, David, Robert W. Downey, and Jonathan Geithner. *Desert Storm Reconstruction Report, Volume X: Reserve Manpower*, October 1991. Center for Naval Analyses Research Memorandum 91-186.

Graham, Amy, Cdr. A. Dale Burns, USN, and Linda Keefer. *Desert Storm Reconstruction Report, Volume XI: Medical*, October 1991. Center for Naval Analyses Research Memorandum 91-187.

Bell, Robert. *Desert Storm Reconstruction Report, Volume XII: Naval Special Warfare*, October 1991. Center for Naval Analyses Research Memorandum 91-188.

Brown, Alan, Lester Gibson, and Alan Marcus. *Desert Storm Reconstruction Report, Volume XIII: Training*, October 1991. Center for Naval Analyses Research Memorandum 91-189.

Horne, Gary E., et al. *Desert Storm Reconstruction Report, Volume XIV: Naval Gunfire Support*, October 1991. Center for Naval Analyses Research Memorandum 91-190.

Dittmer, David L. *U.S. Marine Corps Operations in Desert Shield/Desert Storm, Volume I: Overview and Summary*, August 1992. Center for Naval Analyses Research Memorandum 91-227.

Akst, George, Lt. Cdr. Kevin J. Becker, and H. Dwight Lyons. *U.S. Marine Corps Operations in Desert Shield/Desert Storm, Volume II: Ground Force Operations*, October 1991. Center for Naval Analyses Research Memorandum 91-228.

McGrady, Katherine A. W., et al. *Marine Corps Desert Storm Reconstruction Report, Volume III: Logistics Support of Ground Combat Forces*, July 1992. Center for Naval Analyses Research Memorandum 92-58.

Parsons, John D., Benjamin T. Regala, and Orman H. Paananen. *Marine Corps Desert Storm Reconstruction Report, Volume IV: Third Marine Aircraft Wing Operations*, February 1992. Center for Naval Analyses Research Memorandum 91-229.

OTHER CNA PUBLICATIONS

Adams, Gregg W., and Andrew Ilachinski. *Documentation of Possible HARM Fratricide Incidents Reported during Operation Desert Storm*, October 1992. Center for Naval Analyses Research Memorandum 92-9.

Atamian, Michael, and Gregory L. Allen. *Follow-on Analysis of Link-11 Issues Raised during Reconstruction of Desert Storm*, February 1993. Center for Naval Analyses Research Memorandum 92-158.

Brobst, William D., et al. *Navy TACAIR Overland Strike Operations, Desert Storm, Volume I*, October 1992. Center for Naval Analyses Research Memorandum 92-15.

Brobst, William D., and Michael J. Shepko. *F/A-18 Multirole Operations during Operation Desert Storm*, March 1994. Center for Naval Analyses Research Memorandum 93-4.

Carroll, Timothy J. *Multinational Naval Cooperation during Desert Shield and Desert Storm*, November 1992. Center for Naval Analyses Research Memorandum 92-170.

Dezendorf, Peter N., and Michael J. Shepko. *Battle Group Delta Participation in Desert Shield Operations*, July 1991. Center for Naval Analyses Research Memorandum 91-57.

Hirschfeld, Thomas J., *Multinational Naval Cooperation Options: Final Report*, March 1993. Center for Naval Analyses Research Memorandum 95-44.

Holliday, Mary Robin, et al. *Overview of the Performance of the Tomahawk Weapon System in Real-World Operations*, December 1995. CNR 95-216.

———. *TLAM Performance during Operation Desert Storm: Assessment of Physical and Functional Damage to the TLAM Aimpoints, Volume I: Overview and Methodology*, March 1994. Joint CNA/DIA Research Memorandum 93-49.

———. *TLAM Performance during Operation Desert Storm: Assessment of Physical and Functional Damage to the TLAM Aimpoints, Volume II: Leadership and C3 Targets*, March 1994. Joint CNA/DIA Research Memorandum 93-50.

———. *TLAM Performance during Operation Desert Storm: Assessment of Physical and Functional Damage to the TLAM Aimpoints, Volume III: Air Defense, Electric Power, and POL Targets*, March 1994. Joint CNA/DIA Research Memorandum 93-51.

———. *TLAM Performance during Operation Desert Storm: Assessment of Physical and Functional Damage to the TLAM Aimpoints, Volume IV: Chemical and Missile and Airfield Targets*, March 1994. Joint CNA/DIA Research Memorandum 93-52.

Lyons, H. Dwight, Jr., et al. *The Mine Threat: Show Stoppers Or Speed Bumps?* July 1993. Center for Naval Analyses Occasional Paper 96-138.

Mikolic-Torreira, Igor, et al. *TLAM Performance during Operation Desert Storm: Patterns and Factors in Missile Performance, Volume I*, September 1994. Center for Naval Analyses Research Memorandum 94-72.

———. *TLAM Performance during Operation Desert Storm: Patterns and Factors in Missile Performance, Volume II*, September 1994. Center for Naval Analyses Research Memorandum 94-73.

Ossege, W. Todd. *Operation Desert Storm: Reconstruction and Analysis of the 25 February 1991 Silkworm Missile Attack*, September 1991. Center for Naval Analyses Research Memorandum 91-157.

Perin, David A. *Some Observations on the Sortie Rates on Land-Based and Sea-Based Tactical Aircraft,* March 1995. Center for Naval Analyses 96-017900.

Perla, Peter P., et al. *The Navy and the JFACC: Making Them Work Together*, April 1993. Center for Naval Analyses Report 202.

Shepko, Michael J., et al. *Navy TACAIR Overland Strike Operations, Desert Storm, Volume II*, October 1992. Center for Naval Analyses Research Memorandum 92-20.

———. *TACAIR Effectiveness against Bridges during Operation Desert Storm, Volume I*, March 1994. Center for Naval Analyses Research Memorandum 93-218.

Shepko, Michael, Sandra L. Newett, and Rhonda M. Alexander. *Maritime Interception Operations*, February 1991. Center for Naval Analyses Research Memorandum 91-26.

Siegel, Adam B. *Eastern Exit: The Noncombatant Evacuation Operation (NEO) from Mogadishu, Somalia, in January 1991*, October 1991. Center for Naval Analyses Research Memorandum 91-211.

Siegel, Adam B., Stuart G. Dunn, and Lt. Cdr. Patrick C. Rabun, USN. *Case Study of a Tactical Ballistic Missile (TBM) Attack: Al Jubayl, Saudi Arabia, 15–16 February 1991*, August 1996. Center for Naval Analyses Research Memorandum 95-158.

Swider, Gregory M. *Communications for Joint Air Operations*, April 1993. Center for Naval Analyses Research Memorandum 92-223.

———. *The Navy's Experience with Joint Air Operations: Lessons Learned from Operations Desert Shield and Desert Storm*, July 1993. Center for Naval Analyses Research Memorandum 92-166.

Wigge, Maureen A. *The Joint Force Component Commander: Theory and Practice*, March 1993. Center for Naval Analyses Research Memorandum 92-195.

INTERVIEWS

[Rank listed is that on the date of our last interview. We list the positions held during Desert Shield and Storm in parentheses.]

Admiral Stanley "Stan" R. Arthur, USN (Ret.), 15, 26, and 29 June 1995; 4 June 1996; 12 December 1996. (ComUSNavCent, 1 December 1990 to April 1991).

Brigadier General David Baker, USAF, 7 May 1996. (Director of Operations, 4th Tactical Fighter Wing).

Rear Admiral Stephen H. "Steve" Baker, USN, 6 May 1996. (Operations Officer for Carrier Group Eight on the USS *Theodore Roosevelt*).

Captain Thomas "Tom" Barnett, USN (Ret.), 23 July 1996. (Commanding Officer of the USS *Horne*).

Rear Admiral David "Dave" Bill III, USN, 7 August 1997. (Commanding Officer of the USS *Wisconsin*).

General Walter "Walt" Boomer, USMC (Ret.), 11 December 1996. (ComUSMarCent).

Captain Thomas "Tom" Connelly, USN, 21 November 1994 and 1 May 1996. (ComUS-NavCent Judge Advocate).

Rear Admiral James C. "Cutler" Dawson, Jr., USN, 30 May 1996. (ComUSNavCent Plans Officer).

Admiral Leon A. "Bud" Edney, USN (Ret.), 1 July 1996. (USCinCLant).

Captain Patrick Garrett, USN, 19 April 1996. (Commanding Officer of the USS *Leftwich*).

Lt. Commander Peter Grause, USN, 22 May 1996. (Operations Officer of the USS *Leftwich*).

General Alfred M. "Al" Gray, USMC (Ret.), 20 August 1996. (Commandant of the Marine Corps).

Mr. Richard Haass, 24 August 1995. (Special Assistant to the President for Middle East Affairs).

Admiral Huntington "Hunt" Hardisty, USN (Ret.), 16 May 1991, 23 November 1994, 17 April 1995. (USCinCPac).

Rear Admiral Gordon S. Holder, USN, 22 April 1996. (ComUSNavCent amphibious expert and head of the Naval Offensive Working Group).

Major General Harry W. Jenkins, Jr., USMC (Ret.), 23 July 1996. (Commanding General 4th MEB, Commander, Landing Force).

Admiral David Jeremiah, USN (Ret.), 10 October 1995. (Vice Chairman of Joint Chiefs of Staff).

Captain Robert "Bunky" Johnson, Jr., USN, 15–17 May 1996. (ComUSNavCent Operations Officer).

Admiral Frank Kelso II, USN (Ret.), 29 July 1996. (Chief of Naval Operations).

Vice Admiral John "Bat" LaPlante, USN (Ret.), 14 and 24 May 1996. (Commander, Amphibious Task Force).

Vice Admiral Conrad C. "Connie" Lautenbacher, Jr., USN, 18 and 19 April 1996. (NavCent-Riyadh from November 1990).

Vice Admiral Anthony A. "Tony" Less, USN (Ret.), 23 August 1996. (Acting Deputy, Chief of Naval Operations, Plans, Policy, and Operations, OP-06).

Mr. William Manthorpe, 17 July 1996.

Rear Admiral Thomas F. "Tom" Marfiak, USN, 18 April 1996. (Antiair Warfare Commander in the Persian Gulf, Commanding Officer of the USS *Bunker Hill*).

Admiral Henry H. "Hank" Mauz, Jr., USN (Ret.), 15 May 1991, 14 March 1996, 30 October 1996, and 1 November 1996. (ComUSNavCent, August 1990 to 1 December 1990).

Captain Glenn Montgomery, USN (Ret.), 29 April 1996. (Commanding Officer of the USS *Curts*).

Dr. William Morgan, 28 May 1996. (Center for Naval Analyses representative with CTF 156, Rear Admiral LaPlante).

Captain Dennis "Denny" Morral, USN, 5 January 1996. (Commanding Officer of the USS *Nicholas*).

General Colin Powell, USA (Ret.), 16 January 1997. (Chairman of the Joint Chiefs of Staff).

Rear Admiral William L. "Bill" Putnam, USN, 10 and 11 June 1996. (ComDesRon 35, "November Sierra," and "Harbormaster").

Rear Admiral Grant Sharp, USN, 21 and 22 May 1991. (USCinCCent Plans Officer).

Mr. Adam Siegel, 21 December 1995. (Center for Naval Analyses representative with ComPhibGru Three, Rear Admiral Clarey).

Rear Admiral Bernard J. "Bernie" Smith, USN, 23 April 1996. (ComUSNavCent Chief of Staff).

Admiral William D. "Bill" Smith, USN (Ret.), 25 April 1996. (OP-08).

Lt. Commander Brian Smith, USN, 19 April 1996. (Operations Officer, USS *Curts*).

Colonel Frank Wickersham III, USMC (Ret.), 25, 30, 31 May and 2 June 1995. (ComUS-NavCent Fleet Marine Officer).

Vice Admiral Timothy W. "Tim" Wright, USN, 21 May 1996. (NavCent-Riyadh August–November 1990).

Admiral Ronald "Zap" Zlatoper, USN, 22 April 1996. (Antisurface Warfare Commander for Persian Gulf Battle Force).

Index

About the Author

MARVIN POKRANT has been a military operations research analyst for more than 20 years. After joining the Center for Naval Analyses, he had field tours with Commander-in-Chief Pacific Fleet, Commander Third Fleet, and Commander Seventh Fleet. After Desert Storm, Dr. Pokrant coordinated CNA's reconstruction of Desert Shield and Desert Storm with the Seventh Fleet staff. Later, as Director of CNA's Fleet Tactics and Capabilities Program from 1992 to 1994, he oversaw many follow-on analyses of issues raised during Desert Storm. Dr. Pokrant is now retired.